A visit to Colonial Williamsburg...

...is a rendezvous with one of the most important chapters in America's history and with an entire community that existed more than two centuries ago. Known worldwide as the nation's largest outdoor living-history museum, the restored 18th-century capital of Virginia is presented in the 173-acre Historic Area. It contains 88 original buildings and hundreds of other reconstructed buildings, most of which sit on their original foundations. Visitors step back into time to encounter trade demonstrations, dramatic vignettes, interactive programs and talk with "people of the past" in homes, public buildings and shops.

For information and reservations, visit the official web site at www.colonialwilliamsburg.org or call toll-free 1-800-HISTORY.

Lanny Wadkins

The Golden Horseshoe Golf Club at Colonial Williamsburg is proud to announce Lanny Wadkins as its PGA touring professional.

A Virginia native, Wadkins joined the PGA TOUR in 1972 and was named Rookie of the Year. He won three tour events in 1985 and was recognized as PGA TOUR Player of the Year. Appearing in seven Ryder Cup matches as a player, Wadkins served as captain of the 1995 Ryder Cup Team. Wadkins now represents the Golden Horseshoe on the Senior PGA TOUR and won his debut at the ACE Group Classic on Feb. 13, 2000. For information on Colonial Williamsburg's resort facilities, including our award-winning golf courses, visit the official web site at www.colonialwilliamsburg.org or call toll-free 1-800-HISTORY.

Williamsburg Inn

World-class ambience, elegant lodging, exquisite dining and attentive personal service await guests at the Williamsburg Inn. Reminiscent of early 19th-century England, the Regency-style Inn surrounds guests today with the same sense of hospitality and luxury that Colonial Williamsburg benefactor John D. Rockefeller Jr. envisioned when the Inn was built in 1937 during the restoration of Virginia's colonial capital. The Williamsburg Inn is one of five hotels of the Colonial Williamsburg Company Hospitality Group, a subsidiary of the Colonial Williamsburg Foundation. Profits support the foundation's educational programs and preservation of the Historic Area. For information and reservations, visit the official web site at www.colonialwilliamsburg.org or call toll-free 1-800-HISTORY.

Four authentic 18th-century taverns await your dining pleasure in the Historic Area of Colonial Williamsburg. Each offers its own special sense of life in the capital of colonial Virginia. Christiana Campbell's Tavern was favored by George Washington and features seafood, spoon bread and sweet potato muffins. Chowning's Tavern brings to mind an English alehouse. After 9 p.m., you can try your hand at "Gambols," an evening of colonial-style games and performers. The King's Arms Tavern elevates mealtime to memorable heights, reflecting its heritage as the dining choice of 18th-century gentry. Mrs. Vobe may greet you at the door to welcome you to her refined establishment. Shields Tavern was first to open in the 18th century. Today, the gregarious and outspoke. Mr. Shields invites you to sample foods of the 1740s. For information and reservations, visit the official web site at www.colonialwilliamsburg.o or call toll-free 1-800-HISTORY.

Par Excellence

A CELEBRATION OF
VIRGINIA GOLF

JIM DUCIBELLA

PHOTOGRAPHY BY
ROSS D. FRANKLIN

SPORTS PUBLISHING INC.
CHAMPAIGN, ILLINOIS
804 North Neil Street
Champaign, IL 61820

Book design, project manager
Jennifer Layne Polson

Jacket design
Christina Cary

Copy editor
David Hamburg

ISBN: 1-58-261-103-3

Printed in the USA.

Visit us on the web at
www.SportsPublishingInc.com

In loving memory of Marie Ducibella
and to Ruth and Roger Franklin

a c k n o w l e d g m e n t s

In October 1997, I accepted an invitation to play golf at The Colonial in Williamsburg from owner Francis Fenderson. We'd never met, but we hit it off immediately. By the turn, we were sharing personal thoughts about our lives and aspirations.

It was Francis who suggested that I write a book on Virginia golf. He was a constant source of support from the beginning. There's two ways to look at this, Francis: I either can't thank you enough, or this is entirely your fault. Seriously, I can't thank you enough.

There were so many people I depended on to make this book come together and who I owe sincere thanks. There was the late Eddie Crane, who gave me my first job in journalism and who remained a cherished friend. Sports writers John Keim, Rick Snider and Dave Elfin inspired me by the example they set when writing their books. Ann Sjoerdsma, former book editor of *The Virginian-Pilot*, offered invaluable advice from the start. Mike Williams, photographer for *The Virginian-Pilot*, generously offered me his work, which was uniformly wonderful. His widow Margaret graciously carried out that agreement after Mike's death. Former *Virginian-Pilot* photographer Robie Ray made the same offer and was an enormous help. Al Milley, sports editor of the Danville *Register and Bee*, was wonderful in helping me handle material on Bobby Mitchell. Harold Pearson, editor of *The Virginia Golfer*, is as good a friend and sounding board as a journalist could have. So is Jerry Ratcliffe, sports editor of *The Daily Progress* in Charlottesville.

I am especially indebted to Art Utley, the golf writer for *The Richmond Times-Dispatch*. He was a constant source of aid and gave the manuscript such a thorough editing that I always had complete peace of mind.

In research, Jaya Tiwari of Old Dominion University's library rooted through microfilm at all hours of the day and night. Kathy Albers of *The Richmond Times-Dispatch* was someone I could e-mail on a moment's notice with a request that just had to be filled immediately. She always complied. Peggy Haile, city historian for Norfolk, was a huge help early in the project, as was Ann Johnson, the head librarian at *The Virginian-Pilot*. Weymouth Crumpler, curator of the golf museum at the James River Country Club in Newport News, was especially helpful in allowing us access to many of the game's earliest artifacts.

Special thanks go to David Norman, executive director of the Virginia State Golf Association, Butch Liebler at Cavalier G&YC, Andy Giles, pro for the city of Portsmouth and Glen Byrnes, director of golf at Golden Horseshoe in Williamsburg.

Perhaps the most gratifying aspect of this project was the complete cooperation accorded me by all the players. Thanks to everyone who lent us a photo or offered their scrapbook or who called after an interview to offer one final bit of information. Jack and Ann Snead, in particular, couldn't have been more accommodating to Ross and me if we'd been family. Rick Worsham invited a total stranger into his home late one night, then gladly handed him some of the family's most precious keepsakes from his father's life.

Finally, no two people have had as positive an impact on this project as my wife and my father. To my wife, who already makes sacrifices beyond anything found in a "normal" marriage, we *are* kindred spirits, dear, best friends, and partners forever. This never would have happened without your love and understanding.

Dad, this book is merely the latest example of a lifetime of support and devotion you've shown me. Thank you. I'm proud to be your son.

Contents

INTRODUCTION vi
FOREWORD by Arnold Palmer ix

1 MAJOR CHAMPIONS
Sam Snead 2
Curtis Strange 12
Lanny Wadkins 20
Lew Worsham 26
Chandler Harper 32
J.C. Snead 36
Donna Andrews 42
Vinny Giles 46

2 CHAMPIONS II
Bobby Cruickshank 52
Robert Wrenn 56
Bobby Mitchell 60
Mark Carnevale 64
Carl Paulson 68
Bobby Wadkins 72
Tom Strange 76
Tom McKnight 80

3 FOUR ACES
Robbye King Youel 84
Lily Harper-Martin 86
Mary Patton Janssen 88
Jane Mack 90

4 THEY RULED THE GAME
Harry Easterly 92
Bill Battle 96
Tim Finchem 100

5 VIRGINIANS & THE CUP 104

6 THE RESORTS
The Homestead 108
The Homestead—The Cascades 112
The Legend of The Golden Horseshoe 120
Golden Horseshoe—Gold Course 122
Golden Horseshoe—Green Course 128

Kingsmill 130
Ford's Colony 136
The Tides 140
Wintergreen 146

7 CLASSY DESIGNS
Robert Trent Jones Golf Club 152
Farmington Country Club 158
The Country Club of Virginia 164
The Virginian Golf Club 168
James River Country Club 172
Washington Golf & Country Club 176
The Cavalier Yacht and Golf Club 180
Bide-A-Wee 184
Birdwood Golf Club 188

8 FRED FINDLAY:
STROKES OF GENIUS 190

9 MAKING MEMORIES
The Slammer's Magic Wand 194
Long Live the King 198
First for the Last Time 200
U. S. Hoists First Presidents Cup 202
Peete and Re-Peete At Kingsmill 206
Score One for Inkster's Ginty 210
Not Bad for an Insurance Man 212
A Late, Beautiful Bloomer 216
Decker's State Open: No Accident 218
Rollins Rolls in State Amateurs 220
Kandi Kessler, Kid Tiger 222
Moss Beecroft: Better with Age 224

10 THE NEW FRONTIER 226

11 PRESIDENTS AND
VIRGINIA GOLF 234

APPENDIX 242

PHOTOGRAPHER'S
ACKNOWLEDGMENTS
AND CREDITS 242

What's so special about golf in Virginia that it deserves a "Celebration?".

The answer is simple: *Everything.*

Start with Virginia's finest players: Sam Snead, Curtis Strange, Lanny Wadkins, Vinny Giles, Donna Andrews, Lew Worsham, Chandler Harper, J.C. Snead. They have combined to win 16 major championships—Masters, U.S., and British Opens, and PGA Championships.

They and other golfers from the Old Dominion have won nearly 200 official PGA or LPGA events, the latest being Lanny Wadkins' first victory on the Senior PGA Tour in early 2000.

Hot Springs-born legend Sam Snead, as much a part of golf's Mt. Rushmore as Palmer, Nicklaus and Hogan, actually won 135 tournaments. The PGA Tour credits him with just 81, still more than any man ever.

Virginians have competed in the Ryder Cup 27 times. Snead and Richmond native Wadkins have served as team captain four times, with two-time former U.S. Open champion Strange of Williamsburg set to make it five in 2001 at The Belfry.

Giles of Richmond, Kandi Kessler-Comer of Charlottesville and Lynchburg's Andrews have also distinguished themselves in the Walker Cup, Curtis Cup and Solheim Cup, respectively.

In 1995, the U.S. Golf Association instituted a new competition, the State Team Championship. Held in October at Lake Nona Golf Club in Orlando, Florida, Tom McKnight of Galax, Keith Decker of Fieldale and David Partridge of Richmond crushed the competition. Their three-day total of 424, 8-under-par, was nine shots better than second-place Florida.

Even when Virginia golfers fail it is the stuff of legend. Is there a true student of the game who doesn't know that Snead never won the U.S. Open? Or remember Strange at the 1985 Masters and 1995 Ryder Cup?

Giles finished second in the U.S. Amateur three consecutive years. That's more impressive than winning it once, although with Giles there's no need to debate the issue. He won the '72 Amateur in Charlotte, when he was America's best-known amateur.

David Tolley of Roanoke also finished second in the 1982 U.S. Amateur, as did McKnight in 1998.

History buffs know all about the famous wedge shot Worsham holed to win the 1953 World Championship at Chicago's Tam O'Shanter. Worsham, who also defeated Snead in the controversial 1947 U.S. Open in St. Louis, was raised on the Virginia Peninsula. He retired there when his career as pro at Oakmont CC in Pennsylvania was over.

The man Worsham defeated that day, 1950 PGA winner Harper, hails from Portsmouth.

From the moment the game was first "officially" played in this country—1784 in Savannah, Georgia, according to the National Golf Foundation—Virginians have been in there swinging.

Probably earlier.

In Norfolk County, an inventory of the estate of William Young, taken on Aug. 25, 1762, includes an item described as "1 Goff club."

This was reported by Bruce Lenman, a history teacher at the University of St. Andrews in Scotland, in *Colonial Williamsburg*, the journal of the Colonial Williamsburg Foundation.

"Even if this unvalued object was probably a freak survival (sic) from an earlier life on another continent . . . it would be no light decision to take a golf club across the Atlantic," Lenman wrote in the August, 1991 edition.

Later, Lenman revealed that a similar inventory of the estate of Charles West of Accomack County in 1757, recorded a year later, uncovered strong evidence of retail sales. At the time of his death, West had in his possession 18 golf "sticks" and three dozen balls.

The cost of even one featherie was astronomical in the mid-1700s. Lenman wrote that you could hire a servant for six days for the same price as one dozen balls. It would be highly unusual for even the wealthiest gentleman to have 36 golf balls on hand just for personal use.

The last British colonial governor, John Murray, the Earl of Dunmore, was a Scot. According to Colonial Williamsburg, there are informal records indicating that he practiced the game on the grounds of the Governor's Palace in Williamsburg between 1774 and 1776.

Having said that, it's a fact that no one is absolutely certain where in Virginia golf was first played. Because of the regular influx of Scotsmen coming to shore in the Hampton Roads area, there has long been speculation that it started there.

Here's what we *do* know about the birth of golf in the Old Dominion:

In 1892, The Homestead in Hot Springs unveiled a six-hole layout that was indicative of the course-construction "boom" in the U.S. that year. According to the National Golf Foundation, 12 courses opened in 1892, including two in Connecticut, two in Illinois, and two in New Jersey.

Sixteen years later, some members of the sporting elite in Richmond laid out a six-hole course of their own on what is now Monument Avenue, sinking tomato cans into the ground for the holes.

(You can't overestimate the significance of tomato cans to Virginia golf. As a kid, Snead buried them on the family farm, then trimmed the grass around them to create the "greens" on which he learned to play.)

By 1904, there appears to have been eight prominent clubs in Virginia: Norfolk Country Club, Alexandria Golf Club, Hampton Roads Golf and Country Club (now James River CC in Newport News), Roanoke Country Club, Washington Golf and Country Club, Hermitage Country Club in Richmond, Lakeside Country Club in Richmond, and the University of Virginia Golf Club in Charlottesville.

In August 1904, James Hume of Norfolk CC sent a letter to the other clubs inviting them to compete in a tournament on Nov. 25-26 on a course now known as Sewell's Point.

Lakeside, led by Scotsman Fred J.D. MacKay, won the inaugural competition. At a dinner following that first competition, Norfolk, Hampton Roads, Lakeside, Hermitage, Roanoke, and Lexington Golf Club, which apparently didn't compete but was represented, agreed to form a Virginia State Golf League.

In 1921, a formal organizational structure was established, with William P. Wood of Richmond elected as president.

Since then, membership in the VSGA has grown to more than 270 clubs and courses and 85,000 members. The VSGA currently operates more than 100 annual tournament events for players of all ages and skills. Through 1999, the VIP membership program had raised more than $700,000 for scholarships awarded to students attending Virginia colleges and universities since 1985.

In 2001, the VSGA will open the most complete state golf center in the United States. Located along the Chesterfield-Powhatan counties border near Richmond, the centerpiece of the $12.8 million project will be a 7,179-yard, par-72 championship course designed by noted architect Tom Fazio.

Included in this campus-like setting will be a "short" course for children, a 9,000-square foot clubhouse, practice facilities and an instruction center, a dormitory, a museum and library dedicated to Virginia golf history, a turfgrass research center and classrooms.

While the VSGA golf center will make history, one of the most fascinating aspects of golf in Virginia is how so many of its courses intersect with the history of America.

In July 1861, Union soldiers marched to Manassas for the first Battle of Bull Run on a road that passes the entrance to Fairfax National Golf Club. A soldier who was killed in the second Battle of Bull Run, a Sunday School pupil of General Stonewall Jackson's, is buried on course property.

The nines that comprise the 27 holes of Fairfax National are named for major battles in the Civil War: Bull Run, Antietam, and Wilderness.

A friend once jokingly told me that the two most important elements for a successful book on anything related to Virginia were references to Robert E. Lee and ghost stories.

Lee's Hill in Fredericksburg gets its name because the golf course sits on land where Lee's Confederate troops camped during the winter of 1862-63.

Then there's the Somerset Golf Club in Locust Grove, located on the outskirts of the bloody Battle of the Wilderness. From May 5-7, 1864, more than 17,000 Union soldiers and 7,750 Confederates were killed or wounded.

Somerset's 13th hole, a par-4 measuring 268 yards, runs near an old plantation house the Confederates used as a field hospital, and is adjacent to a low point of the Rapidan River Union soldiers used as a crossover point.

Since the back nine opened in May 1999, members have rushed back to the clubhouse with tales of having witnessed bizarre happenings. They've reported seeing it raining on the 13th hole while the rest of the course was bathed in sunshine.

Director of golf Don Kramer was on the 13th fairway with the crew from a local TV station when they heard their clubs rattling in the carts behind them. Kramer says when they turned around, they saw a tiny funnel cloud of wind inside their cart, shaking the cart and the bags.

The funnel cloud passed through the front of the cart, lifting the scorecard from its holder on the steering wheel and carrying it onto the green, where the card fell near the cup.

On July 27, 1999, Somerset officials abolished the club's 13th hole, erecting a tombstone near the tee and renumbering the holes. The 13th is now the 14th. The 14th is now the 15th. Golfers finish on the 19th green.

Two miles from Somerset is Meadows Farms, one of the wildest flights of fancy ever carved out of Mother Nature. Nursery mogul Bill Meadows read dozens of books on golf courses and clipped out the photos he liked best, glued them together, and handed the package to architect Bill Ward.

In addition to being home to the longest hole in the United States—a par-6 of 841 yards—27-hole Meadows Farms includes a hole configured like a baseball diamond. Sand traps form first, second and third base.

The 165-yard eighth hole features a green sitting on the cliff of a man-made waterfall. The whole course is wonderfully insane, and open to the public.

When it comes to crazy, nothing beats the long-forgotten story from the 1930s of J. Smith Ferebee of Virginia Beach.

At the time, America was obsessed with bizarre feats of endurance, dance marathons, flagpole sitting. Ferebee, a self-proclaimed mediocre player, was into golf.

Really into golf.

On Sept. 25, 1938, Ferebee, accompanied by friend and heating executive Reuben Trane, three pilots, a nurse and a scorekeeper, began a quest to play 600 holes in eight cities in four days.

Starting on the West Coast, Ferebee played 84 holes at Lakeside Club in Los Angeles. He then flew to Phoenix in an American Airlines DC-3 that Trane chartered and installed this new thing called air conditioning, where he got in another 81 holes that night at Encanta.

"We had flares at the tees and at the greens," Ferebee recalled in 1985. "In the fairways were two forecaddies with flashlights who watched for the ball."

The next day, Ferebee played 72 holes at Blue Hills in Kansas City and 72 more that evening at Norwood Hills in St. Louis.

On it continued: 75 holes at Tuckaway in Milwaukee; 72 holes at Olympia Fields in Chicago; 72 holes at North Hills in Philadelphia and 72 holes at Salisbury CC on Long Island. He finished the last hole with the help of mobile floodlights before being whisked to the World's Fair in New York City. There he sank the last putt on a specially constructed hole.

Even without benefit of an electric cart, since they hadn't yet been invented, Ferebee averaged 76 minutes per round. His lowest score was a 75, his highest 99. He was assisted by 110 caddies and walked an estimated 180 miles.

The stunt was an amazing success. Ferebee's story was told in more than 400 newspapers—and now in one book celebrating Virginians and the game they hold so dear.

THROUGH THE YEARS

A timeline of Virginia Golf:

1757—An inventory of deceased Accomack County resident Charles West includes "18 Goff Sticks, 3 dozn balls," suggesting retail sales of equipment
1892—Play begins at The Homestead Course, Hot Springs
1894—Play begins at The Washington Golf and Country Club, Arlington
1895—Play begins at Roanoke Country Club
1902—Play begins at Norfolk CC (now Sewell's Point)
1903—Play begins at Country Club of Virginia Westhampton Course
1904—Virginia State Golf Association is founded
1911— William Palmer of Richmond wins first State Amateur
1922—Mrs. J.W. Zimmerman wins first Women's State Amateur, at Roanoke CC
1924—Elmer Loving, Virginia Beach, wins first State Open, at Hermitage CC
1928—Glenna Collett (Vare) wins USGA Women's Amateur, at The Cascades
1930—Portsmouth's Chandler Harper, age 16, wins State Amateur, at The Cascades
1932—Harper wins first of 11 VSGA, VPGA Open titles
1934—Lilly Harper of Portsmouth wins first of six Women's State Amateur titles
1943-45—No tournaments, World War II
1946—Sam Snead of Hot Springs wins first, and only, State Open
1946—Snead wins British Open at St. Andrews
1946—Lew Worsham of Newport News wins first pro event, Atlanta Invitational
1947—Worsham beats Snead to win U.S. Open
1949—Snead wins PGA Championship at Richmond's Hermitage CC (now Belmont)
1948—Fred Gill of Petersburg wins first VSGA Senior Championship
1950—Chandler Harper wins PGA Championship at Scioto Country Club, Columbus, Ohio

1953—Wayne Haley of Bassett wins first VSGA Junior Championship, at Hidden Valley, Salem
1957—Mary Patton Janssen of Charlottesville wins first of six consecutive Women's State Amateurs
1957—Tom Strange wins inaugural Eastern Amateur, at Elizabeth Manor; brother-in-law Jordan Ball finishes second
1958—VSGA, VPGA begin conducting separate State Opens
1960—Future PGA commissioner Deane Beman wins his first of record four Eastern Amateur titles
1962—Vinny Giles wins first of seven State Amateur titles
1964—Lanny Wadkins of Richmond wins first of two VSGA Junior Championships
1966—Lloyd Liebler of Portsmouth wins first of two VSGA Junior Championships
1970—Curtis Strange wins first of two VSGA Junior Championships
1970—Lanny Wadkins wins United States Amateur
1971— Ben Crenshaw wins Eastern Amateur
1972—Vinny Giles wins United States Amateur
1972—Lanny Wadkins wins first pro event, Sahara Invitational
1975—Vinny Giles wins British Amateur
1977—Wayne Jackson of Hampton wins VSGA's first Mid-Amateur title
1979—Curtis Strange wins first PGA tournament, Pensacola Open
1981—John Mahaffey wins first Michelob Championship at Kingsmill (nee Anheuser-Busch Classic)
1983—Miller Barber wins inaugural UVB Seniors Classic, at Hermitage CC
1985—VSGA, VPGA agree to hold one Open, won by amateur Tom McKnight at Farmington CC, Charlottesville
1985—Donna Andrews of Lynchburg wins first of five consecutive Women's State Amateur titles.
1986—Kandi Kessler Comer of Charlottesville is first Virginia woman selected to U.S. Curtis Cup team
1988—Curtis Strange of Williamsburg wins United States Open at The Country Club in Brookline, Mass., in 18-hole playoff with Nick Faldo
1989—Strange becomes first player since Ben Hogan to successfully defend his Open title, winning at Oak Hill in Rochester, New York.
1991—Moss Beecroft of Newport News finishes second at United States Senior Amateur
1991—Kay Schiefelbein of Alexandria wins first of four straight Women's Senior Amateur titles.
1993—Vinny Giles is selected captain of United States Walker Cup team
1993—Donna Andrews wins first pro event, PING-Cellular One championship
1994—Pat Tallent of Vienna crosses the border to win Maryland State Amateur and Maryland State Open
1994—Donna Andrews wins Nabisco Dinah Shore
1994—Inaugural Presidents Cup held at Robert Trent Jones GC, Gainesville
1996—Sam Wallace of Williamsburg advances to quarterfinals of U.S. Senior Amateur
1997—Robbye King Youel of Charlottesville is inducted into the Virginia Sports Hall of Fame
1998—Peggy Woodard of Virginia Beach wins third straight Women's Senior Amateur title
1999—Tom McKnight of Galax is selected to U.S. Walker Cup team
1999—VSGA breaks ground on State Golf Center near Richmond
2000—Lanny Wadkins wins first Senior PGA Tour event

I 'll bet you are as surprised to see my name attached to a book honoring the history of Virginia golf as I was when I was asked to write on the subject.

As you probably know, I am a native Pennsylvanian, not a Virginian.

I attended Wake Forest University in North Carolina, not a university in Virginia.

I live in Pennsylvania and in Florida, not in Virginia.

Yet the truth is that Virginia and Virginia golf have a special place in my heart.

The last time I won was in Virginia, at the 1988 Crestar Senior Classic at Hermitage Country Club outside Richmond. I beat Lee Elder, Jim Ferree, and Larry Mowry by four strokes.

Back in the 1950s, when I'd drive home to Latrobe from Wake Forest, I'd pass the old Hermitage Country Club, which was located at the intersection of U.S. 1 and Hilliard Road. So many times I wished I could have turned into the parking lot and played. It would have been the ideal way to break up what was often a miserably long journey.

Although I won the Crestar Senior Classic on the "new" Hermitage course, I had a sense of comfort that week that came, in part, from my familiarity with the Hermitage name.

I have done design work in Virginia, building the Plantation Course at the Kingsmill resort in Williamsburg and undertaking an extensive renovation of the Keswick Club outside of Charlottesville. I'm now in the middle of two more course projects in the Old Dominion—Indian River Plantation in Virginia Beach and Bay Creek in Cape Charles, which overlooks the Chesapeake Bay on the Eastern Shore.

The Cape Charles project is unique. I'm designing the first 18 holes, and an old pal of mine—Jack Nicklaus—is designing the second 18. When you visit there, we'll even let you mix-and-match nines so you can let us know which you like better.

As far as Virginia golfers are concerned, they are some of my favorites—not to mention fellow alumni. Curtis Strange, along with Richmonders Lanny Wadkins and Robert Wrenn, all attended Wake Forest on the Buddy Worsham Scholarship, which I founded.

My daughter Peggy attended the College of William & Mary in Williamsburg, just up the road from what may be the finest golf museum in the world. It's located in the clubhouse of the James River Country Club in Newport News. There's plenty more about the museum on these pages. Suffice it to say that if you wanted to play a round with the oldest known club and oldest certified ball in the world, you would find both at the James River CC museum. Best of all, the museum is open to the public and is free.

When I think of Virginia golf, I think of the Worsham family. Bud played a crucial role in my decision to attend Wake Forest. We roomed together there and were close, close friends. Brothers, really. There's no telling what Bud could have accomplished as a player had he not been killed in an auto accident while we were still in school.

Of course, his older brother Lew enjoyed a great career. He was the head pro at Oakmont in Pittsburgh from 1947 to 1979. When he wasn't taking care of his members, Lew was out winning the 1947 U.S. Open (beating that Virginia legend Sam Snead) and the 1953 World Championship at the Tam O'Shanter Club in Chicago.

There, he laid one on another fellow Virginian, Portsmouth's Chandler Harper, when he holed a shot from the 18th fairway for an eagle in the first tournament ever televised.

When I think of golf in Virginia, I think of old pro Bobby Cruickshank, who had a much-deserved reputation as a great teacher. Bobby spent most of the 1930s and 1940s working in Richmond before moving to Chartiers, a fine club just outside of Pittsburgh in western Pennsylvania—my neck of the woods—in 1949.

Cruickshank was at least as good a player as he was a teacher. He finished second in three U.S. Opens, with one of them a playoff loss to Bobby Jones.

When Chartiers threw a dinner to honor Bobby in October 1965, I was there, holding the microphone for him while he addressed his friends and admirers. There were plenty of both in attendance that night.

When I think of Virginia, I see what may be the finest example of the phrase "the family of golf."

Consider this: Sam Snead hired Tom Strange to work for him as an assistant pro at The Greenbrier in West Virginia. Tom and wife Nancy had three children, including identical twins Curtis and Allan. When Tom died in Virginia Beach at the age of 38, Curtis was only 14, but already gaining a reputation as someone with a possible future as a pro.

Chandler Harper, the 1950 PGA champion, offered to pick up where Tom's instruction with Curtis had ended. Judging from Curtis' career, he turned out to be in excellent hands.

As for those considered to be the greatest players ever to come out of Virginia, that's one of the main reasons for this book: to acknowledge their accomplishments and share them once again with golf fans everywhere, not just in the Old Dominion.

Sam Snead. Curtis Strange. Lanny Wadkins. Vinny Giles. Donna Andrews. Lew Worsham. Chandler Harper. J.C. Snead. I'd put them up against any group from the other 49 states and feel confident that they would be hard to beat.

Among them, they have won 16 major championships: three Masters, three U.S. Opens, five PGAs, one British Open, two U.S. Amateurs, one Senior Players Championship, and one Dinah Shore. Vinny Giles also won a British Amateur.

Virginians have competed in 27 Ryder Cups—four times as captain—eight Walker Cups, and two Solheim Cups.

Two Virginians, Bill Battle and Harry Easterly, served as president of the United States Golf Association. Another Virginian, Tim Finchem of Virginia Beach, is the current commissioner of the PGA Tour.

It would be difficult, maybe impossible, to find players and administrators from one state whose impact on golf has been as great as those who have hailed from Virginia.

I am delighted that someone has decided to tell the story. Enjoy.

Par Excellence

A CELEBRATION OF
VIRGINIA GOLF

major champions

Sam's most famous pose: seated on the 9th green
at Augusta National during the 1938 Masters.

MAJOR CHAMPIONS

SAM SNEAD

The man who hung the moon.
That's what former Masters winner Bob Goalby once called Samuel Jackson Snead.

It's certainly more stylish than calling Snead one of the great golfers of all time, which only a fool would argue. It's softer on the ear than identifying Snead as the game's first "personality." It's more artful than saying that while people today are enthralled with Tiger, no one has forgotten that Sam Snead was a different breed of cat.

In a workshop so stuffed with clubs and oversized bags that a visitor can barely see the walls, Snead grabs a wedge, flips on the radio, then dances a quick couple of steps, a delighted grin on his face. Music has always played a major role in his life. He played a little guitar, blew some trumpet. Sometimes when he was closing in on yet another victory, he would hum the "Merry Widow Waltz" or another favorite tune.

"Like classic plays and symphonies, Sam Snead doesn't just belong to a generation," five-time British Open champion Peter Thomson told *Golf* magazine in 1992. "His mark will be left on golf into eternity."

How many tournaments did Snead really win? It depends on who's answering. Snead says 165, including regional events.

Independent record-keepers call it 135.

The PGA Tour, which didn't keep track of such things until 1947—13 years after Snead turned professional, a decade after he joined the touring circuit—credits him with 81.

In any event, that's more than any golfer in PGA history.

In 1959, Snead became the first modern player to break 60, shooting a 59 at the Sam Snead Festival at the Greenbrier Resort in West Virginia. It isn't in the record books because the PGA Tour deemed the tournament's purse too small for it to qualify as an official event. Never mind that the field included some of the biggest names of the day, including Gary Player.

At Quad Cities in 1979, Snead, then 67, became the youngest Tour player ever to shoot his age. It was no fluke. The next day he came in one stroke lower!

Snead played on eight Ryder Cup teams, and was captain in 1951 and '59.

He won the Vardon Trophy for lowest scoring average in 1938, '49, '50, and '55.

Sixty years later, Sam mimics his famous pose, this time behind the 18th green of The Homestead's Cascades Course.

Born Samuel Jackson Snead in Ashwood, Virginia, on May 27, 1912, he is shown here at age nine as a caddie at The Homestead.

In 1998, the PGA Tour honored him with a Lifetime Achievement award.

Snead brought his warm, homespun personality to everything he did. When his putting became even more problematic than usual, Snead described himself as having the "yips." The term is now an accepted part of a golfer's lexicon.

In the late 1960s, he began putting out of a croquet-style stance, straddling the ball with his legs and holding the top of the club in his left hand and placing his right hand well down the shaft.

When the PGA issued a rule that a player had to position both feet on one side of the ball, Snead adjusted again. He positioned the ball to the right of both feet, but stood with his body square to the line, not parallel to it. The "sidesaddle" approach was thus born.

Snead didn't care that no one else employed it. It was uniquely his, and it worked, enabling him to remain competitive for another few years.

Even now, people want to know how Snead could swing so effortlessly, yet so powerfully. What was he thinking? Could it be duplicated?

"Make your arms feel oily," he'd say. Or "Hold the club as if you were holding a baby bird." Or "Swing loose, like you're going to melt."

No matter how much he talked, or how much people listened, no one ever matched the grace and power of Snead's self-taught swing.

In 1994, *Golf* magazine attempted to help its readers duplicate Sam's swing. Its advice was to make practice swings while holding a beach ball between your knees. At the top of the swing, your knees should pinch the ball, holding it tightly. On the downswing, your knees should separate, dropping the ball before they come together again at the finish.

It all came naturally to Snead, which is why there's nothing like the real thing.

Snead was born in tiny Ashwood, Virginia, on May 27, 1912—three months after Byron Nelson, three months before Ben Hogan. The youngest of Henry and Laura Snead's six children, Snead grew up on a 250-acre farm just a couple of miles from the Cascades Course in Hot Springs. He still lives there part of the year, in a house that sits atop a hill overlooking a pond in full view of motorists using the one-lane road to The Homestead.

His first memories of golf start at age seven, when he'd go out into the fields and shag balls for his brother Homer. When the 19-year-old Homer balked at sharing his clubs with Sam, Snead had a plan. He tied an old club head to the end of a buggy whip and began swatting rocks around the property.

Not long after, Snead cut a stick out of the woods, trimmed the knots and all but a dozen inches of bark that he used as his "grip," and attached another old club head.

From the time he swung one of his homemade clubs, Snead expressed a preference for playing the game in his bare feet. He always felt that he could anchor himself better by digging his toes into the dirt.

One area where bare feet didn't help was in caddying. Snead started when he was nine and weighed 75 pounds. He kept the job throughout his teen years, walking the Cascades course barefoot—even in the snow—until a case of frostbite nearly cost him a couple of toes.

Unable to get onto the course to play, Snead took a couple of his mother's tomato cans and buried them in the pasture. Those became his "greens," and he spent hours hitting short shots at those cans, honing a wedge game that in later years was maybe the best in the business.

To improve his driving, he'd wallop rocks or balls over fence posts on the farm. After a while, distance didn't intrigue him as much as accuracy, so he began aiming at the fence posts. Soon, he could hit them with regularity.

And his famous draw was born out of necessity. On the family farm, there were mud puddles along the right side. If he hit too many balls over there, and came home too muddy, odds were he'd get a spanking.

Snead didn't buy his first set of clubs until he was 22 years old, and not all at once. He purchased his Bobby Jones Spalding irons one at a time, for $5 each, from the head pro at the Cascades. At the time, Snead was earning just $20 a month there as a "club mate," maintaining other people's clubs. But the job, seven days a week, 12 hours a day, afforded him a chance to play as much golf as he desired.

In 1936, the Cascades Hotel announced it was hosting an "open" golf tournament. Snead entered and finished third, earning $358.66. Watching the tournament was Fred Martin, manager of golf at The Greenbrier in White Sulphur Springs, West Virginia.

He offered Snead a job, only later admitting that he brought Sam to the resort with the idea of getting him the money to try the tour. It was the start of a relationship between Snead and the resort that exists even today.

A year after accepting Martin's offer, Snead joined the pro circuit. The game would never be the same.

"I started from nothing," Snead said. "I went to California with $300 in my pocket. Johnny Bulla told me, 'You're going to have to write home for some more money.'

"I said, 'What money?'"

At the 1937 Oakland Open, Snead found the Izett driver he used until 1970 in Henry Picard's bag. He swung the stiff, steel-shafted club a few times and Picard gave it to him. Snead joined the tour without a putter, picking one up out of barnstorming pro Leo Wallop's bag after Wallop challenged him to a friendly putting contest. Wallop sold it to him for $3.50.

THE SNEAD PERSONA

No one could tell stories like Snead. No one had more stories told about him.

Comic legend Bob Hope, a close friend of Snead's, once addressed Snead's longevity by quipping, "While I don't know the exact year he started,

I do know that at Sam's first pro tournament he was paid in Confederate money."

Rooming with Snead in Boston, Bulla once said that he spent half the night watching Snead walk across the floor on his hands. Why? He was hoping that by forcing more blood to his head, his follicles would be stimulated and he'd regain some of the hair he had lost at a relatively early age.

Whether true or not, Snead soon began wearing a snap-brim palmetto hat. It became his trademark and he rarely is without it, even today. It is so much a part of his makeup that, bareheaded, he could pass for any other fit, virile octogenarian. But once he reaches for that hat, something seems to come over him. He *becomes* Sam Snead, golf legend.

"A lot of con men walked off with pockets stuffed full of my money," Snead once wrote of his hair's early departure. "But none of them got a single strand to stand up and take notice."

At the awards ceremony following his victory in the 1949 PGA Championship at Hermitage Country Club in Richmond, Snead stunned the crowd by removing his palmetto when he was presented with the champion's diamond-studded gold medal. Behind him crept a photographer, anxious to get a rare shot of Snead's dome.

At the last minute, Snead sensed the man's presence and quickly replaced his hat. It was only after the embarrassed photographer told Snead, "OK, Sammy, I'll lay off," that Snead took it off again, drawing a huge roar of approval from his fans.

Cary Middlecoff walked in on Snead one day as he was polishing his golf shoes in the locker room. It was a task Snead gladly performed daily, but something other successful pros left to the clubhouse help. That was the beginning of Snead's legendary reputation for pinching pennies, as best summarized by agent and promoter Fred Corcoran:

"Walter Hagen is the first man to make a million dollars in golf and spend it. Snead is the first to make a million—and save two."

Sam stands behind seven of his Ryder Cup golf bags in his Hot Springs home. The walls are lined with photographs and other memorabilia of his amazing golf career.

Sam, left, with Johnny Farrell and Johnny Burke at the Cascades in Hot Springs in 1935.

THE '42 PGA:
A MAJOR BREAKTHROUGH

The 25th annual PGA Championship, being held at Seaview Country Club outside Atlantic City in 1942, would be America's only major tournament that year. All U.S. Golf Association events had been canceled because of World War II.

The week before, Snead stood in line at a Navy enlistment center. He had already passed his physical and was waiting to sign his papers. Although he had won 27 official tournaments, including the Bing Crosby Pro-Am three times, the first of six Miami Opens, and the first of a Tour-record eight Greater Greensboro Opens, none were considered majors.

Suddenly, Snead dropped out of line and approached a recruiter.

"I have a big golf meet next week. I want one more shot at a title before I go."

"We'll give you a pass for that, don't worry."

Snead eyed him warily. He had wife Audrey to think about, also a clause in his contract with Wilson Sporting Goods that paid him a $2,000 bonus for each major victory. He decided to postpone enlisting for a week.

Seaview was located near Fort Dix Army Base, and the GIs had several favorites in the field, including Cpl. Jim Turnesa.

Snead qualified for match play by shooting 73-71–144, six shots worse than medalist Harry Cooper. He made five consecutive birdies in the first round to defeat former New York Yankees outfielder Sam Parks 7 and 6. He beat Willie Goggin 9 and 8 in the second round to set up a quarterfinal match with PGA president Ed Dudley.

The match was spectacularly tight. Tied playing the final hole, Dudley's drive down the right side of the fairway hit a spectator on the head, then ricocheted into the trees. He had no chance to reach the green.

Snead pushed his drive as well, but played the ball safely back to the fairway, then onto the green.

After lagging a putt close to the hole, Dudley told him, "That's good, Sambo," and the match ended 1-up.

In the semifinals, Turnesa needed 37 holes to eliminate Nelson, while Snead took care of Jimmy Demaret 3 and 2.

In the final, with 7,000 soldiers rooting him on, Turnesa had a three-hole lead at the end of the morning 18, a cushion he maintained for the first five holes of the afternoon round.

On the 24th hole, Turnesa hooked twice into the rough and made bogey 5. Snead made par and closed to within two. Two holes later, Snead made birdie 3 to Turnesa's par. When Snead birdied the 520-yard ninth hole, 27th of the match, the two stood even.

Not for long. Snead gained the lead for the first time since the fourth hole of the morning round when he parred the 10th hole and Turnesa made bogey.

The momentum had shifted for good. Snead's tee shot on the 146-yard 12th hole was too strong, but hit a spectator standing behind the green and stopped rather than flying into the woods. Snead salvaged par; Turnesa made bogey and Sam led by two.

That was as close as Turnesa got. Snead made birdie by chipping into the hole on No. 17. He then conceded Turnesa's 40-foot putt for birdie to officially post a 2-and-1 victory.

"To me, that was the most satisfying tournament I ever won—and that includes the British Open and the Masters," Snead said. "I didn't know what was going to happen with the rest of my life. I didn't know where they were going to send me. I might be on ship. I might get knocked off. It could have been a once-in-a-lifetime experience."

Snead quickly returned to the recruiter to sign in and report for duty. He was curious. Would he really have been given a pass to play in the PGA?

"Negative, Snead."

Snead won the PGA on two other occasions,

in 1949 at Hermitage Country Club in Richmond (see "Making Memories") and in 1951 at Oakmont Country Club in Pennsylvania, where he beat Walter Burkemo 7 and 6 for the title.

The '51 victory was not without controversy. Snead and Marty Furgol were locked in a tight second-round match. On the 14th green, Snead suddenly bent over and began staring at his ball. Then he waved his hand over it. Seconds later, he blew on it.

When Furgol walked over, Snead calmly explained that he was shooing away a fly. Furgol shrugged and walked off—until they finished the match tied. Then he approached a rules official, claiming Snead had committed a violation by chasing the fly. He even filed a protest.

Although it was ruled that Snead had committed no violation, Furgol waited 30 minutes before dropping his protest and continuing play. Snead beat him by holing a five-foot birdie putt on the third extra hole.

BEATING THE BRITISH

In 1946, officials at Wilson Sporting Goods, who had Snead under contract, decided that he should pursue an international title. With the British Open being staged at St. Andrews, Snead felt pressured to enter, though his heart was hardly in it. He had been to England twice before, once for a British Open, once for Ryder Cup matches. Neither experience had been pleasant.

Huge crowds—"including women with perambulators," noted Reuters—descended on St. Andrews. In an unprecedented move, one the USGA wouldn't implement until the 1954 U.S. Open at Baltusrol in New Jersey, spectators were forbidden from walking the course with the players. Instead, Nazi war prisoners constructed high-rise bleachers that afforded patrons views of the course.

In another twist, the tournament was staged on two courses. Not only was the Old Course employed, the "new," or Egan, Course also saw service.

Snead opened with a 1-over-par 74 on the Egan Course. Reports of his round said that he had trouble judging his approaches, mis-clubbing much of the time. There was a reason for that, Snead said.

Sabotage.

"This man knew this woman who had some money," he recalled "And he went to her and said, 'Would you like to make some money real quick?' She said yeah, and he said, 'Bet on Snead.' That got to my caddie—Old Scotty—right away.

"We came to this par 3 and I said, 'What do you think?' And he says, '5-iron.' I said, 'That don't look like no 5-iron,' but he just says, '5-iron.' And if you don't take what the caddie tells you to, he just drops the bag. But I took an 8-iron and I put it about seven or eight feet from the hole.

"That sort of thing kept happening and this guy in the gallery finally tells me, 'Snead, that guy's trying to booger you.' I gave him a pound for the round and he didn't show up the next day."

Playing the Old Course the next day—and with his second caddie—Snead led all Americans with a 75 and 36-hole total of 149. That was four shots behind the medalist, Australian star Norman Von Nida.

In the following day's first round, pre-tournament favorite Bobby Locke fired a record-setting 4-under-par 69. Von Nida and Henry Cotton were one shot back; Snead, Johnny Bulla, and Joe Kirkwood trailed by two.

Cotton led Snead—now employing his third caddie—by one stroke heading into the 36-hole final.

"I finally got a guy and I told him, 'Son, I don't want you to tell me how far it is. I don't want you to tell me where the wind is. I don't want you to even open your mouth. All I want is for you to have my clubs at my ball when I get there.' "

High winds the final day sent scores soaring. Snead kept his shots low and true and came home at 1-over-par 74 in the morning, 2-over 75 in the afternoon, to whip Bulla and Locke by four shots. Snead was brilliant down the stretch, playing the final nine holes in 2 under par.

Sam Snead checks a grip on his club during his first U.S. Open in 1937.

Disgusted with his poor putting, Snead developed and started using the croquet-style method during the 1966 PGA, and immediately started putting better. In 1968, the USGA outlawed the practice, so Sam adopted the sidesaddle stance.

Prize money was a mere 150 pounds ($600 at the time). Snead estimates that it cost him $2,000 for the trip, which made appearing at another British Open a moot point. And one final incident with a caddie just underscored in Snead's mind that he and the British Open weren't meant for each other.

"When the final round is over, the caddie begs me for the ball," Snead remembered. "So I give it to him and he says, "Oh, thank you, I love this. I'll never forget you.'

"The next morning, there's this guy sitting in the hotel lobby. It isn't even light yet. He's got my ball and he says to me, 'Would you please sign this? I paid the caddie 50 dollars for it.' "

OPEN WOUNDS

Anyone with even a passing knowledge of golf knows that Snead never won the U.S. Open. It is the game's single most compelling tale of futility. But what isn't nearly as well known is his overall record in the event. In 31 appearances over a 40-year span, he finished second four times, third once, fifth twice, and in the top 10 on five other occasions.

More than one of those heartbreaking losses has taken its place among the most dramatic events in the history of the sport.

Entering the 1937 Open at Oakland Hills in Michigan, Snead was the second-leading money winner. Even though he'd played in just seven pro tournaments, he had won two—Oakland and the Crosby.

Tied for second heading into the final round, Snead finished with a 72-hole total of 283 after an eagle 3 on the 18th hole. In the clubhouse, Tommy Armour told him, "Laddie, you've just won yourself a championship worth more than a seat on the Stock Exchange."

But Ralph Guldahl, playing many groups behind Snead, also eagled the final hole to come in at 281, a record Open score that wouldn't be touched until Ben Hogan's 276.

"I never went up to the U.S. Open again without thinking, 'Now don't look like the fool you did

in 1937,' " Snead wrote in 1986. "And every time, that way of thinking beat me before I got to the first tee. If I had won that '37 title, I believe I'd have knocked over my other three close calls and likely a few more besides."

Two years later, on the Spring Mill course of Philadelphia Country Club, Snead needed to par the final two holes to take home the trophy. Or so he thought.

The on-course scoreboard hadn't been invented yet. Word of mouth was a player's only way of knowing where he stood in relation to the field.

Snead guessed that his primary competition was Johnny Bulla, who led by one after 54 holes, Byron Nelson, Craig Wood, and Denny Shute. Nelson was in the clubhouse at 284, higher than Snead calculated. Wood and Shute were playing behind Snead and floundering. He had no way of knowing that. Preparing to tee off on 17, a par 4, Snead had taken only 272 swings.

Playing aggressively, Snead put his approach shot into the rough and made bogey.

The 18th was a 550-yard par 5. There were no fairway ropes. Hundreds of spectators streamed toward him from the clubhouse, creating a jam on the fairway that Snead estimated took 30 minutes to clear. Despite the delay, he still didn't know Nelson's score. No one in the gallery informed him, though Snead said someone told playing partner Ed Dudley.

Mistakenly thinking that he needed a birdie to avoid a playoff with Nelson, Snead hooked his drive into rough that had been trampled by the gallery, 260 yards from the green. Instead of playing out into the fairway, Snead gambled, and lost. He didn't get his 2-wood cleanly on the ball, catching only the top half. The ball splashed down just beneath the lip of a fairway bunker 100 yards from the green.

Snead entered the bunker with his 8-iron—and proceeded to leave the ball in the trap, embedded between two freshly laid pieces of sod. His blast out traveled only 60 yards, into another bunker. He lay four.

Only then did Snead become aware of Nelson's score. Now he had to get down in two to force a playoff. Shaken and angry, he splashed his shot onto the green, but 40 feet past the cup.

The putt for a playoff slithered three feet past. Snead admitted he went numb. He finished the hole with a triple-bogey 8. Nelson won the title by beating Wood in a playoff.

"That was my most disappointing one," Snead said. "All those people and no one said a thing."

That infamous 8 at Spring Mill clung to Snead like lint, surfacing in triumph and tribulation. The night Snead won the 1949 Masters by three shots over Lloyd Mangrum, Atlanta columnist O.B. Keeler wrote: "The story behind it all dates back a decade, to the United States Open at Spring Mill . . . I was there, and I wondered if Sammy Snead could ever come back after that."

Spring Mill may have been the most disappointing, but there were a couple other near-misses that were every bit as dramatic.

One happened 10 years later at St. Louis Country Club against another Virginian, Lew Worsham. (That tournament—the famous "tape measure" Open—is covered in the "Major Champions" section on Worsham.)

In the 1949 Open, Snead had a chance to tie Cary Middlecoff and force a playoff at Medinah outside Chicago.

Middlecoff finished the final round at 2-over-par 286, right about the time Snead was making the turn at 4 over and tied with Clayton Heafner.

Although he had been mired in a putting slump, Snead suddenly caught fire with the blade. He birdied two of the first five holes to grab a share of the lead. After making pars on the 15th and 16th holes, Snead faced the dangerous 17th, a 230-yard par 3, most of it over water.

This day, it played into the wind. Snead hit a good tee shot, but the ball hung in the air and landed on the front of the green, then sucked down an incline and off the putting surface.

He faced a choice: putt or chip. He chose to putt through the apron, slowing the ball as it reached the hole. Historians later said the ball was sitting in a small depression Snead never noticed. Some say he would have played the same shot anyway and just missed it. Either way, the ball popped into the air, flew over most of the apron and rolled eight feet past the hole. He missed the par-saver coming back and now needed to birdie 18.

He couldn't do it, as his approach bounced through the green and his chip back stopped a couple of feet short. He tapped in for par and 287, one shot more than Middlecoff.

In 1953 at Oakmont Country Club near Pittsburgh, Snead was second by a stroke to Ben Hogan entering the final round, but shot 76 and lost by six.

Give the man credit. He never stopped believing he could do it.

Chandler Harper tells how, in 1971, he recruited Snead to represent the United States in the World Seniors Championship at the Bide-A-Wee course in Portsmouth, Virginia. Snead agreed, but asked that a clause be placed in the contract.

He wanted to be allowed out of his appearance if he qualified for the World Series of Golf. The only way Snead, then 58 years old, could qualify was to win one of the four majors that year.

"I don't reckon it's impossible," Harper, then 56, said at the time, "but it seems that way to me."

Back at Oakmont in 1973, the 61-year-old Snead made the cut and shot 295, 16 strokes behind winner Johnny Miller. At Winged Foot in 1974, Snead was so pleased with his practice rounds that he talked confidently of winning. Then he began having severe chest pains and thought he was having a heart attack. Tests revealed he was playing despite two ribs broken in an accident at his farm in Hot Springs.

He played his final Open in 1977 at Southern Hills in Oklahoma on an exemption from the USGA, which wanted to commemorate the 40th anniversary of his first Open appearance.

"I never understood it. I'd get a bad kick, or this, that, or the other," Snead said in 1999. "Oftentimes, things happened that were beyond my control. Palmer never won the PGA. Nicklaus never won at L.A. I guess there's always one."

A MASTERS TO REMEMBER

Maybe it was the way he endured the misery of those many Open close calls. There is no picture of Snead in defeat in which he isn't wearing a game smile or extending warm congratulations to his opponent.

"I always thought of myself as a case of predestination," Snead said in a 1999 interview. "If I won, fine. If I lost, that was fine, too. I wasn't going to let it eat me alive. That's what it did to a lot of players, and they were never much good after that."

Maybe it was that loose, fluid swing, or the way it sent the ball scalding farther down the fairway than almost anybody. Maybe people believed all those homespun stories, though many were undoubtedly true.

"They love him, maybe, because he misses those 10-inch putts when the pressure is on, just as the rest of us do," wrote columnist Ed Danforth. "Snead is less of a machine than his fellow practitioners of the fairways and therefore closer to the thundering galleries."

Whatever the reason, Snead was the fan favorite during the early part of his fierce rivalry with Ben Hogan.

That changed in 1949 after Hogan's near-fatal auto accident on a foggy road in West Texas. He worked tirelessly to regain the strength in legs that had been crushed in that collision with a bus. Still weaker than his doctors would have liked, Hogan nonetheless shocked the golf world when he entered the 1950 Los Angeles Open, just 11 months after the crash.

Remarkably, Hogan finished at 280, 4 under par, and appeared to have won the tournament. The fans were ecstatic. Then Snead birdied the final two holes to force a tie, beating Hogan in a playoff that was delayed a week so everyone could play in the Crosby.

Snead may have won the playoff. Hogan won the public's heart.

Snead had the greatest season of his career in 1950, winning 11 tournaments and leading the tour in earnings with $35,000. His stroke average for 96 tournament rounds was 69.2.

Hogan won only once, albeit at the U.S. Open. Nonetheless, he was named player of the year, an award for which Snead figured to be a shoo-in.

"I just couldn't do any better than I did that year," Snead said. "The way things happened took a little of my heart out of the game."

It didn't show, especially during Masters week.

Snead had won at Augusta National in 1949. Hogan had won in 1951. Snead won in '52. Hogan won in 1953.

Then came 1954, and perhaps the greatest Masters ever.

Snead got off to a shaky start, posting a 2-over 74 to trail 31-year-old amateur Billy Joe Patton by four shots and Hogan by a pair.

Patton, a father of three who worked in the lumber business, set a record the next day when his 36-hole total of 144 made him the first amateur to hold the Masters lead at the midpoint.

Hogan was just a stroke off the pace. Snead had closed to three behind after a 73 that included three consecutive three-putts on the front nine.

Hogan, "the man with the white hat and the porcelain personality," as one writer described him, took the lead after 54 holes with a 69, the first sub-70 round of the tournament. Patton ballooned to a 75. Snead moved into second, three shots off the pace.

Patton didn't quit. After making bogey 5 to open the final round, the North Carolinian played the next eight holes in 5 under par that included a hole-in-one on No. 6. Patton was tied with Hogan, both three ahead of Snead.

Patton made bogey 4 after hitting his tee shot over the green on No. 12. Then he collapsed. With the gallery beseeching him to go for the green with his second shots on the par-5 13th and 15th holes—and Patton exuberantly shouting back to them, "I am! I am!"—he put both shots in the water. He made double-bogey at 13, bogey at 15, and finished one shot out of the Snead-Hogan playoff that was created when both finished at 289—still the highest winning score in Masters history.

Called "the match of the century" by the press, it may well have been.

Neither man enjoyed more than a one-stroke lead.

There were six lead changes.

Hogan missed one green. Snead missed just two, including one at what turned out to be the pivotal hole of the match.

The 10th hole at Augusta National is a 485-yard par 4 with the green tucked in the far back left. They were tied when Snead's approach with a 6-iron flew slightly over the green. Hogan was on, figuring to make par and take the lead. But Snead, hitting the 6-iron again, slammed a pitch-and-run into the cup for birdie and what became a one-stroke lead.

In an unprecedented display of emotion, Hogan watched Snead's shot fall, then turned away and gave a barely perceptible laugh.

"I chuckled when Snead chipped in for birdie, but I'm afraid the chuckle was insincere," Hogan said. "Where it looked like I had the advantage, it was a great lift for Snead. It not only allowed him to withstand what pressure I tried to apply, but fixed him where he could turn the pressure on me."

A crowd estimated at 8,000 was awed by the precision shot-making of the two men. Both went for the green in two at 15, Hogan requiring a 4-wood. Snead used a 3-iron. Both made birdie.

On the par-3 16th, Hogan almost made an ace, the ball just missing the pin but rolling about 15 feet past the hole. Snead's tee shot stopped 25 feet from the flag, and his lag putt left him seven feet from par.

Then Hogan blinked, literally stubbing his putter into the ground before making contact with the ball. His putt was three feet short.

Now it was Snead's turn.

"I'm standing over that putt, about to take the club back, and someone suddenly yells from across the water, '*Miss it!*'" Snead remembered. "And everyone—everyone—turned to look at this guy to see who would do such a thing. I had to back off and start all over.

"I looked over at that guy and I muttered, 'You mean son of a gun,' but I tapped it in."

Hogan's turn. He blinked again, missing the par-saver.

"I was so intent on the line of the putt that I made a faulty stroke, hitting the ground behind the ball," Hogan admitted later. "Then I just missed again."

Now Snead led by two shots with two holes to play.

At the 400-yard 17th, Hogan hit a poor drive, just past the Eisenhower Tree, leaving him a long iron to the green. Snead blew the ball past his competitor but was shocked to find that it had rolled into a deep, dry divot.

Instead of the half-wedge he normally would have played, Snead used a 6-iron to burrow through two inches of sod and dirt before making contact with the ball. He gouged it out brilliantly, putting it in the center of the green, 18 feet from the hole. Both made par, Hogan leaving a 10-foot try for birdie seven inches short.

Snead dodged another bullet at 18. His tee shot landed just short of a water sprinkler in the middle of the fairway. When he reached it, the ball was covered with mud. Putting his foot down on the other side of the sprinkler, water rose over the top of Snead's shoe. He couldn't stand near the ball without water bubbling to the surface, but when he backed away, it subsided. Snead sought relief from an official.

"You must see water, Sam, not make water," Snead recalls being told. He argued, to no avail, then hit a 3-iron shot that bounced on the right side of the green and skipped into a bunker. Hogan was 25 feet short of the green with his approach, chipped up to seven feet, and made par.

When Snead executed a splendid blast to within five feet, he could afford the luxury of a two-putt bogey. With it came his last "major" title, though it was hardly the end of the story.

"The finest exhibition of precision shot-making you ever saw," Masters founder and legend Bobby Jones said at the awards ceremony, drawing a loud ovation. "I saw the play on every hole, and I never saw two golfers give a finer performance under severe stress."

Five years before the epic showdown with Hogan, Snead made Masters history of another kind.

After beating Johnny Bulla and Lloyd Mangrum by three shots, Snead was shocked when he was helped into a green jacket during the winner's presentation. It was the first time the Masters' champion had been so honored. Before that, only members of Augusta National wore green jackets, so that they could be easily spotted by patrons seeking help.

Although Snead captured the Masters three times, he received just one green jacket—at least initially.

"Somehow, my first coat was misplaced," he recalled. "I wore Bobby Jones' coat from then on. The sleeves were about four inches too short, so I finally got a new one in 1994."

A REALLY BIG SHOW

The 1965 Greater Greensboro Open at Sedgefield Country Club was dedicated to Snead in recognition of his 25th appearance. He had won the inaugural event in 1938 and on six other occasions.

At a testimonial banquet the week of the tournament, 800 patrons heard television star and master of ceremonies Ed Sullivan describe Snead as a man "with the color that distinguishes champions."

Snead, 52 years, 10 months old, told the audience that he didn't expect to win, but he warned the younger players, "You better watch out."

By the 36-hole cut, they knew exactly what he meant. After rounds of 3-under-par 68 and 2-under 69, Snead shared the midway lead with Billy Casper. Snead's putter was working as well as it had in years. He rolled in a 40-foot putt for birdie on the 11th hole and a 45-footer for birdie on No. 12.

"Anytime I three-putt just once in 36 holes, it's wonderful," Snead exclaimed. "I'm just hoping that my putting will hold up until I get the rest of my game smoothed. It's a little jerky."

No problem.

Snead made only one bogey Saturday in shooting a 3-under 68, two strokes better than rookie Labron Harris Jr. and four ahead of Casper and Phil Rodgers.

Sunday was the perfect Sam Snead Day in Sam Snead Week.

A 3-under-par 68 gave Snead an 11-under total of 273, five shots ahead of the rest of the field. He had just become the oldest player to win a PGA Tour event.

"This is terrific, just great," Casper said. "I think it's wonderful to win it at a time like this."

Snead all but clinched the tournament in the sweetest manner possible, holing a 60-foot putt for birdie on the 13th hole, just when Casper, Harris, and Rodgers seemed to be gaining on him.

"I'm about as far from the pin as you can get—from China to Japan," said Snead, who had three-putted 10 and 11 and worried that he wouldn't have enough touch to last the round. "I just wanted to get up close. I just wanted to get down in two. I whacked that thing and when it went in, I just said, 'Holy cow.'"

It was his last official PGA Tour triumph, but it was just the beginning of yet another amazing chapter in Snead's life.

Starting in 1964, Snead would win 14 Senior PGA Tour titles. None of them count toward his victory total. All of them helped the Senior Tour become one of the most remarkable success stories in sports history.

At the 1973 PGA Senior Championship in Palm Beach Gardens, Florida, Snead fired four sub-70 rounds for a 20-under score of 268 and a 15-shot spread over runner-up Julius Boros.

The margin of victory, like Snead and his illustrious career, has never been matched.

The scorecard from Sam's record 59, shot at the Greenbrier on May 16, 1959.

major champions

Curtis and wife Sarah snuggle up to the trophy from
Strange's 1988 U.S. Open victory.

CURTIS STRANGE

Curtis Strange received golf's equivalent of a lifetime achievement award on Oct. 25, 1999, when the PGA of America named him captain of the 2001 Ryder Cup team.

While it was just reward for a 20-year career in which he became the first player since Ben Hogan to win back-to-back U.S. Opens with his triumphs at The Country Club in 1988 and Oak Hill in '89, Strange's achievements are more diversified than that.

After all, since the Ryder Cup began in 1927, five players have won two or more U.S. Opens and *not* been asked to be captain.

Strange, born in Norfolk, raised in Virginia Beach and Portsmouth, and now the touring pro for Kingsmill Golf Club in Williamsburg, has won 19 other tournaments throughout the world.

Before turning pro in 1976, Strange won the 1974 NCAA championship and All-American honors at Wake Forest University. He won the prestigious Western Amateur. He won the North & South at Pinehurst No. 2. He was a member of the victorious 1975 Walker Cup team.

In Virginia, he won the State Junior Championship in 1970 and 1972 and the State Amateur in 1974 and 1975.

Strange played on five Ryder Cup teams. In 1988, he became the first player to win more than $1 million in a season. He holds the record on the Old Course at St. Andrews with a 10-under-par 62 recorded in the 1987 Dunhill Cup.

"His dedication to the game of golf, the impact he has made in major championships, his Ryder Cup experience, and his relationship with players makes him the ideal individual to captain," PGA of America president Will Mann said in introducing Strange.

"He possesses a combination of intensity and courage that will serve as an example for his team in golf's most compelling competition."

During his remarkable two-year reign as Open champion—and, many said, the world's best golfer—Strange's life story was well documented.

His father, Tom, won the State Open five times and is enshrined in the Middle Atlantic PGA Hall of Fame and the Virginia Sports Hall of Fame.

Once an assistant to Sam Snead at The Greenbrier in West Virginia, Strange

Curtis pauses at home on the practice range at
Kingsmill Resort in Williamsburg.

Curtis Strange takes a seat during a round at the Anheuser-Busch Golf Classic (now the Michelob Championship) in 1989.

brought his family back to Hampton Roads to take over the White Sands Country Club in Virginia Beach. Now a public course known as Bow Creek, the place holds many fond memories for Curtis and identical twin Allan.

"I enjoyed everything I did when we went to the golf course," Strange said. "We always had a bunch of juniors to hang out with. We had fun. Dad was big into junior golf. Golf as a kid by yourself is kind of boring and slow, but to have people to spend your time with, that was a lot of fun."

Strange smiles wistfully when he says he liked to think, "I practiced 10 hours a day . . ."

He didn't. Oh, he got in plenty of golf, but Strange also did fun things. He worked around the pro shop. He foraged for lost balls and sold them to his father for some spending money. He ran carts. He raked traps. He learned what it was like to be a local golf pro from the ground up.

When Strange was 14, his father died of cancer. By then Curtis was in love with golf, though not ready to devote himself entirely to it. His mother, Nancy, phoned Chandler Harper, winner of the 1950 PGA Championship and family friend, and asked if he would continue teaching her son where Tom had left off.

"I remember I was so nervous waiting to hear what he said," Strange said during a visit to Portsmouth in 1989. "He told her he would be glad to do it."

Today, Harper downplays his sphere of influence. He took the fundamentals Tom Strange already had ingrained in his son and reinforced them.

14

"All he needed was the confidence that comes from winning," Harper said. "He had everything else."

He certainly had the desire.

"Even back in high school, you could see that burning desire in his eyes to succeed," said Richard Tucker, a teammate on the 1972-73 Princess Anne High School golf team that won the state title. "When Curtis was 13 or 14, he'd practice at Princess Anne Country Club for hours and hours. I'd see him on the practice range when I'd go out to play 18 holes. He'd still be there, hitting balls, after I finished my round."

The other great influence in Strange's life was Wake Forest coach Jesse Haddock. Friend and fellow Virginian Lanny Wadkins recruited Strange to Wake Forest, dangling the Bud Worsham Scholarship begun by Arnold Palmer.

Haddock knew how to shape the teen's thought process and his discipline. Strange considers his guidance to have been invaluable.

"He was the perfect guy at the time for me," Strange said. "For three years, he was a father figure for me. He disciplined me when I was away at school, kept me on the straight and narrow. We were college kids, and he was the true trainer for the rest of our life.

"He'd say and do things I still remember. He was good for me psychologically, which I didn't know at the time. I didn't know how good I could be. I think he knew I could be good, but he also knew I couldn't stray too much. He was good for how you thought on the golf course and for how you handled pressure."

Strange's appreciation of golf as a team sport, an essential in his role as Ryder Cup captain, grew from his relationship with Haddock.

"Wake had had tremendous teams over the years and never won an NCAA title," Strange said. "So when I won the individual and we won the team, we were as happy for the team as I was for me.

"He instilled in us that you had better be thinking about the team, none of this individual stuff. I made a mistake my freshman year when I asked him how the individual part of some tournament stood. That was the last time I ever did that. That was good, because there's more than enough individual stuff later on."

Strange still calls college golf "the most fun I've ever had." His victory in the NCAA tournament at Wilmington Country Club in Delaware as a freshman featured the epitome of the clutch pressure shot. On the final hole, Strange hit a 1-iron eight feet from the cup and made the eagle putt that gave him and the Demon Deacons a one-shot triumph.

"I didn't think much about it then, but down deep, I knew I could play with the best," he said. "The NCAA is as tough a tournament as there is to win."

The following week, Strange arrived in Benton Harbor, Michigan, for the Western Amateur. Strange was medalist after 72 holes of stroke play. After the 72 holes of match play that followed, he was champion.

"That was a grand two weeks for me," Strange said. "I think everyone who gets to the college level and progresses starts to think about the pros. I can't point to a specific day I started thinking about it. It was a gradual feeling, but those two weeks certainly fed into it."

Strange already had won 13 times in his career before the 1988 Memorial. He already had played on three Ryder Cup teams. He already had won PGA Tour money titles in 1985 and '87. He was an accomplished, veteran professional in the midst of a memorable career.

In general, that isn't how people saw him. Their memories were stuck on the 1985 Masters. After opening with an 80 that left him 75th in a field of 77, Strange roared back into contention with an unforgettable 65 on Friday and a 68 on Saturday.

Four holes into the final round, he took the lead. By the time he reached the back nine, he had played his last 45 holes in 15 under par to open a four-shot advantage.

Then he bogeyed the 10th and the par-5 13th when he hit his second shot into Rae's Creek. They were damaging blows, but nothing like the next par 5, the 15th.

Only 200 yards from the green with the wind at his back, Strange striped a 4-iron so solidly that he told himself, 'You're not supposed to hit shots this good.'"

But the ball never made it to the green. It landed short and in the water, leading to another bogey and, ultimately, a two-shot loss to Bernhard Langer.

Not long after, Jack Nicklaus told Strange the '85 Masters would either make or break him. Strange answered the question by winning eight times leading up to the 1988 Memorial Tournament in Dublin, Ohio.

Then he fired a 5-under-par 67 in the final round to win that tournament by two shots over Hale Irwin and David Frost.

"He's absolutely the best player in the world right now," Irwin volunteered to the media. He likened playing against Strange to "running into a buzz saw."

Frost's opinion was slightly more temperate.

"It's a toss-up between Curtis and [Greg] Norman," he said, when asked who was best.

That was not something the golf world necessarily wanted to hear. Nicklaus spoke the obvious when he said Strange was a terrific player "but he has to win a major. I think he will."

Strange was completely at ease with the argument, but he dodged it like a man trying to walk across a Los Angeles freeway.

"Sure, some people questioned it, and rightfully so," Strange said. "How could I be the best player in the world when I hadn't won a major? It was something I'd been leading up to for a couple of years, but I hadn't done it."

Three weeks later, Strange arrived at The Country Club in Brookline, Massachusetts, site of the famous 1913 Open in which Francis Ouimet beat back the British charge of Harry Vardon and Ted Ray.

Curtis celebrates his Open victory at The Country Club in Brookline, Massachusetts, in 1988.

Strange immediately fell for the place, calling it "a great place to play golf every day. It really flowed."

Most of his memories of 1988 begin on the last few holes of regulation on Sunday. Strange, paired with Britain's Nick Faldo, took the lead with a par at the 16th hole.

At the par-4 17th, he hit a 9-iron approach 12 feet from the hole. The only problem was that he was 12 feet *above* the hole. He hadn't putted from there all week, even in practice.

"Hubert Green told me a couple of weeks later that he knew I was in trouble when I put it there," Strange said. "It was a new green, and it was actually faster than the other greens. The putt got away a little, but I never thought it would go four or five feet past.

"I openly admit I was in shock after that."

He lapsed into something worse than shock after he missed the comeback putt for par, tossing away his hard-earned lead.

"I missed the next putt because I broke one of the first rules I ever learned," he said. "I didn't forget—I couldn't forget—about the previous putt."

Strange's tee shot at 18 landed in the rough. Preferring to be in a bunker guarding the front edge of the green than hit over the green and have a tricky downhill chip for a third shot, Strange chose a 7-iron and found the sand.

Meanwhile, Faldo was on in two, 35 feet from the hole.

"That bunker shot was the most critical shot of my life," Strange said. "If I don't hit that, I don't have a chance to hit any good shots on Monday because I lose."

Strange said the bunker shot was not as difficult as it looked on television, at least not physically.

Mentally, he might as well have been trying to climb a mountain with a toothpick.

"The only thing not easy about it is that it was on the 72nd hole of the U.S. Open and I'm tied for the lead," he said.

In the time it takes to turn off a lamp, Strange calmed himself. An inner voice kept reminding him that he had played this shot hundreds of times, that he was playing well, that it wasn't far-fetched to think he could hole it for a birdie.

With a single, precise stroke, Strange sent the ball flying from the sand to tap-in range for an easy par and a tie. He and Faldo would return on Monday for another 18 holes.

Strange never trailed in the playoff, taking a two-shot lead through 11 holes. That's not to say that there weren't some anxious moments.

Faldo birdied the 12th to narrow the deficit to one. Moments later, Strange faced a delicate 30-foot downhill putt for birdie on No. 13. He envisioned it breaking right to left, then tensed up when the ball drifted left of the hole almost immediately after he hit it.

"I got a little lucky," he said. "It suddenly straightened itself out and got back on the path to the hole. You're not trying to make 30-footers in the U.S. Open. I was just trying to get it close."

Moments after the ball plunged into the hole, Faldo missed a par-saving putt. In a wink, Strange's lead had ballooned to three, which is how it finished.

"I remember how supportive the people of Boston were," Strange said. "I'd gotten a couple of phone calls Sunday night telling me not to be disappointed when there weren't too many people out there for the playoff."

Instead, 25,000 golf fanatics played hooky from work to follow Strange and Faldo. There was emotion there that Strange never expected, and he fed off it.

"I have to thank my dad," Strange said at the start of a brief victory speech. "This is for him—and that's all I can say. I've waited a long time to do that. I screwed up the '85 Masters, and I'm as disappointed by that as anything."

The next year at Oak Hill was a totally different experience. Again, Strange loved the course. He

Not long after he finished play in the 1999 Michelob Championship at Kingsmill, Curtis Strange was named Ryder Cup captain for 2001.

had performed well there in the 1980 PGA Championship that Nicklaus had captured by seven shots.

"All I asked was to give myself a chance," Strange said. "I didn't go in there the hot prospect. I went in as the defending champion, a guy playing decent golf. The media hype about repeating wasn't that big because it had been so long since someone had done it. It was like, 'Hey, if Nicklaus, Palmer, and Watson weren't able to do it, why should he?' "

Strange trailed by four strokes after the first round, then got everyone's attention with a sizzling 64 on Friday that pushed him to a one-shot lead.

"I never thought Oak Hill had a 64 in it, honest to God," he said. "Not in me, not in anybody. I just got going and, as we all say, it should have been better. Even so, it was a special day, one that put me in position to close at the end."

In tying the course record set, amazingly, by Hogan, Strange posted nine 3s on the par-70 Robert Trent Jones design. He hit 16 greens in regulation and made his sixth career eagle in Open competition by holing a shot from 115 yards.

However, Saturday wasn't such a special day. Oak Hill had taken so much rain that some of its fairways were flooded. The U.S. Golf Association was forced to call in the Rochester Fire Department to pump water from the fairway into a creek that ran away from the golf course.

"My recollection is that this is the worst string of days we've ever had," said USGA executive director P.J. Boatwright, who referred to the eighth fairway as "the Mississippi River. I've never seen a course as damaged as this one."

Strange wasn't up to fighting the conditions, or a cranky putter. He shot a sloppy 3-over 73 and trailed Tom Kite by three shots with 18 holes left.

What worried Strange about his position wasn't that he trailed, but *whom* he trailed. He respected Kite's game. He thought the bespectacled Texan was destined to win a major. Past experience had taught him that Kite wasn't the type to give tournaments away.

"I thought it would be tough to beat him," Strange said.

He was right about all but the last part. Kite took himself out of the Open with a final-round 78 that included a triple-bogey 7 on the 405-yard fifth hole.

Two holes ahead of Kite, Strange had just made par when he heard the unmistakable groan that comes when the gallery following the leader has just witnessed a disaster. As he made his way to the eighth tee, Strange overheard someone mention the word "triple."

"I asked [caddie] Greg Rita if it was true that Tom had tripled, and he said he would try to find out," Strange said.

Rita waited until after Strange hit his tee shot on No. 8 before confirming Kite's plight.

"We just sort of buttoned down then and said the game was on," Strange said. "Tom had played right into my hands."

While Kite continued to fade, new challengers surfaced in Chip Beck, Ian Woosnam, Mark McCumber, Jumbo Ozaki, and Scott Simpson.

Strange held them off by grinding out par after par, protecting a one-shot advantage until the 16th hole. There, he rolled in a 15-footer for his first birdie in 36 holes.

"That gave me so much more confidence to play 17, the toughest hole on the course," Strange said. "I hadn't made par there all week, but I made par that day."

Armed with a two-shot lead and with all of his closest competitors already in the clubhouse, Strange made an "intentional bogey" at the home hole to win by one over Beck, Woosnam, and McCumber.

"Move over, Ben," an elated Strange said, causing a mild stir among purists who thought the comment was flippant.

"I meant it in good fun, not as any sort of disrespect," Strange said. "I was answering the first question I was asked (What would you say to Ben

Curtis Strange warms up for an exhibition at the redesigned Bide-A-Wee in Portsmouth, on which he consulted.

Hogan if he was here?). I got more than a few letters about it from people who said they were offended."

His '88 triumph was a tribute to his father and the past. His '89 victory was reserved for the present.

"This one's for Sarah, Thomas, and David," Strange said, referring to his wife and their two sons. "They're as much a part of my winning this golf tournament as anybody because you sacrifice a lot to play this Tour. I've made sacrifices being away from them; they've made sacrifices having me be away."

It's easy to play "what if," but Strange came amazingly close to winning four Opens.

In 1987 at Olympic Club in San Francisco, he was in contention entering the final nine holes and finished tied for fourth.

"A good friend of mine was on the 10th tee," Strange revealed for the first time after his 1988 win at The Country Club. "I felt like if I would have shot even par the last nine holes, I would have been very close. But when I got to No. 10—obviously, the Open ends on Father's Day each year—my friend said to me, 'Win this for your dad.'

"Well, I went to the 10th tee with tears in my eyes. I didn't want that to happen again. I was not going to let it slip away for reasons I could control, and I could control my emotions."

All he needed was a decent final round at the 1990 Open at Medinah Country Club to put himself in contention for No. 4. Instead, he shot 75 and later said that he knew it was over midway through the back nine when he missed the green with a 4-iron shot he normally would have nailed.

"I didn't have it that last day," he said. "People can never grasp what went through me leaving Medinah that night. I had a legitimate chance to win three straight Opens."

Strange has long admitted that something inside of him flickered and died that final day at Medinah. He hasn't won since then, though he rebounded strongly enough in 1995 to finish 49th on the money list and make the Ryder Cup as Lanny Wadkins' captain's choice.

Losing the critical match to Faldo turned out to be the second-most disappointing experience of his career, right behind the '85 Masters.

Yet his career has been much bigger than a couple of Open triumphs or a couple of mind-numbing, heartbreaking defeats.

"Your priorities change," Strange said before the 1999 Open at Pinehurst. "It's no longer No. 1 in your life. It's still hard to accept, but you can't fight it all the time. You can't live your life fighting it.

"This isn't a sad story, a feel-sorry-for-Curtis story. This is a happy story."

A young Curtis Strange gets some hardware after winning the 12-13 age group at the 1967 Virginia State Junior Tournament.

major champions

Lanny Wadkins had an auspicious debut on the PGA Senior
Tour in 2000, winning the first tournament he entered.

LANNY WADKINS

Lanny Wadkins attacks golf as though it were a game of Monopoly. He rolls the dice, gobbles up as much as he can as quickly as he can, makes his opponents pay for their mistakes, and gives nothing away.

From 1972 to 1999, Wadkins rode that daredevil philosophy to a brilliant career that included winning the 1977 PGA Championship in the first sudden-death playoff in a major championship. He also captured 20 other tournaments on courses considered the toughest on Tour to tame.

He appeared in nine Ryder Cups, including one as captain in 1995. He won nearly $7 million and a well-deserved reputation as a fierce competitor. And he crashed the Senior Tour in February 2000 with a victory in the first event he entered.

"My greatest strength was my tenacity," said Wadkins, who was born and raised in Richmond. "I stayed after it. I won a lot of tournaments from three, four, five shots behind. I played medal-play golf with a match-play mentality. If I got the lead by two, I wanted to lead by three. If I got to three, I wanted to lead by four."

He began the last round of his final PGA Tour victory, at the 1992 Canon Greater Hartford Open, five shots behind Donnie Hammond. He shot a 5-under-par 65 to swoop past Hammond, Nick Price, and Dan Forsman and win by two.

He birdied five of the last nine holes to force a sudden-death playoff he won in 1973 at the Byron Nelson Classic at Preston Trail in Dallas.

In 1982, he overtook Tom Kite by shooting a 7-under-par 65 in the final round to win the Buick Open with what was then a tournament-record 15-under 273.

The following year in Greensboro, Wadkins again birdied five of the last nine holes to clobber defending Masters champion Craig Stadler and Dennis Watson by five.

"Lanny hit some of the most incredible shots I've ever seen," Watson said that day. "I thought he was going to pitch everything in."

That's funny. Most of the time, Lanny did, too.

Three weeks after beating Stadler in a playoff at the 1985 Bob Hope Classic,

Lanny Wadkins, a Richmond native, represents Williamsburg's Golden Horseshoe on the PGA Senior Tour.

Wadkins fired a 7-under-par 64 at Riviera in Los Angeles. He finished with a seven-shot win and a tournament record of 20 under par.

At the time, he was just the ninth golfer in PGA Tour history to pass $2 million in career earnings.

"I never let up if I had the lead," Wadkins said. "I'd set little goals for myself from hole to hole, knowing that if I could accomplish those goals, I would definitely win the tournament."

Those goals, short-term and long, began at a tender age. So did the rapid-fire pace with which he liked to make his way around a course. Wadkins played as though he was being chased by a tiger or was late for a date with a movie star.

Other players talked about waltz tempos. Wadkins was totally rock 'n' roll.

Friends remember seeing Wadkins, barely taller than his putter, hitting golf balls at Meadowbrook Country Club after a snowstorm. Whether or not it's true, it certainly is indicative of Wadkins' undeniable fire.

"I was fortunate," Wadkins said. "Meadowbrook was brand new when my parents joined, and there weren't many members. There were no restrictions on us—kids—playing it. Saturdays. Sundays. Anytime.

"It wasn't unusual to play 36 holes by lunch, eat, go swimming, then play nine more later in the afternoon. Kids can't do that today. I'm the first to admit that a lot of it was being in the right place at the right time."

Virginia golf was in one of its most competitive periods during the 1960s, though you'd never know it by looking at some of the results.

Wadkins won four Richmond City Junior titles. He won the 1964 and 1965 State Junior Championships.

The University of Houston wanted him so badly that it scheduled his recruiting visit the same weekend that the basketball team was welcoming some visitors from out west in what remains a watershed American athletic event.

Lin Hairfield, right, president of Elizabeth Manor CC, and David Whitener, co-chairman of the Eastern Amateur Tournament, honor Lanny Wadkins after his 1969 victory.

Wadkins was in the Astrodome with 52,693 others in January 1968 when Elvin Hayes and the Cougars ended the 47-game winning streak of Lew Alcindor and UCLA.

But that was nothing compared to being offered the Arnold Palmer "Bud Worsham Scholarship" by Wake Forest, where Wadkins felt more comfortable.

After playing on the U.S. Walker Cup team in 1969, he interrupted a two-year championship run by Vinny Giles to win the 1970 State Amateur, beat-ing his brother Bobby 6 and 5 in the final. The next year, he lost a 3-and-2 final to Giles, though by then the State Amateur was small potatoes.

That's because Wadkins, then a rising junior, had already grabbed the big prize in 1970, the United States Amateur.

Wadkins arrived at Portland's Waverley Country Club as one of the favorites, along with defending champion Steve Melnyk, Allen Miller, Giles, and Tom Kite of the University of Texas. Wadkins had already captured the Southern and Western Amateurs, and a lot of people figured he'd overpower Waverley's short par-70 course, which measured just 6,496 yards.

He made his supporters look like prophets, opening with a first-round Amateur-record score of 3-under-par 67. He was the only player not to make a bogey.

However, that changed the next day. Playing in the rain, Wadkins faltered to a 3-over-par 73 to fall four shots behind Kite.

"I putted so bad today," Wadkins said, "I hated being on the course."

He wasn't much happier as he neared the end of the third round. When he made a double-bogey after hitting out of bounds on the 15th hole, Wadkins trailed Kite by five strokes.

Then came the pivotal sequence of events, which occurred over two days.

Wadkins made an eagle 3 at 18 when he holed a wedge shot from 70 yards. Kite made bogey, a three-shot swing in Wadkins' favor, giving him momentum heading into the next day.

While Wadkins and Kite were running away from the rest of the field, Wadkins drew even with Kite with birdies on Nos. 2 and 3. Although Kite would twice regain the lead, Wadkins wouldn't be shaken.

He took the lead for good when Kite bogeyed the 15th after hitting his approach shot over the green. Both players birdied the 16th, double-bogeyed the 17th, and came back to birdie 18, Wadkins from 20 feet.

"There just aren't enough adjectives to describe this," Wadkins said. "I could have jumped through the sky when that last putt fell. I knew that was it."

Meanwhile, back in Richmond, friends and family were jumping for joy, too.

Wadkins' father, Jerry, who quit his job with a transportation company to work for Meadowbrook pro James "Popeye" Lumpkin, was "busting out proud" of his oldest boy when the match was over.

"Lanny telephoned me from Portland last night and told me he was going to win it," Mr. Wadkins

told the *Richmond Times-Dispatch*. "These were his exact words: 'Daddy, it's my tournament and I'm going to win it. Make sure you stay in front of the television set and watch me win.' "

The following day, Wadkins returned to Richmond and found a hero's welcome. Several hundred well wishers gathered at Byrd Airport, including Mayor Thomas L. Bliley, who naturally made a speech.

Later that year, Wadkins accepted an invitation to play in the Heritage Classic at Harbour Town GC in South Carolina. Although still an amateur, he finished second to Bob Goalby by four shots.

The following year at Merion GC, Wadkins finished 13th in the U.S. Open. He saw little sense in hanging around campus.

"I had done some things that told me I could play well against the Tour guys," Wadkins said. "It wasn't a surprise to me when I won."

By the time he came to the 1972 Sahara Invitational in Las Vegas, Wadkins had already accumulated a couple of second-place finishes, one a playoff loss to Homero Blancas. He was behind, entering the final round, but rallied to beat Arnold Palmer by one stroke.

"I remember Arnold wasn't too happy because I was still supposed to be in school," Wadkins said, smiling.

He also might not have been so happy because anyone looking at Wadkins' record that year knew there was a new star emerging. In 33 events, Wadkins made the cut 27 times.

In addition to beating Palmer, Wadkins finished second twice, third once, in the top 10 eight times, and in the top 25 on 18 occasions. He was 10th on the money list and an easy choice for rookie of the year.

The following season, Wadkins won twice, something he would accomplish five times, and finished fifth on the money list with nearly $200,000.

Everyone thought Wadkins' career was set to zoom. Instead, it was headed in the opposite direction.

Lanny Wadkins watches a putt during his 1969 victory at the Eastern Amateur.

In December 1974, Wadkins underwent surgery on both his gall bladder and his appendix. That year, he played in just 26 events, with only two top 10 finishes. The 1975 season was about the same: Two more top 10s, but only $23,000 in earnings.

Although he mounted a mini-comeback in 1976 with four top-10 finishes in 29 events, he entered the 1977 season on a three-year winless streak and with lots of unanswered questions.

The PGA Championship was conducted at Pebble Beach that summer. Wadkins had to endure a qualifying round just to make the field.

Wadkins, here finishing a round at the Kemper Open, has won on many of the game's finest courses.

There was little doubt about the sentimental favorite: Gene Littler, a popular 47-year-old Californian who had won that state's Amateur in 1953, the Crosby in 1975, and 29 other tournaments during an illustrious career.

Littler, whose sweet, smooth swing had earned him the nickname "Gene the Machine," also was a medical marvel. He had beaten cancer in 1972 after doctors removed malignant muscles, nerves, and bone from under his left shoulder. However, Littler had been away from the Tour for five weeks just prior to the PGA with severe back pain. He had gotten out of bed just long enough to test his back before deciding to join the field.

"Compared to a couple of weeks ago, I feel like Tarzan," the normally reserved Littler joked.

Actually, it was hard to tell which was in worse shape, Littler's back or Pebble Beach. The course was one huge patch of brown after a two-year drought in Southern California.

"The condition of the course, and the fact that it is Pebble Beach, dictates that you must approach it with a very conservative attitude," said Jack Nicklaus, who opened with a 3-under 69, two shots behind Littler.

Wadkins, too, was at 69, though he might have been tied for the lead had his second shot on the 565-yard, par-5 14th hole landed on the green instead of a few feet short. Wadkins pitched his third shot to within eight feet of the hole, then started to walk up the hill to mark his ball before coming to an abrupt halt.

The ball was rolling back in his direction. Now 30 feet away, Wadkins chipped again, this time to three feet. Again the ball rolled back at him. A third chip, two putts, and Wadkins' short birdie possibility had turned into a double-bogey.

"I probably hit the best shots on that hole and look what I wind up with," he groaned later.

Littler came back on Friday with another bogey-free round, a 3-under 69 that gave him a 2-shot cushion over Jerry McGee. Nicklaus and Wadkins

remained tied, but now were four behind the leader, who confessed that he didn't think windless Pebble Beach was playing all that hard.

"Ah, listen to that guy," contender Joe Inman said. "The rest of us are out here grinding and sweating and working ourselves to the bone every week, and along comes Gene the Machine, who hasn't hardly had a club in his hands for weeks, and shoots Pebble like it was nothing."

Although "The Machine" finally proved he was human by making his first bogey of the tournament during the third round, Wadkins didn't play as well as he had the first two days, either. His even-par 70 left him six shots behind Littler.

For much of Sunday, Wadkins didn't look like he would mount the charge needed to get back in the game, although he overcame three bogeys with a pair of eagles. But a birdie at 18, accomplished when he struck a wedge three feet from the cup, suddenly gave Wadkins a front-row seat at the dramatic finishes of Littler and Nicklaus.

"I looked at the leader board coming to 16 and saw that Gene was 8 under and I was 5 under, but I didn't give it much serious thought," Wadkins said. "It wasn't until about 15 minutes after I holed out on 18 that I really started thinking about it. That's when Jack bogeyed 17. I thought Gene could bogey it, too."

Littler didn't, but he had inflicted enough damage with bogeys on five of the first six holes on the back nine. While Wadkins and Littler advanced to the historic sudden-death conclusion, Nicklaus went home after his 3-iron off the tee at 17 kicked the wrong way, leading to a bogey.

"I figured I'd be lying in the weeds, and when the numbers started to fall off the board, I'd step out," Nicklaus said. "Only 'I' turned out to be Lanny Wadkins."

On the first hole of the playoff, Littler was just a couple of feet away from the cup and victory. Wadkins was 20 feet away, facing a severe downhill putt, needing a miracle.

He got it, stroking the ball into the heart of the cup.

"He might hit 40 shots from there and not make one of them," said Littler, a sentiment with which Wadkins agreed. "He had to hit the perfect putt."

Both men birdied the second hole, a par 5, reaching the green in two and two-putting. Both missed the green with their approach shots on the 368-yard third hole. Littler was short. Wadkins was long.

Littler's chip caught some deep grass and barely made it onto the green. Wadkins pitched to six feet, made the putt, and went airborne in unbridled joy.

"I can't even explain what winning means to me," he said. "I can't express it. I went from a non-exempt player to 10 years of exemptions."

Three weeks later he made another jump, whipping Hale Irwin and Tom Weiskopf by five shots in the World Series of Golf.

"That PGA win stands out for its timing as much as anything else," Wadkins said. "It got me back on top instead of stuck in the middle of the pack. And I stayed there for a long time after that."

Although he never won another major, Wadkins compiled a remarkably consistent record in those events.

He had five top 10s in the Masters, including three third-place finishes. He also had five top 10 finishes in the U.S. Open, including a second to Ray Floyd at Shinnecock in 1986 after shooting a final-round 65.

Wadkins had a pair of top 10s at the British Open, and he nearly won the PGA Championship again in 1982, '84, and '87. Each time, he was second.

"That's impressive, but I would have liked to have won more majors," he said. "If there's anything missing from my career, it's that I should have won more majors. If I had the putting stroke I have now, that probably would have happened."

Wadkins conquered some of America's greatest

Lanny Wadkins gets a congratulatory handshake from fellow Virginian Curtis Strange as the two walk up the 18th fairway at the end of the final round of the 1990 Anheuser-Busch Golf Classic at Kingsmill. Wadkins won by five shots.

challenges: Pebble Beach, Doral, Riviera, LaCosta, and Firestone. He won in every area of the country: Arizona, California, Ohio, Massachusetts, Florida, Texas, and Virginia, where he beat Curtis Strange at the 1990 Anheuser-Busch Golf Classic in Williamsburg.

Although he suffered through as many injuries as anyone on Tour, he refused to make excuses.

"I don't think they held me back," he said. "The body's not built for the golf swing and the daily grind of practice. You're going to have some ailments. You have to expect it. It's a matter of how you handle them, whether you can handle them.

"I won in front of my family and friends a lot, which is neat. There's a lot of pressure involved in that. I've played a lot of meaningful golf with other Virginians: Walker Cups with Vinny Giles, a World Amateur with Vinny and Curtis.

"When I won the Anheuser-Busch, Curtis and I were in the last group. That was very special to me."

Wadkins grinned.

"And there was no way he was going to get me that day, either."

In his prime, Lew Worsham competed in two of
golf's most famous tournaments and won them both.

LEW WORSHAM

Bobby Thomson hit his home run. Max McGee had his Super Bowl touchdowns. Mike Eruzione worked a miracle for American Olympic hockey fans.

It's a common theme in sports: Good, but not necessarily great, athletes step up when they are needed most to deliver a performance thought to be beyond their skills. They are admired, even revered, for making that day extraordinary.

Lewis Elmer Worsham Jr.—nicknamed "The Chin" by his buddies on the professional golf circuit for his square, protruding jaw—had two moments so spectacular that no one with a passion for golf lore could dare not treasure him and them.

Lew Worsham was born on Oct. 5, 1917, on a tobacco farm in the town of Alta Vista, between Lynchburg and Danville in the south-central portion of Virginia. He moved with his family to Hampton when he was a young boy, played golf at Hampton High School, and worked as a caddie and repaired clubs under pro Jack Isaacs at the Old Dominion Golf Course.

PGA of America records say he turned pro in 1935, when he was just 18. In 1936, Worsham moved to the Washington, D.C., area and worked at Kenwood Country Club before accepting an assistant's job at Chevy Chase Club in Maryland.

He didn't have much faith or confidence in his game at the time and told head professional Bob Barnett that he wanted to tear his swing apart and start over.

"Just keep hitting the ball the way you do now," Barnett advised, "and someday you will have a good game."

A year later, Worsham became head pro at Burning Tree CC in Maryland. He returned there after serving in the Navy in World War II, then joined Congressional Country Club in Maryland. He was hired as an assistant to famous pro Wiffy Cox, although the idea was to put him out on the tour in the fall of 1946.

"I was lucky," Worsham told *The Senior Golfer*. "I won the Atlanta Open in just my second start."

The controversial "Tape Measure" ruling during the 1947 U.S. Open at the St. Louis Country Club. Fellow Virginian Sam Snead, left, watches as Worsham, with putter, and two USGA officials measure to see which player will putt first on the last hole of an 18-hole playoff. It was Snead, who missed. Worsham made his to win the playoff by one stroke.

Lew Worsham shares a laugh with baseball great Babe Ruth during the 1940s.

THE TAPE-MEASURE OPEN

Worsham arrived at St. Louis Country Club for the 1947 U.S. Open in an upbeat, energetic mood.

Six weeks earlier, he had won his third Middle Atlantic PGA championship. The final round had been played on his father's birthday, and he was proud to have been able to offer his dad the best present imaginable.

He had just named head pro at prestigious Oakmont Country Club in Pittsburgh, replacing the famed Emil Loeffler. His death had left the post vacant months before, but the selection committee labored over finding his successor. Worsham finally signed to report for work there on July 1.

It was debatable how much he would enjoy St. Louis. Flood waters rolled down the Mississippi and Missouri rivers. Streetcar crews were on strike.

At the course, which measured a meager 6,532 yards long, players were sounding an old refrain about the lengths the U.S. Golf Association had gone to make the layout more challenging. Officials had taken already narrow, rolling fairways and made them even tighter by allowing the rough to grow to five inches high.

"You hit your tee shot down the middle and it'll kick right into the rough," Jimmy Demaret groused. "That's the trouble with the Open. They take a good golf course and diddle-dump it all up. Just for the Open. That's why so many dark horses win the Open. They fix the course so a guy like Ben Hogan—the greatest golfer in the world—doesn't have a chance unless he's very lucky."

Hogan either wasn't very lucky or very good that week. He finished 72 holes at 289, seven shots off the pace set by Worsham and Sam Snead.

Both men had a chance to avoid what turned out to be one of the greatest playoffs in golf history.

Worsham, whose best showing in five previous Opens had been 24th, bogeyed two of the final four holes in the last round. Included was a putt for par on 17 that hung on the lip of the hole but refused

Worsham was popular with his fellow pros.

They liked his friendly, frequent smile.

They admired his game, and the tenacity with which he played, regardless of the circumstances.

Once, in a 90-hole tournament in Boston, Worsham was 19 over par after two rounds. He finished the tournament under par.

They appreciated his integrity.

Worsham was leading the 1947 Jacksonville Open by a shot on the final day and addressing a putt on the 18th green when the ball moved. Calling a one-shot penalty on himself, Worsham fell into a tie with Clayton Heafner. He lost the playoff.

Disappointing as that was, there would be a victory later in '47 that would forever change Lew Worsham's life.

to fall. At 18, Worsham was barely off the green, 30 feet from the cup. Choosing to putt, he nudged the ball at the hole, and the crowd that had gathered to watch rose and began to cheer, so certain were they that the shot would fall.

It didn't, veering away at the last possible instant.

Behind Worsham was Snead, a year removed from his big victory at the British Open and one of the game's best draws for a decade.

At 17, Snead's five-foot putt for birdie 3 stopped three inches short of the hole. That left him in need of a birdie at 18 just to tie and force an 18-hole playoff the next day.

Snead's tee shot was a winner, 300 yards down the middle of the fairway. His approach, while good, considering it was played over a hump to a green the player could not see, wasn't as close as he would have liked. The ball stopped some 18 feet from the hole.

But with Worsham watching intently, Snead waited calmly for playing partners Dick Metz and Bud Ward to finish their business. Already struggling occasionally with that mysterious putting malady he would later call "the yips," Snead stepped to the ball and sent it rolling straight into the heart of the cup.

Worsham rushed onto the green to congratulate Snead. They were friends who shared a passion for hunting and fishing and had played together on several previous occasions before joining the Navy. The Slammer beamed.

Scot Tommy Armour, in the clubhouse drinking tea, watched Snead draw back the blade and told a writer friend, "You've just seen one of the very great putts of golf."

The two came back the next morning for an 18-hole stroke-play confrontation.

"Worsham is the type of golfer that's hard to beat," Snead said the night before. "He's steady under pressure and I can't blow a single hole if I intend to win."

Snead took a one-shot lead with a birdie on the first hole, then extended it by another stroke with a birdie 4 on the fifth.

Worsham retrieved both shots on the next hole when Snead made double-bogey 6.

Snead regained a two-shot edge when he sank a 30-foot putt for birdie on No. 8 while Worsham made bogey after hitting his tee shot into the rough.

Worsham made a seven-foot birdie putt on No. 9 to reduce his deficit to one stroke at the turn.

On 12, a 180-yard par 3, Snead's tee shot landed 30 feet from the hole, and his birdie putt trickled past by inches. Worsham hit the better tee shot, to 12 feet of the cup, and made the birdie to draw even.

After 15 holes, Snead again led by two, but at the par-3 16th, Worsham holed a 22-foot birdie putt to halve his deficit. Snead bogeyed the 17th when he hit into heavy rough at the edge of the green and couldn't make a seven-foot par putt. Worsham, meanwhile, missed a birdie by inches but settled for the par and even status in the match.

The 18th hole at St. Louis was a 418-yard par 4. Snead and Worsham each bombed long, accurate tee shots, with Worsham's finishing two yards ahead of Snead's.

Snead's approach shot landed on the green, 18 feet from the hole and at about the same position from which he had holed out to force the a playoff the day before. Worsham was just off the green, inches from some of the thickest rough on the course, inches from being immersed in grass so tall, it would have been impossible to play a finesse shot.

Hitting first, Worsham was a bit too firm with his chip, but the ball hit the cup and stopped about two feet past.

"I'm glad it hit the cup," Worsham admitted later. "It was going too fast. Of course, had it been a little nearer the center, it would have dropped in."

Snead, putting downhill on a slick green, played a poor shot, leaving it short. Though it was a tricky putt—the kind that had given him so much trouble lately that he had publicly threatened to retire just

two weeks before—Snead marched to the ball and addressed it for his next stroke.

"Wait a minute," Worsham called to him. "Are you sure you're away?"

Snead stood up and argued that it didn't matter. Once he had begun the act of putting, he had the right to finish.

Worsham continued to disagree.

"Not if I'm away," he said firmly.

Isaac B. Grainger, chairman of the U.S. Golf Association rules committee, was standing on the edge of the green. He joined the conversation, and sided with Worsham. The player whose ball was farthest from the hole would putt first.

But there was no way to make that call with the naked eye. Grainger called for a steel tape measure. He stretched the tape from the cup to Snead's ball, then to Worsham's.

Snead's ball was 30 inches away. Worsham's was 29 inches.

Snead would putt first.

There are no reports on how long it took to decide this confab, not that it matters. Clearly, Snead's concentration was broken.

Snead's downhill attempt, which broke left to right, did not hold the line and stopped two inches outside the hole.

Worsham, whose putt was on much more of a straight line, rolled his par-saver into the cup to win with a 2-under 69 to Snead's 1-under 70.

"That's just the way it goes," Snead said later, emptying the contents of his locker into a bag. "Just when I needed a putt, I didn't get it. I'd rather have blown it yesterday than this way today."

Snead never accused Worsham of gamesmanship, because he never considered it such. The two were close friends and would remain that way for 40-plus years, sharing each other's company on fishing trips.

Worsham won just $2,500, although the Open champion traditionally was able to command a whopping $500 per exhibition, or about $50,000 the year

After his famous "shot heard round the world" win at the 1953 World Championship of Golf, Lew Worsham is all smiles. He beat fellow Virginian Chandler Harper.

after his triumph.

Worsham always claimed that the Open win over Snead was the greatest of his career. That would seem a typical and obvious position were it not for something that happened six years later in Chicago.

THE SHOT HEARD ROUND THE WORLD

George May's World Championship of Golf was like none other on the circuit.

In the late 1940s and early '50s, pro golfers faced a difficult decision. There was glory to be had playing the circuit, putting one's game to the test against Ben Hogan, Sam Snead, Byron Nelson, and a countless number of highly skilled players bursting onto the scene in postwar America.

But the money, at least enough to buy a house and feed a family, was back home, at the country clubs and pro shops and lesson tees.

Worsham's deal with Oakmont allowed him to play in the Open, the PGA Championship, and a select few other "name" events. He was the pro there in the summer; during the winter, he was pro at Coral Ridge Country Club in Fort Lauderdale, Florida.

The one stop where a pro could really line his pockets was May's World Championship.

The 1953 tournament carried a purse of $75,000, with $25,000 going to the winner. May also guaranteed that his winner would play in a series of exhibitions he would arrange throughout the year, each of which paid $1,000 plus expenses.

Remember, Worsham had pocketed just $2,500 for winning the '47 U.S. Open.

The ever-innovative May had worked out the first national TV deal in golf history. The camera was trained on the 18th hole, where Harry Wismer and Jimmy Demaret provided commentary.

Worsham had been on the verge of a victory in the '46 World tournament. He had a four-stroke lead with nine holes to play, then started the back nine with a birdie.

"I was thinking of all the ways I could spend that money," he said years later.

Then he bogeyed two of the next three holes and compounded matters by hitting his next two tee shots out of bounds. He limped home with a 77 that ended any thoughts of a big payday.

One year later, on Aug. 9, 1953, he was back in the thick of the competition. With one hole to play, he trailed Chandler Harper by a stroke, though Harper had just energized the gallery by hitting a 9-iron to 20 inches from the hole for a certain birdie.

Worsham laced a 306-yard tee shot on the 410-yard finishing hole. A gallery of 10,000 walked step-by-step with him, officials finally parting them to either side of Worsham so that he could have a clear shot to the green.

Playing by feel because of encroaching darkness, Worsham pulled a wedge from his bag.

Meanwhile, Harper was fielding questions from Demaret, who had already proclaimed him the winner, and trying his best to keep the silversmith stationed behind the green from prematurely adding his name to the huge trophy.

"I kept telling him, 'It isn't over until everyone's played his last shot,' " Harper recalled years later.

Worsham swung, the ball flew over the river that guarded the green, bounced on the front edge 35 feet beneath the cup, and began rolling.

It crossed a ridge and didn't stop until it nicked the flagstick and fell into the hole for an eagle 2 and a miraculous one-shot win.

"I hit it well," Worsham would say later, "but I didn't think it was anything unusual. Jimmy Demaret said the ball was trying to bite, that it had a lot of backspin. But it didn't. It kept going."

The crowd, at first stunned, ran for Worsham. A couple of men hoisted him onto their shoulders and carried him across the bridge to the green.

Demaret, forgetting that he was on live television, shouted into his microphone, "Goddam, it's in!"

"At that point, I'm not thinking of beating him," Worsham said in a 1984 interview. "I'm hop-

News clippings of top Virginia golfers of the 1940s and 1950s including Lew Worsham, Sam Snead, and Chandler Harper. That's Arnold Palmer holding the trophy with Lew in the photo in the lower right hand corner.

ing maybe for a tie, that's all. To have it go in, that was like catching lightning in a bottle. It was the luckiest shot I ever had in my life. I'm sorry I had to do it to my good friend Chandler Harper."

Suddenly, golf fans and experts had something to debate: Had Worsham just hit the game's greatest shot ever?

Harper surely thought so.

"There has never been a more fantastic finishing shot before or since in the history of golf," he said.

The only serious other candidate at the time was Gene Sarazen's 220-yard double-eagle on the 15th hole of the 1935 Masters. That pulled Sarazen into a tie with Craig Wood, whom he beat in a playoff.

Now, Tom Watson's chip-in on the 17th hole at Pebble Beach in the 1982 U.S. Open would be a strong candidate. Another would be Payne Stewart's 15-foot par putt to win the 1999 U.S. Open at Pinehurst No. 2 in North Carolina.

Then again, Worsham won with the last swing on the last hole, and from the middle of the fairway, not five yards from the cup.

Initial reports estimated Worsham's shot at 140 yards, but Worsham knew he couldn't hit a wedge that far. Using film from the broadcast, he finally was able to determine that the "shot heard round the world" had actually traveled 104 yards.

Amid the chaos after Worsham's ball fell, a friend asked him if the shot had been skill or luck.

"Skill? Luck? Heck, what came first, the chicken or the egg?" Worsham answered, flashing one of his trademark grins.

Worsham finished as the leading money-winner of 1953, totaling $34,002 in official earnings. He later figured that he earned an additional $35,000 from exhibitions.

After 32 years as head pro at Oakmont, Worsham and wife, Virginia, bought a home in Poquoson, near Hampton.

A member of the Virginia Sports Hall of Fame and the Middle Atlantic PGA Hall of Fame, Lew Worsham died on Oct. 20, 1990.

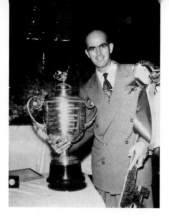

major champions

Chandler Harper poses with the trophy he received for winning the 1950 PGA Championship at Scioto Country Club in Columbus, Ohio. In his left hand is the key to the City of Portsmouth, his hometown.

CHANDLER HARPER

Sam Snead was celebrating his 75th birthday at his restaurant in Hot Springs when a visitor mentioned Chandler Harper's name.

"The man could get it up and down from inside a shoe box," Snead said, shaking his head in amazement.

Ben Hogan was equally impressed with Harper's short game. A mutual friend once told Harper than Hogan considered him the best player in the game from 150 yards in.

Yet, there was more to Harper's game than just pitching and putting. He won 11 times on the PGA Tour, including the 1950 PGA Championship at Scioto Country Club in Columbus, Ohio.

In the 1954 Texas Open, Harper's last three rounds—63-63-63—189—remains the PGA Tour record for lowest consecutive 54-hole score.

Harper, a lifelong Portsmouth resident, earned a spot on the 1955 Ryder Cup team, accumulating his qualifying points in just 19 events. That, by the way, was the most he ever played on the PGA Tour. Harper divided his time between the Tour and his duties running Glensheallah, Elizabeth Manor CC, and Bide-A-Wee Golf Club, which he built.

"I was told that I was probably one of the best putters out there. I was a good putter, but I always thought chipping was the best part of my game," Harper said. "I could have been more consistent had I had some early instruction and had I been able to play full-time."

In 1968, Harper captured the World Seniors title at Dundee, Scotland. Later, he would bring that event to Bide-A-Wee.

At 16, Harper was the youngest player ever to win the State Amateur. At 56, he was the oldest player ever to win the State Open, an event he dominated with 10 victories from 1932 to 1970.

Between 1950 and 1955, Harper won seven times and finished second another seven times. Four of them were by one shot, including Lew Worsham's famous victory from the 18th fairway at the 1953 World Championship at Tam O'Shanter in Chicago.

"Grantland Rice wrote that I was the victim of the pangs and barbs of outrageous fortune," Harper said. "I guess I was."

If Harper, who received the nickname "Old Bones" in appreciation of his long, angular frame, was bothered by these setbacks, he had a funny way of showing it.

Not long after Worsham's miracle shot, Harper's wife, Essie, was given a cocker spaniel puppy for her birthday. The couple named him "Wedgie," a constant reminder that Worsham had fashioned his astonishing triumph by holing a wedge from 104 yards on the final hole.

Harper hit his first golf ball at age nine at the Portsmouth Country Club. It was a six-hole course designed by the vice president of a local bank. He was chosen for the job because he had actually *played* golf a few times in other cities.

That was 1923, the same year that Harper saw an exhibition given by Gene Sarazen and Walter Hagen at Princess Anne Country Club in Virginia Beach.

"I was hooked," he said. "To this day, I have never forgotten what a thrill it was watching those two great American players."

By 1929, Harper had already won the Portsmouth City Championship twice, once beating his brother in a final that lasted 23 holes.

Harper turned professional in 1937, five years after he had captured the State Open as an amateur. Although he and Herman Keiser teamed to win the 1942 International Four Ball Championship, Harper didn't find individual success on the touring circuit until the 1950 Tucson Open.

The victory was highlighted by Harper's remarkable putting exhibition in the third round. He used just 20 strokes, then a PGA Tour record, in shooting a 63.

Harper was still wielding his 10-year-old, wooden-shafted blade putter when he arrived at Scioto Country Club in Columbus, Ohio, for the PGA. Although the course, famous as Jack Nicklaus' home

A 1998 photo of Chandler Harper at his home in Portsmouth with his favorite set of irons.

33

layout, was relatively short and well suited to Harper's game, no one took him as a serious contender.

Defending champion Sam Snead, who had won at Richmond's Hermitage CC the year before, was the favorite, along with Lloyd Mangrum, Jimmy Demaret, and Johnny Palmer.

Harper beat Fred Annon in the first round and Dick Metz, once the touring pro for the Cavalier Yacht & Golf Club in Virginia Beach, in the second round. After disposing of Bob Toski, Harper faced Mangrum in what he called "the best single match I ever played."

Harper raced to a 4-up lead after the morning 18 of what were then 36-hole quarterfinal, semifinal, and final matches. He was 2 under through 14 holes in the afternoon round and should have been cruising.

However, Mangrum blistered Scioto after lunch. He played the first 14 holes in 6 under to tie Harper and assume momentum in the match.

The 17th at Scioto is a par 3. The 18th is a long par 5 on which Mangrum's length off the tee was a huge advantage. Harper had to win 17 if he was to advance.

Hitting first, Mangrum knocked his tee shot 20 feet from the hole. Harper, who put his shot 15 feet from the cup, said he immediately knew what Mangrum was going to try next.

"I don't know why, but I got it in my mind that he was going to putt it short and I'd be stymied," Harper said.

The stymie went out as strategy later in the '50, but it was one of the most powerful weapons a golfer possessed in match play. The concept emerged from the game's earliest fundamental edict: Play it where it lies.

That was the rule, even if an opponent's ball was directly between yours and the hole. Faced with a stymie, you had two choices. You could try to pitch the ball over your opponent's towards the hole, or take an additional stroke by playing around the other ball.

Mangrum did as Harper predicted, leaving his first putt directly in Harper's line, slightly right of the hole. Harper, knowing he wasn't likely to win the 18th hole, grabbed his 9-iron, chipped his ball short of Mangrum's, and then saw it hop over his opponent's and into the cup for a birdie 2 that restored his lead.

"That's dirty pool," a shocked Mangrum mumbled in Harper's direction before breaking into a smile.

Chandler Harper tees off at the 1950 PGA Championship at Scioto Country Club in Columbus, Ohio. He won by defeating Lloyd Mangrum, Jimmy Demaret, and Henry Williams (final), all in match play.

At 18, Mangrum hit driver-driver and reached the left side of the green, 76 feet from the hole. Unfortunately for him, he putted it just 75 feet, the ball stopping dead on line with the hole.

Again Harper answered the challenge, holing a 12-footer for birdie to preserve the hard-fought victory.

Against Demaret in a 2-and-1 semifinal victory, Harper again caught fire with his short game. He was 1 up at the conclusion of the morning round after a 2-under-par 70. He increased his advantage to 3-up with birdies on the second and third holes of the afternoon round.

Demaret wasn't through, making birdies on the next two holes when Harper inexplicably lost his touch and missed birdies from four and six feet.

The two halved the next six holes before Harper inched to a 2-up lead with a 15-foot birdie on the 33rd hole of the match.

Demaret seemed certain to climb back into the competition when his tee shot on 17 found the green while Harper's flew into a bunker. The Portsmouth pro then hit another clutch shot, closing out the match by blasting to tap-in distance while Demaret missed his birdie attempt.

The final, against Henry Williams Jr. of Secane, Pennsylvania, was barely competitive, though Harper conceded that he wasn't nearly as sharp as before.

The final was broadcast live back to Tidewater by radio station WLOW. Harper won the first three holes and led 4 up through 11. Williams couldn't control his tee shots, spraying them everywhere. He didn't even take time out for lunch, dashing to the practice range in a desperate attempt to find his swing.

He didn't. Harper played conservatively after lunch and eased home with a 4-and-3 triumph.

"After I got past Dick Metz in the second round, I felt that I could win," Harper said later. "I still had Lloyd Mangrum and Jimmy Demaret in my way, but I thought I could get past them because I was playing consistently."

He was playing better than consistently. Harper finished the match-play portion 23 under par, and never trailed at any time.

In addition to the $3,500 winner's check, Harper received a $250 bonus every time he entered a pro tournament.

"Well, there's a bank down home that'll be glad to hear I'm making a little money," Harper joked.

Harper didn't win on the circuit again until 1953 in El Paso.

"I never was consistently good, because I never had the game Snead had, or Byron Nelson had, or Hogan had," Harper conceded. "But I felt that when I got it going, I could beat them. I could win. When I was at the top of my game, I could shoot the scores that could win—and I did."

He proved that at the '54 Texas Open in San Antonio, although it didn't start out that way.

Harper went out in 39 and had to hole a 40-foot putt on No. 9 to do that. Dejected, Harper told playing partner Horton Smith that he was going to withdraw.

"Oh, no," Smith said. "Don't do that. Play some more. See what happens."

Harper stayed because the 6,400-yard municipal course was one of the easiest on the circuit, enhancing the chances of a comeback.

Immediately, things improved. Harper came home in 31 to finish with a respectable 1-under-par 70. He was still nine shots behind leader Rudy Horvath and tied for 68th overall. There was no sense thinking about anything but making the cut and a decent check.

Harper's 63 in the second round was lost in the uproar over Johnny Palmer's 62. Palmer's 36-hole total of 127 was a PGA record.

Harper birdied the second, third, fourth, and ninth holes going out. He birdied 10, 11, 13, and 18 coming home, sinking an 18-foot putt, by far his longest of the day, on the closing hole.

Still, 63 players broke par the second day. Harper had plenty of work left.

Palmer, who hadn't won in two years, all but wrapped up the tournament—or so said the press—Saturday with a 7-under 64 that set the 54-hole PGA record for low score at 191. Only three players didn't lose ground on the North Carolina native, among them Harper and Lionel Hebert, who were tied for second, five shots back.

"Palmer had the oldest tournament on the winter circuit all wrapped up Saturday and ready for delivery Sunday," one newsman wrote. "All Palmer has to do today is shoot a 4-under-par 67 for an all-time national PGA record for 72 holes."

It would be Harper's name that would be etched into the record book. His third consecutive 63 gave him a 72-hole total of 259, one shot better than the Texas Open record of 260 set by Jackie Burke in 1952. It tied the all-time record for 72 holes held by Hogan and Byron Nelson.

His consecutive-round score of 189 remains the PGA Tour record, although Harper shares it with John Cook, who did it in the first three rounds of the 1996 FedEx St. Jude Classic.

Palmer, who would finish second, lost the lead early. His putting touch, which had been brilliant, deserted him. He three-putted two of the first three holes and made a bogey at No. 7 when he drove into the woods. Although he righted himself to shoot 3 under on the back nine, Harper blew by him.

Feeling confident, Harper birdied the third, fourth, and seventh holes and polished off the front side with an eagle 3 on the ninth.

But he wrapped up the victory by hitting what everyone who saw it described as one of the greatest shots in the 27-year history of the tournament.

Harper's drive on the 375-yard par 4 hit a spectator and bounced behind some trees to the left of the fairway. Battling against overhanging limbs, Harper hit a punch shot that flew into the creek that crossed the fairway.

"I could see the ball, but barely," Harper remembered. "I thought that if I took a six there, I'd lose so much ground I wouldn't be able to make it

up." Harper removed his shoes and socks and stepped into the water, which rose above his ankles. Using his wedge, he swung as hard as he could and arched the ball onto the green, 14 feet from the hole.

As if nothing extraordinary had happened, Harper calmly dressed, walked to the green, wiped the muck off his ball and holed the putt to save par. He would win by two shots.

"It was one of those shots you know can't happen but it just comes off," Harper said at the time.

In 1955, Harper won the Virginia Beach Open by four shots and the Colonial National in Fort Worth by eight. He finished second in Kansas City. Overall, it was a spectacular season, although Harper spent as much time in Portsmouth, presiding over the construction of Bide-A-Wee GC, as he did competing.

"After I got back and stayed at the club for a year, I wasn't playing very well after that," Harper said. "It just kept going like that and after a while, I wasn't too concerned about entering any more tournaments until I was a senior. That didn't take very long."

In January 1968, Harper captured the American Teacher Seniors Championship at Palm Beach Gardens, Florida, beating Snead by four shots. That put him into the World Seniors championship against Max Faulkner of England on July 7.

Harper won the scheduled 36-hole final 2-up in a cold, driving rain. The critical hole was his eagle-3 at the 31st hole at 6,872-yard Downfield in Dundee, Scotland. They were even at the time, but Harper took control with a driver and 4-wood to within 18 inches on the 521-yard hole. Faulkner lost the hole with a birdie.

Harper was 2-up after 16, saw the lead trimmed in half when Faulkner made a birdie, then won with a conceded birdie after Faulkner put his tee shot at 18 into the woods.

Harper was elected to the PGA of America Hall of Fame in 1968, and the Virginia Sports Hall of Fame in 1973.

J.C. Snead plays out of the sand during his victory at the
1976 Kaiser International Tournament in California.

J.C. SNEAD

The victory was doubly sweet for J.C. Snead.
Not only did he win one of the PGA Senior Tour's major championships—the first of his career—at the 1995 Senior Players Championship, he did
it at the scene of what he called "the biggest disappointment of my athletic
career."

He had played the first 36 holes of the same event in 1992 in a record 13
under par and had a two-stroke lead with one hole to play in the final round.

Then he made a haunting, disastrous play. Using a 3-iron, Snead hit his tee
shot into the water on the 18th hole at the TPC of Michigan in Dearborn. The
resulting double-bogey handed Dave Stockton a one-stroke victory.

"That was a real choke job, or whatever you want to call it," Snead said
seven years later. "That was the first time I ever felt that I gave something away.
Normally, I didn't relinquish much when I had something. It took me a while to
get over that deal in Michigan."

Three years later, Snead and Jack Nicklaus finished 72 holes of the same
event tied for first at 16 under par. The playoff began at the 450-yard, par-4 18th.

"I really felt pretty calm," Snead said. "I walked up on the tee, Jack was
standing there, and I looked at him, laughed, and said, 'Well, big boy, let's get it
on.' And he just laughed back and said, 'Let's go.' "

While he had replayed his 1992 collapse over and over in his mind, Snead
came to the playoff actually having just finished rehearsing what turned out to
be his victorious strategy.

Needing a par on 18 to make the playoff, Snead had boomed a drive down
the middle, 182 yards from the hole. Five-iron in hand, he told his caddie that he
was going to aim his next shot at the corner of a TV tower located behind and
to the right of the pin.

"And I hit it exactly there," he said. "I kind of laughed after I hit it. I told
my caddie, 'If I had known I was going to hit it that good, I'd have shot it at the
pin.' "

After the two-putt par, Snead opened the playoff by drilling another perfect tee shot—and again had 182 yards to the pin.

"It was amazing," Snead said. "I was about four feet from where I'd hit it

J.C. won eight times on the PGA Tour and ranks among the top 20 all-time money winners on the senior circuit.

J.C. Snead with his uncle Sam Snead in a park on the outskirts of Richmond. J.C. has won 11 PGA and Senior PGA Tour events. Sam's accomplishments speak for themselves. They make quite a family duo.

the first time, but the exact same distance. Now I tell the caddie, 'I'm going right at it. If I blow it, I blow it, but I'm going right at it.' "

This time, Snead's 5-iron shot was even better, stopping four feet from the hole for an easy birdie and a redemptive first major.

While it is his fondest memory of what has been a highly successful stint on the Senior PGA Tour, it is just one of a slew of highlights in what has been a fascinating 35-plus years in pro golf.

Though often engulfed by the giant shadow cast by legendary uncle Sam Snead, J.C.'s career deserves respect on its own merits.

A regular on the PGA Tour from 1968 to 1990, Snead won eight tournaments and $2.2 million. He played on three Ryder Cup teams and was at his best competing against some of the game's biggest names. Snead defeated Seve Ballesteros in a sudden-death playoff at the 1987 Manufacturers Hanover Westchester Classic.

In addition to his Senior Tour triumph over Nicklaus, Snead beat Raymond Floyd in a playoff for the Royal Caribbean Classic in 1995. He was one shot better than Gary Player and Bobby Nichols in winning the 1993 Vantage at The Dominion.

Since joining the Senior PGA Tour in 1990, the Hot Springs native has won more than $5.4 million, comfortably within the top 20.

That's awfully good for someone who didn't take golf seriously until he was in his 20s and only after his baseball career in the Washington Senators chain was finished.

"Baseball helped by making me strong," said Snead, who batted left-handed and does almost everything as a southpaw except play golf. "I could hit a ball a long way."

Originally, that was one of the most attractive aspects of golf for Snead. Anyone who has ever smacked a golf ball with the fat part of a wooden bat knows the thrill of watching it soar a prodigious distance.

"I was 22 or 23 when I left the minor leagues, and I didn't have any aspirations of being a Tour player," Snead recalled. "Hell, I didn't even play golf! That would have been insane. When you play baseball, you're geared to how far you can hit it. You sit in the dugout and dream of hitting one over the stands, over the trees, over that hill. In golf, you're literally hitting a ball that far. It was fun just to see how far it would go."

Snead's first stop after quitting baseball was Century Country Club in Purchase, New York, where he worked for three years as an assistant pro for a former employee and friend of Sam's.

"I used to hit drives 340 yards at Century," Snead said, chuckling and shaking his head. "It was ridiculous. I'd come off the course and tell someone, 'I hit driver and wedge to No. 8, which was a par 5.' And they'd say, 'Yeah, what'd you make?' And I'd say, 'Hey, we're not talking about that part.' "

Snead quickly fell in love with the nuances and intricacies of the game. Soon, he was on the practice range daily. After his first summer playing the game, some of the members at Century pushed him to attend something new the PGA Tour was trying called Qualifying School.

"I went and, of course, I didn't play very well," Snead said. "But I wasn't disappointed because I didn't expect to qualify. The way I looked at it, every shot I hit, every course I played, every good player I watched, was a chance for me to learn something. I could live with that.

"I started golf in 1964 and I went through 1974—10 years—and never felt like I regressed."

Snead crashed the winner's circle in spectacular fashion in 1971, winning twice in three weeks. First, he outlasted Dale Douglass to win by a stroke at the Tucson Open, then held off Gardner Dickinson by one at Doral.

"That was the best golf I ever played," Snead said. "I often think, 'What the hell happened? Why didn't I continue to play that well?' I don't know."

Snead is his own worst critic. He is an unrelenting perfectionist who, yes, has often cursed those things that have prevented him from having been more successful. He knows it. He can't help it.

"I used to hit balls all day long, then go to the driving range and hit balls at night," Snead said. "People don't know that. This game is like any other job. You get out of it what you put into it. I've worked hard because I felt like I had a lot of catching up to do.

"I'm still looking for it. I keep thinking this damn game can't be this hard. Why can't I go out there and hit the ball the way you're supposed to hit it, most of the time? I shot 68 one time at Orlando and Mac McLendon asked me why I wasn't happier. I told him 'I want to hit it 300 yards down the middle of every fairway and I want to hole the second shot. Is that OK?' And he looked at me and said, 'You know what, that's really not all that bad.' "

At the same time, Snead has an endearing sense of humor and a unique way of showing people he knows how to keep things in perspective.

In the early 1980s, Snead made a public announcement that he wanted to be referred to by his full name, Jesse Carlyle. After a few weeks of not playing well, he informed everyone that he was going back to J.C. because "Jesse Carlyle hasn't been playing worth a damn."

Snead admits that some of his search for perfection is floating in the family gene pool. He doesn't try to escape the fact that he's kin to one of the greatest ball-strikers ever. Rather, he embraces the connection, which has left him open to outrageously unfair comparisons through the years.

"I played with Sam in the winter of 1968 and '69 three or four times a week," Snead said. "I watched this man play, and I thought, 'This is how you're supposed to play the game.' Maybe that's why I am the way I am, because I saw the best and I compare myself to him. If he can do it, there's no reason I can't do it."

Like Sam, golf presented J.C. with his share of heartache. Twice he finished second to Nicklaus at the TPC, when it was staged at Atlanta Country Club and at Inverrary in Florida.

He was second to Andy North at the 1978 U.S. Open at Cherry Hills in Denver. He was second to Tom Watson at the '74 Western Open at Butler National outside Chicago. He lost a playoff to George Archer at Hartford in 1971 and finished two shots behind Rik Massengale at the same tournament five years later.

He won three tournaments in 1971, but Nicklaus and Lee Trevino won five times apiece.

"I competed against more good players when they were in their prime," Snead said. "I had Trevino. I had Johnny Miller. I had Watson. I had Jack Nicklaus. I had Gary Player. From tee to green, I could probably hit the ball as good as those guys. But those guys beat me to death on the greens. I never was a bad putter. I never was a good putter. I could two-putt from anywhere. But I just don't make that many putts."

Putting had little to do with what he considers the most bizarre second-place finish of his career, to Tommie Aaron at the 1973 Masters. His downfall started when his tee shot on the par-3 12th hole spun back off the green and into the water. However, Snead says there's a lot more to the story than that.

"In my mind, the reason I lost that golf tournament is that I hit a bad golf ball," Snead said. "There was something wrong with the ball, and it was something that didn't dawn on us until several weeks later."

Snead, who no longer represents that equipment manufacturer, said that he used to play one new ball every three holes. When he got to the 10th tee at Augusta National that year, he introduced a new ball into play. Although he had a bad drive and a weak approach, he two-putted from 20 feet for par to maintain a two-shot lead with eight holes left.

Snead loved Augusta's par-4 11th. Something about the way the hole set up gave him tremendous confidence off the tee, and he remembers cracking what he thought was a perfect drive. His playing partner, Peter Oosterhuis, had been having trouble keeping up with Snead off the tee, so when Snead found two balls in the fairway, he immediately walked to the one that was 40 yards closer to the green.

J.C. Snead lines up a putt at the 1995 U.S. Senior Open at Congressional Country Club in Bethesda, Maryland.

It belonged to Oosterhuis.

"I had been hitting anything from a 6-iron to an 8-iron on that hole; now I'm 210 yards away and I just murder a 3-iron, trying to cut it for the center of the green," Snead said. "And it lands short and pops on. I'm 90 feet away, I lag it to a couple of feet from the hole and make par."

Twenty-six years later, Snead still shakes his head in disbelief that the light inside his head never came on.

Something's wrong.

Snead had had problems with the famous 155-yard par-3 12th hole all week. He'd always remembered what Sam had warned him: You could make bogey hitting it over the green, but odds were long, real long, that you could make bogey hitting it short.

Snead drew a 6-iron, only to have his caddie remind him that he had been knocking 7-irons over the green all week. He decided to hit an easy 7, then was appalled after his swing because he thought he'd hit it much too hard.

"But I'd hit it right over the pin, and as I'm watching, it starts to come down, and now I'm thinking, 'Hell, this might go in.' "

It went in, but not where Snead thought. The ball landed on the front edge of the green, then rolled back into the water.

"It was like somebody took a knife, stuck it in my stomach, and pulled my intestines out," Snead said. "It was just awful."

Sticking to his routine, Snead tossed the ball out of play after 12 and immediately birdied the par-5 13th to pull to one of Aaron.

That's the best he could do. A poor drive at the par-5 15th kept him from making birdie. He had a slick 15-foot downhill putt to tie Aaron on 18 but couldn't get it to fall.

"And that was my Masters week," he said with a shrug, "my really good chance at winning. I did the best I could do. I played well. You have to do your thing and hope it's good enough."

Snead's best was plenty good in 1987. Then 46 years old and without a victory since the 1981 Southern Open, Snead conquered one of the world's greatest stars, Seve Ballesteros, in a playoff at the Manufacturers Hanover Westchester Classic.

Snead moved into contention with a third-round 65 that left him three behind Mike Reid to start Sunday. His 1-under 70 the next day, accomplished by making birdies on the last two holes, made him the man to beat.

Ballesteros answered the challenge, also making birdies on the last two holes to force sudden death. Snead won with a par after Ballesteros sent his tee shot behind a pine tree on the first extra hole.

Snead didn't just beat other players. His victories were often meteorological miracles.

His '93 win over Player and Nichols came in a fluke winter storm in San Antonio that sent temperatures plunging into the low 20s—in March.

At the '95 Senior Players Championship, the opposite was true. The temperature at the golf course rose beyond 100 degrees every day. Players who steadfastly refused carts before were driving them all over the TPC of Michigan.

That included Snead.

"I got sick a couple of times," he said. "I normally never ride in a cart, and I rolled my pants legs up and rode down the fairways as fast as the cart would go on a couple of holes, just to get some air on them. I was OK after that.

"Most of my wins were in bad weather, where you really had to hit the ball low, play the wind. There was San Antonio. The Andy Williams in San Diego was wet and muddy. Doral was cold and windy."

Then there was Dearborn and Nicklaus. Even today it amuses Snead how much fuss people made over his beating the Golden Bear.

"Someone asked me how it felt being in a playoff with Nicklaus," Snead recalled. "I said, 'You know what, this wasn't my first rodeo.' "

But it was one of his most memorable rides.

J.C. Snead hits a drive at the 1995 U.S. Senior Open at
Congressional CC in Bethesda, Maryland.

DONNA ANDREWS

In four seasons on the Ladies Professional Golf Association Tour, Donna Andrews thought she had experienced almost everything that could happen to a player, good and bad.

In 1991, just a year after finishing second for rookie-of-the-year honors, Andrews missed the cut in seven straight tournaments.

In 1992, she accidentally hit her ball while taking a practice swing in the first round of the U.S. Women's Open. She penalized herself one stroke, which she assumed was the rule. It was, if you moved your ball back to its original spot. Andrews had not, and was forced to take a two-stroke penalty.

She finished third behind Patty Sheehan and Juli Inkster.

In '93, Andrews was named by *Golf Digest* as the LPGA's "most improved" player. She cracked the winner's circle at the PING-Cellular One Championship. She finished in the top 10 in seven of her final 11 events.

And she came close in another major, finishing in a second-place tie at the U.S. Open.

Now she stood in the 18th fairway of the Mission Hills Country Club during the final round of the 1994 Nabisco Dinah Shore tournament, the first major of the season.

It had perhaps been a day unlike any other for Andrews, a Lynchburg native who in two weeks would celebrate her 27th birthday.

Andrews began with a one-shot lead on Great Britain's Laura Davies and a two-stroke edge over close friend Michelle McGann. In addition to being world-class players, Davies and McGann were the Babe Ruth and Mark McGwire of women's golf, known for driving the ball prodigious, intimidating distances.

Andrews, normally no slouch off the tee, had displayed great discipline and composure in sticking with her strategy, despite always hitting from the shadows created by her competitors.

She had weathered a bizarre mistake on the 14th hole. Andrews reached into her bag for the 6-iron she needed for her shot to the green. She swung, then watched in horror as the ball flew over the putting area.

Donna Andrews used a fine amateur career in Virginia as springboard to success on the LPGA Tour.

She hadn't drawn the 6-iron. She had pulled the 5-iron, an error she survived by pitching to four feet and holing the putt to save par and her share of the lead.

At 17, a poorly played 5-iron led to a bogey. Now she trailed Davies by a stroke with one hole left.

On another day, the 18th at Mission Hills would be the last place Andrews figured to make up a stroke. The hole was a 526-yard par-5. Davies' advantage off the tee was so great that she had played the course's four par 5s in 9-under par, routinely reaching the green in two shots.

What was different this day was the wind. It was blowing in the players' faces. Davies and Andrews knew the long-hitting Brit would have to play more conservatively.

As had been her custom on many holes during the tournament, Davies played a 4-iron off the tee, but she pushed it into the trees down the right side. Andrews hit a 5-wood straight down the middle.

Davies played out with a 2-iron that she busted down the right side, but still in the rough. Andrews hit another perfect 5-wood and had 135 yards to the hole.

Then Davies left Andrews the opening she needed. She hit an 8-iron fat and far left of the hole, 60 feet. Although she still could make par with two putts and find herself in no worse than a playoff, Davies would have to negotiate a putt that went uphill, then downhill, and could be difficult to get close to the hole.

"I didn't dream I'd have a chance to win there until I saw where her third shot went," Andrews recalled. "I knew that was three-putt territory."

Andrews reached into her bag, seeking the 6-iron. This time, she made sure that's what she had before taking one of the most important swings of her career.

"I hit the perfect shot," Andrews said. "I just kept thinking, 'Be the right club . . . Be the right club.' "

It was. Knocked down to burrow through the wind, the ball traveled 135 yards on a line for the flag, stopping five feet from the hole.

As Andrews surmised, Davies needed three putts to hole out. Andrews needed one putt for the birdie that made her a major champion.

"It reassured me that I belonged," Andrews said. "To win a major told me that I had made the right career decision."

No one who watched her grow up in the game ever doubted it.

Donna Andrews was born on April 12, 1967, and grew up in Lynchburg. She doesn't remember how old she was when she took up golf, because she had a club in her hand from the time she was old enough to hold it.

On Sunday afternoons, Barclay Andrews and his wife, Helen, would bring children Jay and Donna to Boonsboro Country Club.

"I had to work at it to keep up with my brother and my dad," Andrews remembered in a 1984 interview.

At E.C. Glass High School, Andrews played basketball and tennis before deciding to concentrate on golf.

"At that point, I remember I had actually decided that it was something I wanted," she recalled.

She spent four seasons on the boys' golf team, playing No. 1 and 2 during her junior and senior years.

"Playing with the guys has helped me," she said as a teen-ager. "I've learned not to be bothered if [an opponent] outdrives me."

By then, she was already established as one of the best women's players in the history of Virginia.

Andrews won the 1983 and 1984 Junior Girls' championships. In 1985, she began one of the most remarkable runs ever seen in Virginia golf, winning five consecutive State Women's Amateur championships.

It was the most dominant reign for any Virginian since Charlottesville's Mary Patton Janssen took

six Women's Amateur titles in a row from 1957 to 1962.

Fittingly, Andrews' last Women's Amateur victory was the most dramatic. Andrews defeated Donna Martz of Broadway in 22 holes at the Cascades Course in Hot Springs.

"She was one of my best friends at the time," Andrews said. "We just had this feeling that, whoever won, it was going to be a great championship."

The two 21-year-olds were even at the turn. They halved 11 holes. Both played the front nine in 3 under par.

Donna Andrews with her winner's trophy from the Women's North South Amateur championship in 1988.

The pivotal hole was No. 16. Martz three-putted for bogey 6 after Andrews put her third shot over the green and scrambled to make bogey. When Martz won the 17th with a birdie to go 1 up, her mistake at 16 was magnified, for she would have closed out the match and pulled off a huge upset.

Andrews evened the match with a routine par at 18.

The two halved the first three holes of sudden death, then Andrews laced her tee shot on the 166-yard fourth hole three feet from the pin. Martz hit her tee shot into a bunker, then blasted to 25 feet. Indicative of the tenacity with which the match was played, Martz made her putt for par.

However, Andrews had no trouble rolling in her birdie try for the victory.

"I'm proud of the way I played," Martz said. "I allowed her to see holes on the back nine she hasn't seen in competition in four years."

That wasn't exactly true, but close. Andrews had beaten Fran Hensley of Martinsville 2 and 1 for the title in 1986. She had defeated Jane Mack of Richmond 3 and 2 in the '87 final. Otherwise, she so dominated the competition that she usually wrapped up her matches in 14 holes or fewer.

"If I had a choice, I would like always to be remembered as a consistently good amateur player who was a nice person and fun to play with," Andrews said. "I suppose I am a tough person on the golf course, but I've never begrudged my opponents' good shots. I have never pictured myself as tough or mean, but I do admit I like to win."

Nothing about her career at the University of North Carolina put that statement in jeopardy. Andrews was a second-team All-American her senior year, graduating in 1989.

In 1985, she received her first lesson from Davis Love Jr., the father of touring pro Davis Love III. They worked together for three years before Love was killed in a plane crash in 1988.

"After meeting him, that's when I decided that if I was going to pursue a professional career, I needed to become more serious about golf," Andrews said.

Intent on winning an amateur tournament with national implications, Andrews flew to Florida two weeks before the 1988 North and South Amateur to huddle with Love.

It was well worth the effort. Andrews, then 21, beat Anne Sander to win the North and South at Pinehurst, the grand North Carolina resort she would soon call home.

"It was like working with a second father," Andrews said of Love. "He treated each person as an individual. He worked with what was best for you. He didn't make all of his students do everything the same way."

Andrews was so devastated by the loss of Love that she went a year without an instructor. Needing help with her short game, she finally chose Jack Lumpkin of Sea Island, Georgia.

She credits Lumpkin with helping her make the late-season charge in 1990 that enabled her to post five top-20 performances. After leading Hiromi Kobayashi in the Rolex rookie-of-the-year race for most of the season, Andrews finished second.

Her '88 victory in the North and South Amateur was significant for one other reason: It came the same week that she met John Reeves.

Reeves, then a teaching pro at Pinehurst, had his eye on Andrews. When he asked her for a date, Andrews cut a deal.

"I told him that if he helped me with my golf game, I'd go to dinner with him," she said. "It worked out that we were in a tournament a week later and I got to spend a lot of time with him, got to know him better as a person. Then, with me at Carolina, we were only an hour away from each other."

Andrews began play in the '94 Dinah Shore with a sense of calm and confidence that she felt would give her the extra edge that can be the difference in victory and a good performance.

Before the tournament, she and Lumpkin had worked vigorously on knockdown shots and shots from the rough.

Then there was Reeves. In 1991, he took a leave of absence to caddie for Andrews. He was on her bag at Mission Hills. By then, the two had been married for five months.

Andrews was two shots behind Nancy Lopez after the first round at Mission Hills. She was one shot behind McGann and Davies after 36 holes.

She moved into the lead after the third round by firing a 5-under-par 67. Her 10-under 206 was one stroke better than Davies and two shots better than McGann.

Reeves provided a crucial moment of comic relief during Saturday's third round. Andrews had just pulled into the lead by making five consecutive birdies. However, she had lost her touch on No. 11, missing a 20-foot putt for par.

Reeves looked at her with bemusement and said, "It's just as well you missed one. The fans were getting bored."

Andrews has frequently said that she thinks of herself and the other pros as entertainers. With the gallery egging her on after the Sunday putt that beat Davies, Andrews did an "entertaining" dive into the lake guarding the 18th green, a Dinah Shore tradition.

"I wish Dinah had been with me," Andrews said, barefoot and wringing the water from her golf shirt. "But I know she was here in spirit."

Since the '94 season, Andrews has been one of the LPGA's marquee players, despite injuries that have kept her from perhaps reaching her full potential.

A series of back problems ruined any chance of a strong 1995 season. Although she played in 24 tournaments, Andrews' best finish was a tie for 20th at the Star Bank LPGA Classic.

Aided by a program of physical therapy, Andrews bounced back the following season to finish a more respectable 39th, then got back in the winner's circle in '97 at the Welch's Circle K Classic.

The 1998 season was a huge success, to a point. Andrews won the Longs Drugs Challenge in California and compiled 14 top-10 finishes and more than $700,000 in prize money.

Donna is a study in concentration as she surveys this birdie putt.

From early-May to mid-June, Andrews finished second four times, including sudden-death losses to Barb Mucha and Annika Sorenstam. She was in prime contention at the U.S. Open at Blackwolf Run in Wisconsin when she heard a "pop" in her hip as she struck a shot during the third round.

In severe pain from then on, Andrews finished tied for 19th.

Doctors diagnosed Andrews' problem as "snapping hip syndrome." A tendon pops over the end of her femur when she extends her hip.

In June 1999, Andrews dislocated her right shoulder in a horse-riding accident near her home in Pinehurst, N.C. She returned to the tour later in the season.

Despite these occasional physical woes, Andrews should just be reaching her prime as a player. There's no reason to believe that her best isn't yet to come.

major champions

Vinny Giles, right, with 1966 State Amateur Championship opponent Nelson Broach on the first tee of The Casacades course in Hot Springs.

VINNY GILES

With the exception of Bobby Jones, perhaps no one has embodied American amateur golf like Marvin Giles III.

Born in Lynchburg, but a longtime resident of Richmond, Vinny Giles won the 1972 U.S. Amateur after finishing second from 1967 to 1969—something no one accomplished before or since.

He won the 1975 British Amateur, beating Mark James, who went on to become the 1999 European Ryder Cup captain.

Giles was just the 11th player in golf history—and the most recent—to win both titles.

He was a member of the U.S. Walker Cup team in 1969, '71, '73, and '75. He played for the United States in the World Cup in 1968, '70, and '72.

He was low amateur at the 1972 Masters.

He was low amateur at the 1973 U.S. Open.

He was low amateur at the 1993, '95, and '97 U.S. Senior Open.

Whether it's his seven State Amateur victories—a record almost certain to stand the test of time—or serving as captain of the 1993 U.S. Walker Cup team,

Giles has either dominated Virginia golf or been its splendid representative on the world stage for four decades.

In 1968, the Virginia State Golf Association changed the format of the State Amateur from match play to stroke for the first time since 1921.

Giles won by 15 shots. The tournament returned to match play in '69 and has remained that way since.

In 1994, when the PGA Tour opened its search to replace retiring Deane Beman as commissioner, the selection committee asked Giles if he was interested in the position. He declined.

The reason was loyalty. The other major impact Giles has had on the game is as president of Pros Inc. He and partner Vernon Spratley began representing professional golfers and other athletes in April 1973. Tom Kite, Lanny Wadkins, Beth Daniel, Davis Love III, and Justin Leonard are just a few of their clients.

While he says his involvement in the business end of the sport created a rift between him and the U.S. Golf Association that led him to distance himself from the national scene in the late 1970s, Giles makes it clear that he wouldn't have done anything differently.

Vinny Giles combines the two things he likes best—cutting deals for his clients and playing golf.

Giles addresses the audience at the 1993 Walker Cup competition at Interlachen Country Club in Minnesota. The U.S. won the competition 19-5.

"A group of players came to Vernon and me initially," Giles explained. "They indicated they felt there was a need for a financial advisor. They trusted us, and you just can't walk away from that. I would have felt like I was abandoning people who put a lot of faith in me from the beginning. I would not have felt right."

It's the same reason, Giles said, that he never gave serious thought to playing the Senior PGA Tour after turning 50 in 1993.

"We have more than a client-agent relationship," he said. "We have a tight friendship that I would never feel right walking away from until I feel like I'm no good at this. And I'm not ready to say that yet."

Giles' involvement in the game began as a boy in Lynchburg. The family lived near Oakwood Country Club and, although they weren't members, the club had no objection to Marvin Giles Jr., who often played to a 1-handicap, and his son "piddling around," as Vinny calls it.

In 1957, Giles won the State Jaycees Junior tournament, then headed off for Episcopal High School in Alexandria—which didn't have a golf team.

Giles played football and basketball and ran track. His attention turned to golf only in summer.

"Golf was expensive," he said. "I never even tried to qualify for the U.S. Junior. We couldn't afford it. But in summer, when I wasn't working, I played every day, 54 holes a day if possible.

"I was blessed with a fairly simple golf swing. I always had a pretty good imagination and an aptitude for the short game. In my most competitive years, that probably carried me. I would never say that I was a great ball-striker. I never remember being a good long-iron player. I was always a good driver of the ball, always a good short-iron player, always a good chipper and always a good bunker player."

Giles began college at North Carolina in 1962 "because that's where I wanted to go to college. I wasn't on a scholarship." Freshmen weren't eligible for varsity competition at the time, but Giles made a mark by winning the Big Four Freshman Tournament, a stroke-play event contested on courses at Duke, Wake Forest, North Carolina, and N.C. State.

When he returned home that summer, Giles won his first State Amateur, a tournament he still considers "the catalyst for everything that's happened since.

"It made me realize that maybe I was better than I thought," he said.

Giles had yet to advance past the third round in four previous trips to the State Amateur. By his own admission, he was playing horribly coming into the tournament at the Cascades Course in Hot Springs. He shot 83 in a practice round and qualified with an 80.

Then something clicked. Giles glided to a 5-and-4 victory over George Beamon of Suffolk in the first round and rallied from a one-hole deficit to defeat Ralph English of Roanoke 2 and 1 that afternoon.

There must have been something about those scores that Giles liked, for the next day he whipped Billy Liles of Roanoke 5 and 4 in the quarterfinals, then survived a penalty stroke midway through the semifinals to oust Jordan Ball of Virginia Beach 2 and 1.

His opponent in the final would be good-natured 23-year-old Sam Wallace of Williamsburg, who earlier in the week had described himself as "the type who doesn't win."

Though Wallace would prove himself wrong by winning State Am titles in 1967 and 1978, he was no match for Giles.

Giles won 6 and 5, missing only seven greens in 31 holes—and one-putting six of them. A 48-foot birdie putt on the sixth hole of the afternoon 18 shattered Wallace's hopes of a comeback.

"I just kept trying, and I just kept getting further in the hole," Wallace said. "Everything I hit was just inches from being good."

Giles played 110 holes in the tournament in 7

over, including a quadruple-bogey 8 on the 20th hole of the final. George Fulton, who refereed the title match, called Giles' performance "the finest since the war."

Giles wasn't the only member of the family to make a splash that week. His father advanced to the final of the State Senior Amateur, which was held a couple of miles away at The Homestead Course. After losing 6 and 5 to Smith Ferebee of Richmond, Marvin, Vinny's mother, Betty, and younger sister Susan drove to the Cascades to check in on Vinny.

Afterwards, when Betty Giles tried to console Wallace, he turned to her and whispered appreciatively, "Someone has to win, Mrs. Giles, and your boy is a grand champion."

An unpretentious man who can be believed when he says he has never spent the first moment thinking about his position in Virginia golf, Giles reveals his life in a winsome, self-deprecating style.

He may have loved college life at Chapel Hill, but he admits he was no fan of academia. Giles left Carolina during Christmas break of 1963. Although he planned to return the following September, he instead continued his college career a little deeper south after receiving a phone call from University of Georgia golf coach H.T. Hollis.

"He said, 'There's a guy on my team who tells me you're pretty good,' " Giles recalled. "Then he says, 'We're losing five seniors, and we'll give you tuition and books for the spring if you come down here in 10 days.' "

At the dinner table that night, Giles jokingly launched into his "you'll never believe what happened to me today" story.

"When I was done, my father said to me, 'Son, how fast can you pack your damn bags?' " Giles said. "One week later I was on a train for the University of Georgia."

The gleam in his eyes says Giles isn't content to end the story there.

"I didn't know where Athens was, and I didn't have a lot of money, so I decided to save three bucks and got off the train in Gainesville rather than go to Atlanta and catch a connector there," he said. "I was congratulating myself for being so smart when I asked the stationmaster when the train for Athens left Gainesville."

"Ain't no train."

"Huh? When's the bus leave?"

"Don't no buses go to Athens."

Five minutes later, Giles stood outside the depot, suitcase, clubs, and shag bag piled on the sidewalk in front of him, and thumb out. Finally, a pickup truck stopped, Giles threw his gear in the back, and climbed in.

"All the time we're driving, I'm thinking to myself, 'Good God, how fast can I get out of here.' "

But he didn't leave until he had a degree and three All-American seasons under his belt.

"Quite honestly, that's where I learned to play," he said. "We had real good players, we played every day, and we'd play $2 Nassau. You lost with any consistency, you didn't have any money. That was your play money, your beer money. You played pretty hard."

He had every intention of turning pro in 1966, but he had promised his father that he would apply to law school.

"I was convinced there was no way I was getting in," he said, shrugging. "My grades weren't all that good."

The University of Virginia thought otherwise.

"When I got in there, I felt obligated to go," he said.

There were other considerations, too. In 1966, total prize money on the PGA Tour was about $6 million. He was a newlywed, and he and wife Key had designs on a family.

"It's so different now," he said. "Most of your travel was in automobiles, and even if you were on a plane, it was a long ride. I went to Australia in 1968, and it took 36 hours from my house to Melbourne. Billy Casper said it was a 9-5 job: Hit balls and play, hit balls and play. I didn't see it that way."

"One of the first things Key said to me was, 'Lord, I don't want to spend the rest of my life in a Holiday Inn.' And those were upscale hotels then.

"The time to have done it would have been '66. I didn't give it much thought when I got out of law school in '69. By then, I had pretty much decided to stay on the amateur side."

There must have been times when he questioned that decision. By 1969, Giles was the dominant figure in Virginia golf, having won the State Am five times and his first of three State Opens. Yet he had been victimized by a series of bizarre, frustrating events in the U.S. Amateur.

Giles began the final day of the '67 Amateur at Broadmoor Country Club in Colorado Springs, Colorado, one shot behind reigning British Amateur champion Bob Dickson.

They remained that way standing on the final tee. Dickson, an army private from Oklahoma who had lost the U.S. Amateur two years before when he was penalized four strokes after calling an infraction on himself for having too many clubs in his bag, launched his tee shot into the woods and had no opening to the green.

When Dickson reached his ball, he claimed that a network television cable prevented him from taking a full swing. He received a free drop, then punched a 6-iron 50 yards from the green. He then chipped eight feet from the hole and converted the par putt.

Giles missed a 30-foot birdie putt that would have given him a tie. The pain in Giles' voice is evident even now.

"I felt it was taken out of my hands by some people who administer the game and don't understand the rules," he said. "They, in my opinion, cost me a minimum of three, and possibly four, shots, with erroneous rulings in the last round.

"At 18, they gave him a drop from the base of a pine tree because his backswing might touch a television cable that was running through the tree. But he couldn't hit the ball in the direction he was swinging because of the trunk of the tree, not the cable. Instead of having to hit it backwards, he hit it down the fairway and got it up for par. Otherwise, he goes backwards and he's 230 yards from the green in two. I'm one shot behind and I'm 130 yards from the green in one."

Moss Beecroft, who was following Dickson closely, caught Giles' attention and flashed him a thumbs-down signal.

"He was telling me that the man had no shot, that he was dead," Giles said. "Next thing I know, he's dropping the ball and hitting it down the fairway towards the green."

Earlier in the round, Dickson got a break Giles found even more outrageous. His opening tee shot sailed out of bounds, struck a blacktop road bordering the fairway, and jumped back into the rough. At least that's the official explanation.

When Dickson and his caddie sought the ball, they found two. Both had identical markings. One was in-bounds, the other out-of-bounds. A couple of caddies came forward and said they had seen Dickson's ball hit the blacktop. Only one ball had a smudge on it, the one in-bounds.

An official ruled that it was Dickson's, after which he made par.

"There were spectators who claimed that his shot ran out of bounds," Giles said. "The rule states that you have to be able to identify your ball. He could not identify his ball.

"I didn't say a word in either case. I had not been around that scene enough. I was a total unknown . . . My feeling, even today, is that I don't get in the middle unless I see something that's so blatantly wrong."

The victory made Dickson the third American golfer after Bobby Jones and Lawson Little to hold both the British and U.S. Amateur titles in the same season.

"I'd be tickled to death under normal circumstances," Giles said that day. "But I felt like I could win it . . . It could have gone either way. It went his."

In 1968 at Scioto Country Club in Columbus, Ohio, Giles trailed 19-year-old Floridian Bruce Fleisher by six shots heading into the final round. However, he had only six players in front of him, among them 21-year-old Hubert Green.

Angry at having kicked away several crucial strokes during Friday's third round, Giles put on a charge unlike any seen before in the tournament. It was made all the more remarkable by the fact that Scioto CC didn't surrender its first below-par score until John Birmingham's 1-under 69 in the third round.

Giles' 5-under 65 remains the lowest final round score in U.S. Amateur history. It is tied for the Amateur's lowest round ever with Kurt Knox's 65, shot at Waverley Country Club in Portland in 1970.

Unfortunately for Giles, almost no one knew it. There was a problem with the scoring system at Scioto, and none of the leaderboards on the course listed a score for Giles.

Playing several groups behind Giles, Fleisher thought he had a four-shot lead with three holes to play and was under no pressure. In reality, Giles was only one behind.

"He told me afterwards, 'Lordy, 'I was on the 18th green 12 feet from the hole when I suddenly realized that I only had a one-shot lead,' " Giles said. "I feel that if he had known at hole 11 or 12 where I stood, it may have affected his game."

Giles finished five shots behind Steve Melnyk in the '69 Amateur at Oakmont, sixth in the 1970 tournament, won by Lanny Wadkins, and third in '71.

"I don't question that at some point the golf gods said, 'Hey, this guy deserves to win one of these,' " Giles said. "I think the golf gods have a lot to say about who wins."

They were chatting up a storm at the '72 Amateur at Charlotte Country Club in North Carolina. Giles, now 29, trailed Mark Pfeil and Greg Stuhler by five shots after the first round, then roared back the next day to fire a 3-under 68 in windy conditions that vaulted him into the lead by one stroke over Bruce Robertson.

Amazingly, it was the first time he'd actually *led* the U.S. Amateur.

"It's the first time I've been this close," Giles said after his bogey-free round. "I like the position. I know some would say they like to catch up, but I like it this way for a change."

Surging, Giles raced to a five-shot lead after 10 holes of the third round, then began giving back strokes. Three consecutive bogeys, and four in his final eight holes, trimmed what had been a comfortable deficit to a more perilous single shot over Mark Hayes. Robertson was two behind, and 20-year-old Ben Crenshaw led a quartet four shots behind.

"I had a great chance to put it away," Giles lamented. "I've opened it up for everybody."

Typical of Giles' career, his breakthrough the next day was anything but routine.

He fell into a tie with Hayes by three-putting the second hole and dropped a shot behind when Hayes birdied from 10 feet at No. 3. When Hayes birdied No. 7, Giles was two behind and only one shot ahead of Crenshaw.

Still trailing by one at the 462-yard, par-4 13th, Giles slashed a 4-iron to three feet of the hole and made the birdie. Rejuvenated, he holed a five-foot birdie putt on the next hole.

Gradually, Giles built the lead to three before making a double-bogey at 15 to bring Hayes and Crenshaw back into it. Giles drove into the rough at 17, knocked it 20 feet from the hole, and "it staggered down in like a drunk" for a monumental birdie that helped him beat Hayes and Crenshaw by three.

"This could have been my last chance," Giles said then. "I know it gets harder every year.

"To be perfectly honest with you, I came down here with less desire than for any other Amateur. I had played more competition, and had gotten to the point where I was tired of playing. I didn't feel I was going to win. I didn't even feel like I was going to

Vinny Giles eyes a tee shot at the 1995 U.S. Senior Open at Congressional CC in Bethesda, Maryland.

have a good tournament. I just wanted to get it over."

Despite the breakthrough in '72, Giles considers 1973 to be the finest year of his career. He was the low amateur at the U.S. Open, playing the first two rounds with Jack Nicklaus. He won the Eastern Amateur, the Porter Cup, played very well in the Walker Cup (a 14-10 U.S. victory) at The Country Club in Brookline, and lost in the (match-play) semi-finals to Craig Stadler the next week at the U.S. Amateur.

When Giles was left off the 1977 Walker Cup squad, the result of what he calls "a running feud with Sandy Tatum of the USGA," Giles turned his back on world-class amateur golf.

"He didn't like the fact that I was making my living at the game, even though he made plenty of living at the game," Giles said, still rankled at the recollection. "In '77, I was at worst the fifth-best player. As an amateur, your only goal is to make an international team. When I didn't make it, I walked away."

Giles found himself in an even more stressful circumstance in the 1972 World Cup in Argentina. It was the anniversary of Juan Peron's return to power. Anti-American sentiments ran high. At the hotel where the U.S. was staying, a radical group somehow rigged a series of bombs that stretched from the second floor to the 24th.

"We were walking towards the hotel when we saw the explosion," Giles said. "It blew the top two floors off the hotel; three or four people were killed, and several more were injured. If we had had a boat or a blank check, we'd have been out of Argentina before the tournament even started."

In 1993, Giles pulled off a seemingly impossible feat. He was 50 years old and hadn't won a State Open since beating Chip Heyl of Sterling on the third playoff hole at Danville GC in 1974.

Yet he opened play at Willow Oaks CC in Richmond with a 4-under 68 followed by a pair of 69s. His even-par 72 the final day was good for a three-shot victory over Bobby Wadkins, Tom McKnight, and Jack Snyder of Palmyra.

"It's one of the highlights of all the golf I've ever played," Giles said. "I went out and beat a lot of people I had no business beating. That's one of the things about my career I'm most proud of. When I was playing my best, I can't think of a time I choked one away."

champions II

Bobby Cruickshank was a three-time runner-up in the U.S.
Open and is a member of the PGA Hall of Fame.

CHAMPIONS II

BOBBY CRUICKSHANK

He was Virginia's first great professional, and it never mattered one bit to purists in the state that Bobby Cruickshank was an adopted member of the Old Dominion.

Maybe that was because there was nothing to dislike about Cruickshank, who was born on Nov. 16, 1894, in Grantown-on-Spey, Scotland, and first swung a club at the age of four.

Depending on who was doing the writing, Cruickshank was either 5-foot-2, 5-3, or 5-4. In any event, his nicknames, "Wee Scot" or "Wee Bobby,' were appropriate.

He was a true hero, having served with the famed Black Watch in World War I. He had watched his brother, standing just yards away, die in battle. Caught in a German ambush, Cruickshank was wounded, captured, and taken to a prisoner-of-war camp for eight months.

There, Cruickshank had saved the life of another POW, Tommy Armour's brother Sandy. Sandy Armour was dying of dysentery but slowly regained his strength after Cruickshank began giving him his rations. As if Cruickshank's

story weren't courageous enough, he escaped from the Germans two days before the armistice ending the war.

Cruickshank was a superb teacher. Among his pupils was Carol Semple-Thompson, the first player to win the U.S. Women's Amateur, Mid-Amateur, and Senior Amateur titles. In addition, she twice has been low amateur at the U.S. Women's Open and has been a member of a record 10 Curtis Cup squads.

"He had a great sense of humor, a real twinkle in his eyes, which worked very well because I was about 10 or 11 when I first went to him," Semple-Thompson said. "He was a real stickler for the short game, and he made me practice it a lot.

"He knew how to tailor his lessons to someone's personality, which is something all good teachers do. He was always getting me to pause at the top of my swing. That fit my personality. I'm sort of slow-moving."

Semple-Thompson said the most important lesson Cruickshank taught her was to be true to herself.

"It was always hard for me to be a 'hitter' as opposed to a 'swinger,' " she

Bobby Cruickshank hits a tee shot during one of his many rounds of golf in Virginia.

said. "That fit with Bobby, who taught an old-fashioned swing."

While Cruickshank was acknowledged by all as one of the game's greatest iron players and putters, he also possessed a damaging flaw.

Armour, who competed with Cruickshank as a kid in Scotland, wrote in a 1967 issue of *Professional Golfer* that "once or twice during the round, he would hit a quick hook. That was his only weakness."

Whether because of his size, his gregarious personality, his style of play, or maybe all of the above, Cruickshank quickly became one of America's favorite players once he came to this country in 1921. Armour once said that he thought Cruickshank had made a mistake picking a career in golf. He was such a great mime and comedian that he could have become a star actor.

"He was the darling of the galleryites," *New York Times* columnist Arthur Daley wrote. "They were the forerunners of Arnie's Army, although they had no name, as does Arnold Palmer's group of loyalists. Maybe they might have been known as Bobby's Brigade—if anyone had thought of it then."

He was a man anyone felt comfortable teasing, even in his moments of greatest triumph.

In a 1967 letter to Cruickshank congratulating him on his selection to the Hall of Fame, U.S. Golf Association executive director Joseph C. Dey wrote:

You have been a great man in golf and a great man for golf all these centuries—I mean, decades. So your selection for the Hall of Fame was, to my mind, just a natural outgrowth of what you are and what you have done in golf. I congratulate you from the bottom of my heart, Bobby. Long may you wave!

By the time Cruickshank arrived in Virginia in 1932 to become head pro at the Country Club of Virginia in Richmond, the stories about him were legendary. His arrival was widely anticipated, and he immediately ingratiated himself to the people of the state.

Back then, the Virginia State Open carried a prize of just $150. But Cruickshank always entered, and he won it six times.

"People would ask why he played in such a [relatively minor] event," 1950 PGA champion and close friend Chandler Harper recalled. "And Bobby said, 'Because I'm a Virginian now; I'd play if there was no prize.' He was a great man."

According to Armour, Cruickshank also was "the unluckiest golfer in the game." One look at his record in the game's major championships supports his claim.

Cruickshank lost 3 and 2 to eventual champion Gene Sarazen in the semifinals of the 1922 PGA Championship. It was the first of two PGA semifinal losses to Sarazen, who would become Cruickshank's roadblock to greatness.

Ten years later, at the U.S. Open at Fresh Meadow Country Club in New York, Cruickshank was firmly in contention, scoring 69 and 68 in the final two rounds. But that was the year Sarazen played the final 28 holes in 100 strokes, relegating Cruickshank to second by three shots.

On the final day of the 1934 U.S. Open at Merion in Ardmore, Pennsylvania, Cruickshank had the lead midway through the morning portion of a 36-hole day. At No. 11, he misplayed his pitch to the green. The ball flew into a brook, then clanked off a rock and bounded onto the green.

The ever-exuberant Cruickshank tossed his wedge into the air, doffed his cap and proclaimed, "Thank you, Lord!" Seconds later, the club came crashing down on Cruickshank's skull.

Dazed, Cruickshank never recovered. He played the final four holes of the afternoon round in 4 over par to finish second, two shots behind Olin Dutra.

Cruickshank won 20 tournaments on the PGA Tour. In 1927, he was golf's leading money winner. But it was his narrow misses for which he was famous, including one in 1923 that became one of golf's watershed events.

BOBBY JONES BECOMES A CHAMPION

Bobby Jones came to the final hole at Inwood Country Club on Long Island, site of the 1923 U.S. Open, with a three-shot lead. He faced a frightening 425-yard par 4 with the narrowest of fairways and a lagoon protecting the green.

He also faced his own growing demons.

Despite the 21-year-old amateur's acknowledged genius, Jones had played in 11 previous major tournament without a triumph.

That finally seemed certain to change. Jones had played the 18th in 2 under par during the first three rounds, and he split the fairway with what looked to be his final tee shot of the tournament.

With a breeze in his face and that ominous lagoon guarding the green, Jones opted to hit his approach shot with a "spoon," or 3-wood, rather than a long iron. He hooked it badly, the ball flying further and further left of the green before finally coming to rest in the rough adjacent to the 12th tee.

Still, he had only to pitch the ball over a pot bunker to reach the green, where even a two-putt for bogey would assure him the championship. Instead, Jones plopped his third shot into the bunker. He blasted out, then putted twice to finish with a double-bogey 6 and a total of 296.

Jones trudged off the course, lowering his head when approached by O.B. Keeler, his friend and future biographer.

"I didn't finish like a champion," Jones murmured to Keeler, who tried to cheer him. "I finished like a yellow dog."

Sarazen, the defending champion and Jones' playing partner, was so convinced that Jones had won despite the brutal finish that he tried to offer him the cup before the rest of the field had finished play.

Jones refused to accept it.

Meanwhile, Cruickshank, who had teed off at least an hour after Jones, finished his final round of regulation with what may have been the most brilliant shot of his career.

Knowing he needed birdie to tie, Cruickshank slashed a mid-iron from the middle of the 18th fairway. It easily cleared the lagoon and stopped just seven feet from the hole. As he arrived at the green, he was greeted by an ovation from a gallery estimated at 11,000.

The 28-year-old Cruickshank, ever the showman, paused, removed his cap, and took a quick bow. Then he knelt behind the ball. Later, he admitted that he was offering a prayer that he would make the putt to force Jones into a playoff, a prayer that was answered.

THE PLAYOFF

Because of Jones' collapse at 18 the previous day, and his 0-for-11 record in major championships, Cruickshank was a 10-to-7 favorite to win a playoff that was among the most thrilling in golf history.

Only three holes were halved, and the two contestants went to the 18th tee still tied.

Unfortunately for Cruickshank, it was here that Armour's analysis of his friend's weakness proved prophetic. Cruickshank, with the honors, hit an ugly top-hook into a much steadier breeze than had blown the day before. The ball, which traveled barely 150 yards, settled in the left rough behind a clump of trees.

Jones hit what began as a beautiful shot, then drifted right and settled onto some loose dirt on the right edge of the rough. A terrible break.

Cruickshank had no choice but to lay up short of the lagoon. Jones then faced a crucial decision: play safe and hope he could beat Cruickshank on the green or in extra holes, or go for the flag and risk losing the ball to the water 195 yards in the distance.

Jones didn't hesitate. He grabbed a 1-iron and sent the ball soaring straight and true across the lagoon. It came to rest six feet from the hole. The 10,000 fans surrounding the green roared their approval. Jones lit a cigarette and began his long-awaited victory stroll.

Still, Jones made only par. Cruickshank, simultaneously awed and devastated by Jones' shot, took a double-bogey and lost by two.

Moments later, the loser gave a gracious, heartfelt concession speech that some said made him almost as many fans as his oft-inspired play.

"I am indeed pleased to have been second, to have been in a playoff with the world's greatest golfer," Cruickshank began. "I have had many illusions slain. But Bobby Jones, to me, is an enduring joy, a dream come true, of splendid youth in love with wonderful sportsmanship, an amateur golfer out for laurels only."

Later, he would call Jones "Harry Vardon at his best, or better than that. To be defeated by him is glory enough."

Jones was practically speechless. He grabbed Cruickshank's arm, hugged him tightly, and whispered in his ear something that sounded like "game old boy."

BACK IN VIRGINIA

From 1933 to 1937, Cruickshank was untouchable in the Virginia State Open. The closest anyone came to beating him was in '37, when Ernie Ball of Charlottesville forced him into an 18-hole playoff at Farmington Country Club. Cruickshank took the playoff by two strokes.

In 1938, Chandler Harper ended Cruickshank's streak at five in a row, but the next year at Danville, the Wee Scot bounced back.

"He was so good that no one could beat him for about six years," Harper recalled. "The only thing that changed was that he got a little age on him."

Cruickshank stayed at the Country Club of Virginia until 1948, then moved to Chartiers Country Club in Pittsburgh. He was there until his retirement in 1969, two years after his induction into the PGA Hall of Fame.

Cruickshank died on Aug. 27, 1975, in Delray Beach, Florida, at the age of 80.

What a foursome! From left: Bobby Jones, Gene Sarazen, Bobby Cruickshank, and Walter Hagen.

champions II

Robert Wrenn grimaces on the 18th green at the 1987 Buick Open
after just missing a birdie pitch that would have tied the record for
the lowest 72-hole tournament score in PGA Tour history.

ROBERT WRENN

Any other week of his life, Robert Wrenn probably would have inter-preted car trouble while driving to a tournament sponsored by an auto manufacturer as a bad omen. That wasn't his mind-set the third week of July in 1987, which is remarkable, considering the circumstances.

He had missed the cut at the Quad City Classic in Coal Valley, Illinois, the previous week, his sixth "MC" in nine weeks. His putting was in total disarray. He hadn't made enough money on the PGA Tour to pay his bills. Now it was late Sunday afternoon, four days before the Buick Open, and the courtesy car carrying him from Detroit Airport to Grand Blanc was stranded on a desolate road, emergency lights flashing.

Wrenn watched as his driver disappeared to find a farmhouse they passed several miles earlier to call for help. He got out and sat on the hood.

"Believe it or not, I thought, 'This is great. I can sit here and relax, watch-ing the sunset,'" Wrenn recalled. "I used the experience as part of a refocusing I had just done in which I was going to make the best of everything that came to me. I wasn't going to get upset at anything. If I hit a bad shot, I was just going to move on and try to hit the next one to the best of my ability.

"That week was one of the few times in my life I was able to convince myself to do it that way, then follow through and execute my plan."

When Wrenn climbed inside another courtesy car one week later, it was as a runaway winner of the Buick Open and a member of an elite group that included Ben Hogan, Lanny Wadkins, Greg Norman, Craig Stadler, Johnny Miller, and John Huston.

Wrenn, then a 27-year-old native of Midlothian whose previous shining moment had been winning the 1983 Indonesian Open, scorched the 7,014-yard, par-72 Warwick Hills Golf and Country Club in 26-under-par 262.

Until Huston posted a remarkable 28-under-par 260 at the 1998 United Airlines Hawaiian Open, the only golfers to better Wrenn's score in a 72-hole event were Hogan at the Portland Invitational in 1945 and Mike Souchak at the Texas Open in '55. Wadkins, Stadler, and Norman needed 90 holes to reach 27-under.

Robert Wrenn has traded in his golf clubs for a microphone, analyzing golf for ESPN.

"What I shot at that tournament was unbelievable," Wrenn said. "I don't know if I'll ever be able to do it again, but what it lets you know is that you're capable of doing it. It was something very special. Not everyone has something like that happen to them in their life."

Wrenn came within inches of joining Hogan and Souchak. His birdie pitch from behind the 18th green perched on the lip of the cup but wouldn't fall. As it was, he finished seven shots ahead of Dan Pohl, eight in front of Scott Hoch, and nine up on Ken Green.

"God couldn't shoot that well," Green quipped.

When Wrenn, who began the final round with a six-stroke lead, walked into the locker room on Sunday, he found a note from Wadkins:

"Take no prisoners"

"That's all he wrote," Wrenn said. "No flowers, nothing. Just 'Take no prisoners.' "

Wrenn had always admired Wadkins, had even followed him to Wake Forest, which both attended on the Bud Worsham Scholarship that Arnold Palmer founded.

"I always liked his attitude on the golf course, but I was always much more conservative than Lanny was," Wrenn said. "Then again, I never considered myself having Lanny's ability from tee to green. Very few players ever have."

With his parents, sister, and some friends looking on after a hasty flight to Michigan Saturday night, Wrenn put Wadkins' advice to work immediately. He birdied the first and third holes, and when Green made bogey on No. 3, Wrenn's bulge was nine. For good measure, he added an eagle and three more birdies.

At the time, Wrenn said, "it was like some outer force took over and led me around." Years later, he sees things differently. There was no outer force. What he achieved was triggered by physical adjustments and from something deep inside of him.

"A second-tier player—and when I was playing my best, I felt I was near the top of the second tier—tends to become too much of a perfectionist in his attitude about how to swing a golf club and how to play the round," Wrenn explained. "If they don't play up to those expectations, they berate themselves.

"I was the king of that. I did it all the time."

Wrenn, who admits his passion for tinkering with his swing has been a detriment, was working with fellow pro Mac O'Grady that week. He stood closer to the ball than usual. He began hitting the ball from right to left, abandoning his customary left-to-right pattern.

More important, he said, a new putting drill he employed worked better than he ever imagined.

"I made more putts that week than I probably have in all the years since then," Wrenn said. "I'd feel my head being very still, very steady, and just work on pushing forward from the ball.

"It was the same routine every time: Hold my head steady and work on pushing forward. Take two looks at the hole, take it back, and feel the push forward. I always had a problem not accelerating through the ball because I always had a fairly long stroke."

Although it may not have mattered in the end, Wrenn points to one shot, one incident, every day that helped him down his triumphant path.

On his final hole Thursday, Wrenn hit his tee shot through the fairway and into an adjoining one. Using a 7-iron, he then rapped the ball 20 feet from the hole and converted the birdie.

On Friday, Wrenn hit his tee shot on the long par-3 eighth hole 20 yards over the green, near a concession stand. He had one shot, and it wasn't high percentage.

"I hit this little bump-and-run shot that dribbled up off all this grass that had been trampled by spectators, dribbled up onto the green, then runs up there about six feet from the hole," Wrenn said. "And I make it for par. I could sit there with a whole

bucket of balls and probably not get more than a few on the green, let alone get it up and down."

That was on his way to a course-record-tying 63.

"On a day like that," Wrenn said, "you have to be a little bit lucky and a whole lot good. Every time I got into trouble that week, I hit a good recovery shot and made a good putt."

After a 5-under-par 67 on Saturday, Wrenn confided to fellow pro Jeff Sluman that he was nervous about the next day.

"Look," Sluman told him, "you were nervous today and look what you did. You are playing as well as anybody in the world. You have to accept that, and not get in your own way. Go out and keep playing like you're the best player in the world right now.'"

Wrenn finished the 1987 season 52nd on the money list with $203,557. He was 52nd the next year as well, with $209,404. And he added a 55th-place money finish the following season with just under $250,000.

"On the one hand, it seems like a 15-minutes-of-fame deal," he said when asked about the Buick triumph. "On the other hand, it set me on a certain platform. It enabled me to do things like my job with ESPN. It set me on a different tier in golf. I always know I've got that one win. I always know I had that one special week."

He would have another, although on a considerably smaller stage.

In 1991, Wrenn entered the State Open, then sponsored by Signet Bank, at the request of a friend. It turned out to be a history-making week.

Wrenn played Willow Oaks Country Club in Richmond with the same precise fury he exhibited at the Buick Open. After opening with a pair or 68s, Wrenn devastated the field with a 9-under-par 63, the competitive course record, to take a 12-shot lead after 54 holes.

"Usually when you shoot 63, you have to make some long putts or hole a bunker shot or something;

Robert didn't have to really even work at it," marveled Charlottesville's Pete Mitchell. He was the professional closest to Wrenn—at 16 shots off the pace. "He hit it in the fairway, he hit his approaches close to the pins, and he made the putts. He made it look so easy."

Wrenn finished off the event with a 69 that gave him a tournament-record 268 and maintained his 12-stroke margin—another record.

Wrenn, who consulted with architect Lester George in the design of The Colonial Golf Course in Williamsburg, is an analyst on ESPN golf telecasts.

THE GOLFERS WHO HAVE FINISHED A PGA TOURNAMENT THE MOST SHOTS UNDER PAR:

- 28: JOHN HUSTON, 1988 UNITED AIRLINES HAWAIIAN OPEN, 260
- 27: MIKE SOUCHAK, 1955 TEXAS OPEN, 257
- 27: BEN HOGAN, 1945 PORTLAND INVITATIONAL, 261
- 27: LANNY WADKINS, 1985 BOB HOPE CLASSIC, 333*
- 27: CRAIG STADLER, 1985 BOB HOPE CLASSIC, 333*
- 27: GREG NORMAN, 1985 LAS VEGAS INVITATIONAL, 333**
- 26: GAY BREWER, 1967 PENSACOLA OPEN, 262
- 26: ROBERT WRENN, 1987 BUICK OPEN, 262
- 25: CHANDLER HARPER, 1954 TEXAS OPEN, 259
- 25: JOHNNY MILLER, 1975 TUCSON OPEN, 263
- 25: TIM NORRIS, 1982 GREATER HARTFORD OPEN, 259

* WADKINS DEFEATED STADLER IN A PLAYOFF AT THIS 90-HOLE TOURNAMENT.

** ACHIEVED IN A 90-HOLE TOURNAMENT

Robert Wrenn blasts out of the sand during his 1987 Buick Open victory, a tournament that saw him shoot a near-record 26-under-par 262 for the 72-hole PGA Tour event.

BOBBY MITCHELL

Bobby Mitchell's life story was so good that he shouldn't have had to beat Jack Nicklaus in the 1972 Tournament of Champions for people to finally hear it.

Mitchell began caddying at Danville Golf Club when he was 11. Two years later, he bought his first club from the son of a farmer on whose land the Mitchells lived. The pitching wedge cost him 90 cents, a pretty good bargain even in 1956.

When he wasn't carrying someone else's clubs, he had hold of his own. Almost daily, Mitchell would sneak onto the course at the fifth hole, a short walk from his house, and play the holes that were hidden from the clubhouse and pro Al Smith's eagle eye.

But you know kids. Mitchell soon grew bold, started playing more and more holes, creeping closer and closer to the clubhouse.

"When I'd get to 17, I'd play fast, because I knew that Mr. Smith could see me from the clubhouse," Mitchell recalled. "He chased me off a few times, and I'm sure there were a few times he looked the other way."

Smith, a wonderful player and a class act who won the State Open three times, must have gotten tired of shooing Mitchell. When Mitchell was 12, Smith hired him to help in the pro shop sweeping up and cleaning clubs.

By the time he was 15, Mitchell had abandoned school and declared his intention to make his living in golf. Smith promoted him to assistant pro.

"He had a great impact on my golf and my life," Mitchell said. "If it hadn't been for him, I probably wouldn't have been in golf. He was such a good teacher around kids, such a good person, that a lot of good players came out of there. He took time with them, always tried to help the better players—and those who weren't so good, either."

With Mitchell, the question wasn't whether or not he was good. The question was how good.

He began revealing the answer in 1965 by winning the Virginia State Golf Association Open at the Country Club of Virginia's James River Course. Not long after, he won the State Open sponsored by the Virginia PGA at Arnolds Ranch in Disputanta. He and Chandler Harper are the only two players in Virginia history to accomplish that feat.

Bobby Mitchell coaxes a putt.

Bobby Mitchell receives congratulations from Jack Nicklaus after beating him in the 1972 MONY Tournament of Champions.

Mitchell had never seen the Arnolds Ranch course. He didn't play a practice round because he was working in the pro shop at Danville GC. Nonetheless, he beat a field that included Harper, Smith, and Tom Strange by three shots.

"This boy has it," exclaimed Jack Isaacs, a five-time State Open titlist and another victim of Mitchell's. "He's the best I've seen in Virginia, strong as a mule. They say he's going on the PGA Tour next year, and he won't have any trouble. Pretty soon, everybody will know who he is."

Mitchell *did* join the PGA Tour in 1966. Isaacs' prediction that it wouldn't be long before Mitchell became famous was another matter entirely.

Mitchell earned just $5,029 during his first two years on the Tour.

"You talk about Lee Trevino being a destitute peon; nobody had a harder time than this guy," said Sonny Ridenhour, a North Carolina pro and friend of Mitchell's. "He came up the old-fashioned way, from the caddy shack and the shop. He came up like Hogan, Mangrum, Demaret and the old-timers did. But he knows the game and he knows what he wants and he goes out and gets it."

Sometimes, it eluded his grasp.

At the 1970 Azalea Open in Wilmington, North Carolina, Mitchell held a four-shot lead with 18 holes to play. He was ahead by two shots with three holes left. He finished by three-putting the last three holes and finished second to Cesar Sanudo.

Six months later, Mitchell entered the Cleveland Open at Beechmont Country Club. After 54 holes, he led by four strokes, exactly the same scenario as in Wilmington.

"I was nervous," Mitchell said. "I woke up five or six times. Finally, I got up around 7:30 and tried to figure out how I was going to play [the round]. I never did come up with anything."

That's not true. Mitchell came up with a 6-under-par 65 that gave him a seven-shot victory over Charles Coody and a nine-stroke spread over Bruce Crampton.

Mitchell's 22-under-par score of 262 was the second-best 72-hole score on the PGA Tour in 15 years. The 28-year-old pro, who had never won more than $36,000 in a season, took home $30,000.

"What I did at Wilmington haunted me a little, and it helped me," Mitchell said. "I didn't let this one get away. My concentration was a lot better. Crampton started the last round birdie-birdie-par. I started birdie-birdie-birdie. I wasn't about to let it get away, and that's what got me into the Tournament of Champions."

He nearly went there as the reigning Masters champion.

Mitchell had finished in a three-way tie for second at Augusta National with Crampton and Tom Weiskopf, three shots behind Nicklaus. Mitchell said there wasn't much doubt that Nicklaus would win; he was comfortably ahead until the last day, when he backed up slightly.

However, had Mitchell done a better job on Augusta National's famous par-3 12th hole, Nicklaus would have had to work a lot harder for what was his fourth green jacket. Instead, Mitchell was 6 over par for the hole during the championship—two double-bogeys and two bogeys.

"Nicklaus played the hole in 2 under," Mitchell said. "He beat me by eight shots on that one hole, and I finished three behind him. If I just could have made a few pars on that hole, I could have won the Masters. My life probably would have been a lot different.

"The funny thing is that I still don't think that hole is that tough. The green is not very big. In '72, the wind wasn't blowing that hard. There was a little breeze, but I just didn't pick the right club. I was never in the water. I was always over the green in the sand trap."

What Mitchell saw after returning to Danville offered no solace. On the cover of a national golf magazine were pictures of Nicklaus, Weiskopf, Crampton, and Jim Jamison, the low amateur.

What about Mitchell? You could say he was

invisible. Mitchell did say that to the press a couple of weeks later after shooting a second-round 65 to grab a four-shot lead at the MONY Tournament of Champions at La Costa Country Club north of San Diego.

"I called myself 'The Invisible Man,' " Mitchell said. "I just felt like I wasn't getting what I deserved [in the press]. I mean, you finish second at the Masters, you deserve something, right? And I told them that I felt like I was invisible. I said, 'Sometimes, I don't even know I'm out there.' "

Mitchell shot 75 on Saturday to fall two shots behind Nicklaus. Nonetheless, they would be paired in Sunday's final round. That morning, Mitchell went to the practice range and watched Nicklaus warm up.

"I convinced myself that I was going to beat him," Mitchell said. "I made a plan—and this is the only time I've ever done this in my life. I made up my mind that I wouldn't watch him hit one shot. I'd played with Nicklaus, Arnold Palmer, Lee Trevino, and if you watched them, you'd lose track of what you were trying to do."

If Mitchell had the honor, he would hit his shot, then move to the side of the tee and stare straight down the fairway. If Nicklaus' shot crossed his line of vision, Mitchell would tell Jack, "Nice shot," then take off for his ball. He never saw a single swing the Golden Bear made.

Mitchell was so focused that he didn't realize until someone told him after the round that Nicklaus had broken his driver on the 16th hole.

"It's uncanny," Mitchell said. "I have tried, but I have never been able to do that again."

Mitchell pulled into a tie for the lead when Nicklaus double-bogeyed the fifth hole. Mitchell surrendered a one-shot advantage when he missed a two-foot par putt on 17. The two wound up in a playoff.

The playoff figured to be a putting contest. With few exceptions, Mitchell and Nicklaus had been drilling them into the hole from all distances and angles the entire day.

"Every time he knocked in a putt, I knocked one in on top of his," Mitchell said. "Finally, on the 13th hole, he said something to me. I'd just knocked the ball in the rough, hit it short of the green, and chipped it long, about 15 feet on the back fringe of the green. Then I went back there and knocked it in the hole.

"We walk over to the next tee, and he looks at me and says, 'Nice putt—*again.*' And all I said was thanks; then I kept going."

The playoff began on the 14th hole, a par 3. Mitchell hit a 3-iron off the bottom of the club, but got enough of the ball to send it onto the green, 20 feet from the hole.

Nicklaus missed the green to the left, then chipped his second shot eight feet past the hole.

Mitchell's putt was downhill and slick, and he would have been more than happy just to get it close.

"But it kept breaking down and down and it caught the lip of the cup," Mitchell said. "It went around the hole, then dropped in the back door."

When the next issue of *Golf World* came out, Mitchell found a pleasant surprise on the cover. Beneath a photo showing him in a powerful follow-through was the headline:

UNDERRATED NO MORE:
BOBBY MITCHELL, GIANT-KILLER

Mitchell won $113,719 that season, 11th on the money list. When he left the Tour after the 1988 season, he had accumulated $422,499 in official earnings.

Bobby Mitchell clinches his 1972 MONY Tournament of Champions win against Jack Nicklaus by sinking this 20-foot birdie putt.

champions II

Mark Carnevale honed his skills for the pro game at
Williamsburg's Golden Horseshoe and in college at
James Madison University.

MARK CARNEVALE

He was the PGA Tour's rookie of the year in 1992. He also may have been that season's most surprising winner.

Mark Carnevale was in a hopeful daze as he walked through the locker room of the Council Fire Golf & Country Club in Chattanooga, Tennessee, on July 19, 1992.

He had just finished off a round of 8-under-par 64 to grab a two-shot lead over Ed Dougherty and Dan Forsman. Both of them were still playing their final rounds of the $800,000 Chattanooga Classic.

"Guys were coming up to me saying, 'Hey, way to go,' and I was like, 'Yeah, yeah, whatever,' " Carnevale said. "I guess I was using negative psychology, thinking that someone was bound to catch me. It was a feeling that I could never explain—how it happened, why it happened. It was an unbelievable experience."

That would keep it in line with the story of Carnevale's career, which is pretty unbelievable.

Carnevale, who taught himself the game while working at the Golden Horseshoe Golf Club in Williamsburg, was 31 years old when he beat Dougherty and Forsman to win $144,000.

He had turned professional in 1983, at age 23, after graduating from James Madison University. From 1983 through 1991, his earnings totaled just $2,584. He even left the Tour in 1990 to take a job with Merrill-Lynch.

On his first day of work, he got into a conversation with a co-worker doing the same job. That person told Carnevale he'd been doing the same thing for eight years.

Carnevale quit that day.

"I decided to go back and do what I knew how to do, with a little better commitment," he said, smiling.

The week before Chattanooga, Carnevale was back in Williamsburg, playing the Anheuser-Busch Classic at Kingsmill. All week, he hit the ball crisply and putted well, but never caught a break.

"I didn't go to Chattanooga thinking of anything other than trying to play well," Carnevale said. "What happened just kind of happened."

It didn't start happening until the third round.

Even then, most of the attention was on Dougherty, a Pennsylvanian with Popeye-like arms. Dougherty started play Saturday 10 shots behind leader Dan

Virginia native Mark Carnevale lets loose with his driver on the first tee at the 1999 Michelob Championship played on the River Course at the Kingsmill Resort in Williamsburg.

Halldorson. But he leaped past Halldorson and everyone else in the field by fashioning a course-record 10-under-par 62.

Carnevale, meanwhile, quietly put himself in contention with a 6-under 66. When he blazed around the front side Sunday in 4 under, Carnevale knew he had a chance to win.

"When I got on the back side, I looked at the leader board constantly," Carnevale said. "I'm the kind of player who is aggressive; I want to know where I am."

He made a birdie 3 at the 10th after hitting his approach a few feet from the cup. He eagled the 536-yard par-5 11th, then made birdie 2 on the next hole.

He was 8 under for the round, with plenty of birdie possibilities remaining. Yet the rest of the way would be anything but smooth sailing.

Carnevale made a bogey 6 on the 13th hole when he three-putted. After a par on the 14th, Carnevale made consecutive birdies on the 15th and 16th holes to put away the win.

"I remember just standing near the green and I had a beer in my hand," Carnevale said, laughing. "I really didn't know what was going on."

Buoyed by the result, Carnevale went on to win $220,922 that season, 70th on the money list.

Winning big-time golf tournaments may have been new to Carnevale, but success in sports certainly wasn't. He'd been around it all of his life.

In 1946, Mark's father, Ben Carnevale, coached the University of North Carolina basketball team to its

Mark Carnevale watches his playing partners tee off on the 10th hole during the first round of the 1999 Nike Dominion Open in Richmond.

first NCAA championship game, although the Tar Heels fell to Oklahoma State.

By the time Mark was born in 1960, Ben Carnevale had moved to the Naval Academy, where he first took his son golfing. Mark was 12 when the Carnevales moved to Williamsburg, where his father served as athletic director at William and Mary from 1972 to 1981.

"I started playing when my father was at the Naval Academy, and there was an immediate attraction," Carnevale said. "As I got older, it provided an opportunity for my father and me to spend a lot of time together."

After Carnevale moved to Williamsburg, Mark worked at the practice range of the Golden Horseshoe Gold Course so that he could play as much as time allowed.

"If I wanted to play in these summer tournaments for juniors or whatever, I had to earn the money for the entry fee," Carnevale said.

Although there have been periods in his career in which he has struggled, Carnevale has never doubted the wisdom of his decision to play professionally. Neither have some of the other people in his life.

Three years after his win in Tennessee, Carnevale was playing in the Merrill-Lynch Shootout at the Kemper Open in Maryland.

"I get to the first tee and who's there but the gentleman who hired me, the man I quit on," Carnevale recalled. "And he comes over and says, 'Mark, you made the right decision.' "

Carnevale's victory at Chattanooga in 1992
is the highlight of his career.

champions II

Carl Paulson confers with his caddie during the 1999
Nike Dominion Open in Richmond, Virginia.

CARL PAULSON

While Carl Paulson would tell you that he loves reading spy novels, the story he liked most had almost no suspense at all.

It's about a professional golfer born in Quantico and raised in Virginia Beach who flirted with success on the PGA Tour, slipped a little, then spent three back-breaking years clawing his way back to the top.

Playing in his 83rd consecutive Nike Tour event—a three-year record for grit and determination—Paulson finally broke into the winner's circle in September 1999 in Sandy, Utah.

He blistered the field and Willow Creek Country Club to win the Nike Utah Classic by six strokes at 22-under-par 266 and collect $67,000.

And he wasn't done.

After taking a week off—"I think I'm entitled," he announced wearily—he returned to the Tour in Boise, Idaho.

He also returned to the winner's circle.

Expecting nothing from himself but his best effort, Paulson cruised through Hillcrest Country Club in 18-under-par 266, four strokes better than fellow Virginian Michael Muehr and Joel Edwards.

"I had been playing well all year, but I finally put the hammer down in Utah," he said proudly.

His winner's share of $58,500 vaulted him into first place on the '99 Nike Tour earnings list with more than $220,000, just the third player in the history of that tour to exceed $200,000 in one season.

When the top 15 Nike money winners began play on the PGA Tour in 2000, as mandated by the rules, Paulson was among them. He might have made it even without his two Western triumphs, though one would be hard-pressed to find someone more deserving of victory than Paulson.

Prior to the Utah Classic, Paulson had accumulated six top 10 finishes during the '99 season. During the final round of each, he shot a round of par or lower, only to be beaten by someone just a little hotter.

"Sometimes it's your week, sometimes it's not," he said after Utah. "It took me a long time to figure that out. Everything just fell into place."

Rather, Paulson put it into place by leaving some unnerving distractions behind him.

Rain caused the postponement of most of the second round. When Paulson

Carl Paulson tees off at the 1999 Michelob Championship on the River Course at Kingsmill.

Paulson's powerful, fluid swing has made him one of golf's longest hitters.

Paulson's victory came with a special perk: an automatic invitation to play in the next day's Ganter Cup Challenge, also at Willow Creek. It was an exhibition featuring PGA Tour stars David Duval, Fred Couples, Craig Stadler, and John Cook versus Paulson and three other Nike Tour players.

Paulson drew Duval, the second-ranked player in the world, and nearly beat him. The two were tied after 13 holes. Then Duval hit a wedge from the rough into the hole for an eagle 2 on the 14th.

Paulson barely missed an eagle 3 on the 17th hole, though the birdie drew him to a shot behind. On 18, Paulson's attempt at a birdie to tie the match stayed out of the cup, enabling Duval to win 73-74.

"Neither David nor I were playing our best golf," Paulson said. "But he made a 2 on a par 4, and that's pretty tough to beat."

The Ganter Cup loss did nothing to diminish Paulson's cheery, confident mood. It only reinforced in his mind what he had been telling himself since leaving the University of South Carolina in 1993 after an All-American career: He belonged at golf's highest level.

There had been evidence of it before.

At the 1995 Fall PGA Tour Qualifying School at Bear Lakes Country Club in Palm Beach, Florida, he birdied the 90th and last hole to win medalist honors over Keith Sutherland and Steve Hart by one shot.

At the '95 Disney Classic in Lake Buena Vista, Florida, Paulson equaled the low round of the season on the PGA Tour, a 10-under-par 62 that helped him finish in a tie for seventh. After two seasons on the PGA Tour, Paulson returned to the Nike Tour in 1997, though he had that special memory to bring back with him.

"You've got to understand: This is a five- or six-year process," he said in a 1995 interview. "When I get into my prime, which is in your early 30s for a golfer, I want to be one of the best players."

Paulson's victories in Utah and Idaho came just a few months shy of his 29th birthday.

arrived at the course on Saturday, he still had 14 holes of his second round to play, plus his third 18.

He responded by posting a second-round 64 to take a two-shot lead. After a quick lunch, he raced back onto the course and literally jogged his way to a third-round 65 and a five-shot advantage.

As darkness approached, Paulson and his playing partners were so determined to complete the third round in one day that they ran to the ball between shots. Paulson didn't have to do much running on 18 after his wedge from 100 yards dropped in the hole for an eagle 2.

"It was perfect yardage, and I knew if I could get it on line, I'd have a pretty good birdie chance," Paulson said.

On Sunday, Paulson's lead was never in danger, though it took a couple of spectacular short-game shots to keep the competition in check.

On the par-3 seventh, Paulson chipped in from 30 feet off the green for a birdie. And at the par-3 11th hole, he faced a 30-foot putt to save par—and made it.

"If he doesn't hit the hole, it would have gone about 10 feet past," said Marco Gortana. "When he made that putt, we were playing for second place."

Carl Paulson was the Nike Tour's player of the year in 1999, earning him an automatic invitation to play the PGA Tour in 2000.

champions II

Bobby Wadkins watches his tee shot on the 17th hole during
the first round of the 1999 Nike Dominion Open in Richmond.

BOBBY WADKINS

Today's athletes are judged by a society that places such a high premium on finishing first that the only notable modern American sports cliché of the past 20 years is that "nobody remembers who finished second."

Under that harshly narrow beam of light, Bobby Wadkins doesn't have much to show for almost 30 years in professional golf.

"Obviously, I would like to have won a tournament," Wadkins said in June 1999 while standing on the practice range at Pinehurst No. 2 in North Carolina. The Richmond native, born July 26, 1952, 20 months after brother Lanny, was preparing to compete in his 14th United States Open. Few others in the '99 field had been there more often.

"I had chances," he continued evenly. "But I wouldn't trade having played in almost 700 tournaments for one or two victories. People don't think I mean that, but I do. I've known a lot of guys who won one or two tournaments, then were gone after 10 years.

"I'd like to be remembered as someone who busted his tail out here for 25 years. To play out here that long, you have to have some talent."

It's not like Wadkins hasn't won a tournament. He just hasn't won a PGA Tour event. In 1978, he captured the European Open. In 1979 and '86, he won the Dunlop Phoenix Tournament in Japan.

In the States, he finished second six times, including playoff losses to Lou Graham in Philadelphia in 1978 and to Bernhard Langer in 1985 at the Sea Pines Heritage Classic.

"I just never got the right break at the right time, although some of that was my own doing," he said. "Sometimes, guys played good enough to beat me. When that happened, I tipped my cap to them and moved on. The times it didn't happen that way are the ones that eat at me, even today. There were a few where I just didn't get it done on 16, 17, and 18. Those eat at you always."

Bobby Wadkins' longevity is remarkable. He turned professional in 1973 and joined the PGA Tour in '74. At the end of the 1999 season, he had played in 613 tournaments during his career—and had made the cut nearly 75 percent of the time.

With approximately $3 million in tournament winnings, Wadkins was

When you've been committed to professional golf since 1973 as Bobby Wadkins has, rain and cold are just minor distractions.

second to Kirk Triplett among players who had pocketed the most money without benefit of a victory. He is No. 102 on the PGA Tour's all-time earnings list.

"In my prime, I thought I was a very underrated player," Wadkins said.

There's no arguing the fact that Wadkins always operated in the shadow cast by his more famous brother. Never mind that Lanny often was incomparable, that Bobby's decision to follow in the footsteps of one of the game's greatest players ever was like trying to swim into a typhoon.

"Some of it was watching Lanny have the success he had at every level: high school, college, whatever, and following in his wake," Bobby admitted. "I watched him and had a tendency to say, 'Gee, if he can do it, I can do it, too.'"

Like his brother, Bobby Wadkins had an intense and diverse interest in all sports until Meadowbrook Country Club opened near his home. That's when he met pro James "Popeye" Lumpkin, who would have a profound influence over both boys' lives.

"Without Popeye, Lanny and I most likely wouldn't be where we are today," Bobby said. "Lanny and I would ride our bikes over there, and he took us under his wing. My parents didn't have any money, and he made sure that we were able to go to the junior tournaments. He made sure that when we went out of town, we had a room in a hotel and a new golf ball to play with. He was a friend from the start, but Lanny and I still talk about the golf lessons he gave us. We'll be standing on the range, practicing, and one of us will say, 'Remember how Popeye told us how to do this?' He was like a second daddy."

In 1972, Wadkins, then an All-American at East Tennessee State University, defeated Curtis Strange 2 and 1 for the State Amateur title at The Homestead's Cascades Course.

It was a moment brother Lanny says was one of several his brother enjoyed that should not go unappreciated, regardless of what has happened since.

"It was a very competitive State Amateur, probably more than in most other states," Lanny said. "Bobby and I, being just about a year apart, grew up together in golf, and we were very competitive. I know people have a tendency to compare everything, but it's really not fair. Bobby had a lot of different interests. I was much more absorbed by golf."

The Wadkins brothers always seemed to have a healthy sense of their position in the Virginia golf community.

A perfect example happened in 1981, when Bobby returned to the state to compete in the Virginia PGA Open at Countryside Country Club in Roanoke. He came at the invitation of Virginia PGA president Peter Hodson, who had been trying to upgrade the field in the $30,000 event.

Standing in front of a scoreboard that showed him trailing soon-to-be-professional Steve Liebler, the reigning Eastern Amateur champion, by three shots, Wadkins mused out loud that the VPGA Open championship had special meaning for him.

When he returned after beating Liebler and fellow pro Bobby Mitchell by two strokes, his explanation of the significance stunned anyone who had ever witnessed sibling rivalry.

"Lanny has won the other Open," he said, referring to the Virginia State Golf Association's event, which would be merged into one in 1985. "We've won the State Amateur. We've won the State Junior. This was the only tournament we hadn't won."

Although he was supposed to be taking the week off, preparing for the following week's Anheuser-Busch Classic in Williamsburg, Wadkins had a feeling it might be a good week when he arrived at his hotel and was handed the key to room 313.

"You know, that's the same room number Jay Haas had last week when he won [the Greater Milwaukee Open]," he said. "For some reason, it never entered my mind that I would lose."

Of the tournaments that got away, none may have been more bizarre than the 1994 Kemper Open at TPC Avenel in Maryland. Wadkins, playing only because of a sponsor's exemption, had a two-shot lead over Mark Brooks, and six strokes over Phil Mickelson, D.A. Weibring, and Mark O'Meara after 54 holes.

Many in the crowd of 50,000—some of whom were trying for the same prize—were rooting for Wadkins to come through. Watching Wadkins sink an eight-foot birdie putt to cap his Saturday round, O'Meara told reporters: "He's a fine player and a really good guy. You want the best for him."

On Sunday, Wadkins held a one-shot lead over Brooks when the two came to the sixth hole, a 520-yard par 5. Brooks already had hit his second shot into the creek that guards the green. Wadkins drove down the right side, his ball coming to rest behind a towering oak, 195 yards from the green.

Wadkins had two choices: Play a conservative shot back into the fairway and still give himself a chance to make birdie, or go for broke with a shot around the tree towards the green.

"I've got birdie on my mind, trying to put more distance between us," Wadkins said later.

Instead, his 2-iron shot hit the tree and ricocheted into the woods. Knowing that under PGA Tour rules ,Wadkins had five minutes to find his ball or suffer a stroke-and-distance penalty for his lost ball, more than 100 people in the gallery following the leaders—even some media members—combed the woods trying to locate it.

Maxfli. Wilson Staff 1. Pinnacle 3. Titleist 3.

Spectators recovered half a dozen balls, all launched by golfers with far less at stake than Wadkins. No one found a Titleist 7, the ball Wadkins was playing.

Meanwhile, Brooks put his fourth shot on the green, 15 feet from the hole, and salvaged par. Wadkins went back to where he hit his second shot and, for all intents and purposes, made the same play.

This time the 2-iron shot just nicked the tree and landed in a greenside bunker. He finished the hole with what he later called "a simple eight."

"If I had it to do over, I would pull that shot off 70 percent of the time," Wadkins said later. "So I'd do it again. The possibility of making an eight never crossed my mind . . . I've hit a lot worse shots than that which got found . . . Only that ball knows what it hit or where it went."

Wadkins finished tied for second, worth $114,400. That would be consolation enough for some, but not for him.

"I've got most of the money I can spend," he said. "I guess my wife can buy more Power Rangers videos for my son. I'd much rather donate the money back to the tournament and have the trophy."

It would be only fitting if one day that happened. Bobby Wadkins deserves that much.

Bobby Wadkins, far right, with older brother Lanny Wadkins at the 1970 VSGA State Amateur Championship Tournament. Lanny beat his brother Bobby in the finals at The Cascades Course at The Homestead in Hot Springs. Here, Bobby receives his runner-up prize from VSGA president Charlie Hancock, as executive director Bunny Blankinship stands off to the left.

champions II

Tom Strange acknowledges the crowd after his win in the
inaugural Eastern Amateur Championship in 1957 at
Elizabeth Manor G & CC in Portsmouth.

TOM STRANGE

Chandler Harper tells a story about Tom Strange that speaks volumes about the man's ability as a golfer and his values as a father.

Strange once asked Harper to arrange a match in Florida that would include Bobby Cruickshank, the famous Scot who had become a darling of Virginia golf fans after coming to Richmond in 1932.

When the match was over, Cruickshank phoned Harper in Portsmouth.

"Where'd you get this fellow?" he demanded. "Why isn't he out playing the circuit?"

Harper explained that Strange was married and had three small children. He had no desire to spend that much time away from his family.

"Then tell him to buy a trailer and take them with him," Cruickshank yelled into the receiver. "This guy's better than 95 percent of the players out here."

Strange played in the U.S. Open several times as a qualifier, but he never acted on Cruickshank's advice. Subjecting himself and his family to life out of a suitcase wasn't for him.

Instead, Strange carved out a distinguished career on the state level while creating an example that his son Curtis used as a roadmap to a pair of U.S. Open titles and 19 other victories worldwide.

Strange, who died of cancer in 1969 at age 38, won the Virginia PGA Open four times and the Virginia State Golf Association Open once. Only Harper, who won the State Open a record 11 times, and Cruickshank, who won it six times, were more successful.

Without question, his finest season was in 1957. It began when Strange became only the fourth amateur to win the State Open since its inception in 1924.

The tournament was held at Ocean View Golf Course in Norfolk and came down to a battle between Strange and Harold "Shorty" Oatman, who was the pro at the Norfolk Naval Station course.

Strange trailed by seven shots entering the final round, but caught Oatman to force an 18-hole playoff. His 6-under 64 the next day enabled him to win by eight shots.

Tom Strange and wife Nancy are all smiles during this photo taken at Elizabeth Manor G & CC. Strange curtailed a possible promising PGA Tour career to stay at home with his family.

Tom Strange shows off his champion's blazer after winning the 1957 Eastern Amateur at Elizabeth Manor G & CC.

Later that summer, Strange fell just short in his bid to capture the Virginia "Grand Slam" when he lost 5 and 3 in the final of the State Amateur to Bob Wallace, a lieutenant commander in the Navy who was stationed in Norfolk.

Strange bounced back to run away with the City Championship, which was conducted on four different layouts in Virginia Beach. In defeating brother-in-law Jordan Ball, Strange shot 69 at Kempsville Meadows GC, Princess Anne CC, and Cavalier Golf and Yacht Club. He finished off a nine-stroke victory with a 73 at Stumpy Lake GC.

He also won the Princess Anne Country Club title for the third consecutive year and captured the

Bide-A-Wee club championship by defeating NFL Hall of Famer Ace Parker 1-up on the 20th hole.

Strange capped the season by winning the inaugural Eastern Amateur at Elizabeth Manor Golf and Country Club in Portsmouth, shooting a 6-under-par 64 in the first round that stood as a tournament record for 30 years.

He and Ball, then the No. 1 player at the University of Virginia, were tied entering the final 18 holes. Playing in a driving rain, Strange beat Ball by two.

A native of Cincinnati, Strange began in golf as a caddie at the Hyde Park Golf Club with close friend Dow Finsterwald. He came to Norfolk in 1951 on assignment from the Coast Guard. Before leaving Ohio, however, Strange made his mark.

He once set a qualifying record of 136 in the Ohio State Amateur tournament. He won the Tri-State Invitational in 1949 and the Cincinnati Four-Ball title in 1948 and '49.

"He was one of the top players ever to come out of Cincinnati," said Tom Nieporte, a frequent competitor of Strange's and the pro at famed Winged Foot Golf Club in New York. "He was a natural. At one time, I think he held the record at every course in Cincinnati."

Strange was on the same kind of path in Virginia amateur circles until 1958.

Widely acknowledged as the state's top amateur, Strange gave it up when officials of Elizabeth Manor Golf and Country Club approached him about becoming their head professional.

"It is a very hard decision for me," Strange said in accepting their overture. "But it is a decision I'll have to make sooner or later, and I feel that eventually I'll follow golf as a career."

Two years later, Strange faced another tough decision that was born out of an invitation he received to play in an exhibition at Ocean View with Sam Snead, Chandler Harper, and Jack Isaacs.

Snead was impressed with Strange's style of play that day and said so. Soon thereafter, Snead offered Strange a job at The Greenbrier Golf Club in West Virginia.

"A smart move for Tom and a smart move for Sam," Harper said. "We hate to lose him, but it is a wonderful opportunity and one he can't afford to pass up."

When he returned to Hampton Roads two years later to become the pro at Bow Creek Golf Course in Virginia Beach, Strange was a more polished player.

"The rounds I played with Snead helped my game tremendously," he said. "I'd watch everything about Snead's swing, and sometimes he'd tell me how to improve my timing and accuracy with the woods and irons. I was a better player for having played golf with him."

In 1968, Strange played 12 official rounds in Virginia PGA-sanctioned or PGA-approved tournaments. His scoring average of 71 was almost three shots better than the next best pro and enabled him to win the Bobby Cruickshank Trophy.

By then, Strange was well established as one of the top teaching pros in the region. He loved devoting time to developing younger players.

"Lanny Wadkins still talks about the clinic my dad gave in 1964, the jokes, the trick shots—shots I can't hit to this day," Curtis said in 1997. "We always had 10 or 12 kids on the course on a Saturday morning. Kids were never restricted from playing."

J.P. Leigh, who won the 1983 Eastern Amateur, the Portsmouth Amateur 12 times, and has been a four-time medalist in the State Amateur, calls Strange an innovator in golf instruction.

"He was the first person I ever saw take Polaroids of someone swinging," Leigh remembered. "Then he'd show them to him to help him visualize what he was supposed to do. You couldn't wait to take a lesson from Tom Strange."

In February of 1969, Strange announced that he was taking over the operation and maintenance of Bow Creek, renaming it White Sands Country Club.

"I'll be busy enough that I'll have to forget about running from tournament to tournament," he said. "We will have a first-class layout. That I can promise you. I'm going to be here to see to it."

But in late June of that year, after a 10-week battle with cancer, Strange died. Reporter Ed Rogers of the *Norfolk Ledger-Star*, at Keswick Country Club in Charlottesville following 14-year-old Curtis in the State Open, relayed the news after receiving a call from Strange's wife, Nancy.

"In the 10 years I had the pleasure of watching and reporting Tom's golfing exploits, I never heard an unkind word cast in his direction," Rogers wrote. "He was loved by all who knew him."

On Nov. 14, 1997, Tom Strange was inducted into the Middle Atlantic PGA Hall of Fame. The next year, he was enshrined in the Virginia Sports Hall of Fame in Portsmouth, not far from where many of his greatest achievements took place, on and off the course.

champions II

Tom McKnight waits for one of his playing partners to
chip onto the green during the 1998 Eastern Amateur at
Elizabeth Manor Golf & Country Club.

TOM McKNIGHT

Tom McKnight, a 44-year-old petroleum salesman from Galax, didn't figure to be much of a factor in the U.S. Amateur Championship—at least not the 1998 version at Oak Hill Country Club in Rochester, New York.

Matt Kuchar of Georgia Tech, whose electric smile and play had dazzled everyone at the '98 Masters, had rejected turning pro to defend his title. Also on hand was reigning British Amateur champion Sergio Garcia of Spain, dubbed "El Nino," and favorably compared to his idol, Seve Ballesteros.

There was Hank Kuehne, once the black sheep of golf's Gen X royal family. His sister Kelli won the U.S. Girls' Junior title in 1994 and consecutive U.S. Women's Amateurs in 1995 and 1996. His brother Trip had a four-hole lead on Tiger Woods after the morning 18 of the 1994 Amateur final, only to lose 2 down.

Hank Kuehne, though generally considered to be the most talented of the three siblings and a second-team All-American at Southern Methodist University, had accomplished nothing like that. What he had was his story, one of a kid who began drinking at age 13. Six years later, he checked himself into a substance-abuse treatment center in Minnesota for three months. He has been sober since 1995.

Among the legion of college hotshots present were Stanford's Joel Kribel, runner-up to Kuchar the previous year; Bill Lunde of NCAA champion UNLV; and 19-year-old Bryce Molder of Georgia Tech, NCAA co-player of the year.

McKnight was a 1976 University of Virginia graduate who was played the J.C. Goosie Space Coast mini-tour before shattering his left arm in a 1980 recreation-league basketball game. He regained his amateur status in 1982, then won the State Amateur in 1984, '85, and '93 and the State Open in 1985.

He also had won three Eastern Amateur tournaments at Portsmouth's Elizabeth Manor Golf & Country Club, one shy of the record set by former PGA Tour commissioner Deane Beman in the early 1960s. His reach had gone beyond Virginia's borders. He had been the medalist in the 1988 U.S. Amateur at the Cascades in Hot Springs. In the '92 U.S. Amateur at

Tom McKnight watches a tee shot during second-round action at the 1998 Eastern Amateur.

At age 44, Tom McKnight debunked the myth that big-time amateur golf is a young man's game, advancing to the final of the U.S. Amateur in 1988.

Muirfield Village, McKnight beat David Duval and Stewart Cink. And in the 1995 North-South Amateur, he had lost in the final to Jackie Nicklaus, with Papa Bear watching anxiously from the gallery.

His seven-shot victory at the '97 Eastern Amateur was thought to be enough to earn him a berth on the U.S. Walker Cup Team. It was a great disappointment when he was instead chosen to be an alternate.

So while it would be wrong to paint McKnight as a complete unknown, among the galaxy of would-be stars gathered at Oak Hill, the man from Galax was most definitely unheralded.

There were no easy verdicts for McKnight once match play started. He was 3 up after four holes against Texan Jim Spagnolo but had to hang on for a 2-and-1 win.

He made the turn 3-up against Georgia's Jedd McLuen and prevailed 3 and 2.

Against J.J. Henry of Connecticut in the third round, McKnight was 1-up through 16. Henry, who had been extended to 25 holes that morning in ousting Californian Tom Johnson, double-bogeyed the 17th McKnight advanced to the quarterfinals 2 and 1.

There, he finally met someone his own age, Sean Knapp of Oakmont, Pennsylvania. McKnight took five of the last six holes to post a 5-and-3 victory.

Next up: Garcia, 18, then the world's No. 1-ranked amateur. Among his earlier conquests had been Kuchar, the defending champion.

Garcia, who at an early age had proclaimed to friends that he wanted to be the best golfer in the world, was seeking to become just the fourth player to win British and U.S. Amateur titles in the same year.

Virtually no one gave McKnight a chance.

"I was asked in an interview before the match how it felt to be an underdog," McKnight said at the time. "I said, 'I don't understand the question. I'm an underdog in some people's minds, but not everybody's.'

"Sergio is a good player, but there are a lot of good players . . . I've seen a lot of things in 30 years in golf. You can't let the moment or the surroundings overwhelm you."

In the end, McKnight wore out Garcia. Every time the Spaniard thought he had the advantage, McKnight would hole a putt or hit a shot that reversed the momentum. McKnight won 3 and 1 when Garcia made a double bogey on the 17th hole.

Meanwhile, Kuehne cruised through the quarterfinals 5 and 4 over Molder. He had an even easier time in the semis, blasting Lunde 6 and 5.

That set up the 36-hole final between McKnight and Kuehne, or as some called them, The Odd Couple.

Although McKnight was exactly twice as old as Kuehne, the two had become best friends. They had played together in nearly every amateur tournament that summer. They had practiced together, eaten dinner together, competed against each other in video games, air hockey, go-cart racing.

At a tournament in Rhode Island, they had gone to a Grand Prix miniature track. McKnight had dared Kuehne to race him. Kuehne won the first meeting, McKnight the next four.

Before the match, they mugged for the cameras like a couple of kids in a drugstore photo booth.

"When we played our practice rounds together, we both said wouldn't it be neat if we could meet each other in the final," McKnight recalled.

Kuehne, one of the longest hitters at any level of the game, was 4 up through 17 holes of the morning match before McKnight started to chip away at his deficit by winning the 18th hole.

"The first 18 holes I played very poorly, but made some great ups-and-downs and was able to salvage something," McKnight said. "I was 3-down, but considering the way I played, I felt that wasn't too bad. I came back in the second 18, and it was like a fresh start."

Feeling some momentum, McKnight closed to 2-down when he sank an eight-foot birdie putt on the second hole in the afternoon. He then squared the match after Kuehne found a fairway bunker on the fourth hole and drove into the trees on No. 5.

One hole later, McKnight led, courtesy of an 11-foot birdie putt.

They halved the seventh hole, before Kuehne would play what he called the critical shot of the match.

Kuehne's drive on No. 8 soared way right and into the trees. Suddenly, it hit a limb and bounded back into the fairway. Kuehne made par, won the hole, and instead of being 2-down, was back even.

"A monkey threw my ball out of the tree," Kuehne said at the time, "and that was a big break, to say the least."

In a cruel twist of fate, McKnight's short game, which had propelled him through the early matches and kept him in the hunt for the national championship, deserted him.

McKnight missed five-foot putts on the eighth and 10th holes, a two-footer on 11 and a seven-footer on the 12th. He made bogeys on 10, 11, and 12, while Kuehne went par-par-birdie. McKnight was 3-down again.

Still, he battled back, winning the 14th when Kuehne made bogey and the 15th when he drained a 30-footer for birdie. Both parred 16, but when McKnight hit his approach shot to 17 into a green-side bunker, then lipped out a 30-foot par-saver, he conceded the match to lose 2 and 1.

"As disappointed as I am for me, I am as happy as I can be for Henry," McKnight said. "It's just great for him and his family. Yes, we're friends, but we were out there trying to beat the tar out of each other."

McKnight was the fourth Virginian to advance to the U.S. Amateur final. Lanny Wadkins and Vinny Giles won the 1970 and 1972 tournaments, respectively, when the game was stroke play. Roanoke's David Tolley fell to Jay Sigel 8 and 7 in the 1982 final.

"Except for a few holes in the final that I didn't play very well, I hung in there," McKnight said. "It

felt like we were in a boxing match, taking each other's best shots. I guess I was the last one down on the mat."

Typical of McKnight, however, he didn't stay down for long. His performance at Oak Hill enabled him to open doors to the world's greatest golf courses in 1999.

First, there was Augusta National. By advancing to the final against Kuehne, McKnight earned an invitation to the '99 Masters. Although he had been offered the chance to play Augusta National on several occasions, McKnight had refused.

"It might seem a little overambitious," he said, "but I'd just decided I wasn't going to play there until I qualified for the Masters. For a while, I was wondering how smart an idea that was."

Although McKnight rented a house near the course for the week, he still good-naturedly spent a couple of nights in the Crow's Nest, taking advantage of the Masters officials' traditional offer to house amateurs on the third floor of their clubhouse.

There, he and three kids he knew pretty well by then—Kuehne, Kuchar, and Garcia—hung out in style, even sneaking a peek inside the Champions Locker Room.

"They're all about the same age as my son, which might seem unusual," McKnight said, referring to 21-year-old Tee, his occasional caddie. "But Hank's one of my good friends. Matt's a good guy and Sergio . . . he's a great kid. Golf helped us bridge the age gap."

McKnight weathered a spectacularly inconsistent second round. On the par-5 eighth hole, McKnight drove into a fairway bunker, then splashed out into the fairway. One hundred fifty-five yards from a green he couldn't see, McKnight then holed his shot for an eagle.

Facing a slick, 14-foot downhill putt at the par-3 16th, McKnight tapped the ball inches past the cup, then watched helplessly as it nearly skittered off the green, coming to rest 40 feet away.

Despite the troubles, McKnight played all 72 holes and finished second-low amateur to Garcia.

"I always dreamed of playing the Masters," he said when he finished. "Time was running out on me. It was great to be here."

It was a sentiment he would soon repeat after finishing play in the British Amateur at Royal County Down in Ireland. He would say it again at Pinehurst No. 2 in North Carolina following the U.S. Open. And again at Pebble Beach after the '99 U.S. Amateur.

Finally, McKnight capped a year to remember the rest of his life when he was named to the U.S. Walker Cup team. Two teams of amateurs, one from the United States, one from Great Britain and Ireland, play every other year for the Walker Cup.

Begun in 1922 at the National Golf Links of America in Southampton, New York, the Walker Cup is named for George Herbert Walker, United States Golf Association president in 1920 and maternal grandfather of former President George W. Bush.

The 1999 event was held in September at Nairn Golf Club near Inverness, Scotland. The par-71 course was designed by Old Tom Morris, Andrew Simpson and James Braid and opened in 1887.

McKnight did not fare as well as he had hoped, losing one foursome and one singles match. Of course, neither did the rest of the American team.

England natives Luke Donald and Paul Casey each won two matches on the final day to rally the Great Britain-Ireland team past the U.S. 15-9. The United States had led 7-5 entering the final day of competition before Donald and Casey, who both played collegiately at American universities, rallied their side.

Still, McKnight could reflect on his spectacular season with an appreciation that came from experience and years of striving for what often seemed to be an unattainable goal.

"The man upstairs has smiled a lot on me this year," he said. "We're talking about playing a lifetime full of courses, places I've always wanted to go, in one year. I never knew any of this was possible."

four aces

Robbye King-Youel won the State Women's Amateur
in 1963, '66, '69, '70, '71, and '72.

FOUR ACES

ROBBYE KING YOUEL

Admiral Ed King had it all planned.

Following a brief but highly successful career, she would marry and regain her amateur status. When the children were older, she would resume an amateur life that would be the envy of her peers.

He wasn't off by much.

In the 20 Women's State Amateur tournaments in which she competed, Youel won six times. She finished second on four occasions. She was third three times.

Between the ages of 19 and 22, Youel played 22 sudden-death matches. She won 21 of them. She was a semifinalist in the 1963 U.S. Amateur.

She became the only player in the history of the region to hold four titles in the same year when she won the Maryland, District of Columbia, Virginia, and Middle Atlantic Amateur championships in 1963.

She played the LPGA Tour, albeit as an amateur.

It is more than tired rhetoric to say that she can be mentioned in the same sentence as Sam Snead, Chandler Harper, Vinny Giles, Lew Worsham, Lily Harper-Martin, and Lanny Wadkins. On May 2, 1997, she became just the seventh golfer enshrined in the Virginia Sports Hall of Fame.

When Youel was 11, her father bought a set of MacGregor irons. Admiral King was a passionate, devoted golfer, intent on making certain that his younger daughter would be a success in everything she did.

"My father looked at all of us and assessed our talents," Youel said. "Given my talents and skills, my generally conservative nature, and the activities that were available for a Navy family, my dad figured, 'golf.' "

Admiral King brought Robbye to the practice range at Army-Navy Country Club in Arlington. Armed with a dog-eared copy of Ben Hogan's *Five Steps to Good Golf*, Admiral King brought Robbye to Army-Navy CC in Arlington. He had one simple rule: She would play *any* golf course until she could execute the basics of the game.

That would take two years. "On the surface, it sounds awful, but it was anything but awful," Youel said. "He made it so much fun to hit a bucket or two of balls.

Robbye King Youel prepares to play at her home course, Farmington Country Club in Charlottesville. A six-time women's State Amateur champion, Youel also finished second in the 1998 women's State Senior tournament.

"I never went through 'breaking 100.' When I got out there, I could hit shots."

In 1961, she began college at Wake Forest, where she would graduate Phi Beta Kappa. There was no women's golf team. Youel would bring her clubs with her each September, set them in a corner of her room, and bring them home to Arlington at the end of the spring semester, dust-covered.

One week after her sophomore year, her father issued a challenge.

"Robbye, we might as well plunge into the deep end of the pool. The Maryland Amateur is next week. You're entered."

She won.

Then she won the District of Columbia Amateur. And her first Virginia Amateur.

And she capped the most remarkable summer in the history of women's golf in the region by capturing the first of her two Middle Atlantic Amateur titles. She's the only one to accomplish the feat.

"That summer, for the first time in my life, I realized I had a reliable, dependable golf swing," she said. "I always thought you had to practice, practice, practice constantly to have that kind of swing. I'm not saying I didn't work, because I did." For two summers while she was finishing college at Wake Forest and graduate school at Virginia, Youel resisted her father's exhortations to turn pro, though she agreed to play the LPGA Tour.

"I would have made money in every tournament in which I played," Youel said. "But at the end of the summer, I was not a happy lady. I told my dad, 'Whether a ball goes in a hole or not is not the purpose of my life.' "

Youel's ideal life was to teach school, which remains her occupation, marry, have a family, and play golf in the summer.

She married in 1968. A year later, she began a streak of four consecutive State Amateur titles, the last a perfect example of grace under pressure.

In April of 1972, Youel gave birth to son David. With the State Amateur scheduled for July, and Youel planning to breast-feed her infant, she already had decided not to go to the Cascades in Hot Springs to defend her crown.

"But I ran into the women's tennis champion at Farmington, who asked me if I was getting ready to defend my title," Youel recalled. "I told her what I was thinking, and she said, 'Having a baby is no reason to not play competitively. Don't go there as a nursing mother. Go there as a competitor.' "

That struck a nerve with Youel. She invited her mother to join her in Hot Springs to help look after the baby. Youel breezed into the final, a 36-hole match against Candy Sibbick of Martinsville.

"I had to feed my baby, and there wasn't enough time to do that in the 30 minutes they gave you between the morning and afternoon match," she said.

Sibbick, an old friend, graciously asked for an extended lunch break. Youel raced back to the hotel, then raced back to the course in time to finish off a 2-up victory.

four aces

Lily Harper-Martin of Portsmouth, shown here with her golfing brother, Chandler Harper, after her 1934 VSGA Women's Amateur Championship win at Cavalier C&YC. It was the first of her seven titles in the event.

LILY HARPER-MARTIN

The sad truth is that two things kept diminutive Lily Harper-Martin from irrefutable claim as Virginia's greatest female amateur: World War II and the premature death of her husband.

Lily, who weighed barely 100 pounds and was dubbed "The Tiny Typhoon of Portsmouth," was the younger sister of Chandler Harper.

Lily won the State Amateur title for the first time in 1934. That same year, Chandler was the men's champion for the third time. They repeated the feat in 1940; only by this time, Chandler had turned pro and moved on to the State Open.

That's where the similarities between the two stopped.

Lily hated to practice golf and preferred softball; Chandler was a workaholic. Yet she won the Women's State Amateur a record seven times from 1934 to 1941, including four in succession. Six weeks after her marriage to Carl Martin, her only stumble came in 1938 at the Country Club of Virginia in Richmond, where she didn't even reach the final.

"People said, 'That's it,' " she remembered in a 1981 interview. " 'She won't win again because she's married.' But I showed them the next three years."

She ripped off three in a row—at Princess Anne CC in Virginia Beach, the Chamberlain Country Club in Hampton, and the old Hermitage Country Club, now Belmont, in Richmond.

Harper-Martin also won the 1936 Mid-Atlantic Women's Amateur the only time she entered. It took some intestinal fortitude. Harper-Martin won her quarterfinal match in 23 holes and made a 25-foot birdie putt on the 19th hole of her semifinal match.

"She was a natural, if ever I saw one," Chandler said. "She wasn't that interested in golf. She had the game, and didn't care for it."

Her brother certainly wasn't the only one who thought Lily "had game." Sam Snead proclaimed that he thought Lily was a better player than Chandler.

There was no course Lily couldn't tame. Her first six State Amateur titles came on markedly different layouts, from the flatlands of Cavalier G&YC in Virginia Beach to the mountainous Homestead Course in Hot Springs. She won twice at the old Hermitage in Richmond, including her seventh title in 1941.

Lily Harper-Martin is shown here with some of her amateur championship trophies. She won seven State Women's Amateur Championships from 1934 to 1941.

Husband Carl, who worked for a machinery company in Norfolk, was a passionate golfer. Although unskilled at the game, he fueled her desire to compete.

In the 1941 final, Harper-Martin and Mrs. George Owens of Petersburg were even through 13 holes before Harper-Martin pulled ahead to stay with birdies at the 14th and 15th.

Harper-Martin was forced to make birdie on the 16th just to halve the hole and maintain her lead. She then wrapped up her final victory with a par 5 on 17.

There were no state tournaments from 1942 to 1945 because of World War II. In 1945, her husband Carl, then just 34, died of a heart attack, leaving Lily a widow at 28.

She never remarried. Not only did she never play competitively again, her brother says she never even held a club.

"You couldn't get her to even grip one," Chandler said, shaking his head. "I tried to get her to come back, many times. I told her, 'Hell, Lily, you can still play!' I told her I'd get her a job as an assistant pro. The only thing she'd ever say is, 'I'm just not interested.'"

Lily Harper-Martin was inducted into the Virginia Sports Hall of Fame in 1995. She had died six years earlier at age 73.

four aces

A familiar pose for Mary Patton Janssen, holding a
championship trophy moments after another win.

MARY PATTON JANSSEN

Mary Patton Janssen came to golf late in life and abandoned her competitive career early. In between, no woman in Virginia history may have accomplished more in her sport.

Between 1957 and 1962, there wasn't a player in the state who could keep pace with Janssen. She won six consecutive State Amateur championships, five by astronomical margins.

She beat Madelyn Egenroad of Arlington 6 and 5 at Princess Anne CC in Virginia Beach in 1957. In 1958, she met Egenroad at the Cascades in Hot Springs and triumphed 12-and-11.

The following year, she whipped Donna O'Brien of Richmond 13 and 11 at Hermitage Country Club in Richmond, where she played the par-75 course in 6-under 69.

In 1960, she returned to the Cascades to dispose of her rival from Farmington Country Club, Sydney Elliott, 15 and 13. Her fifth title in a row was 8 and 6 over Connie Gorsuch of Roanoke at Farmington.

Her last victory, at age 37, was her closest, 1-up over 19-year-old Robbye King.

"I was very aggressive," Janssen said in a 1964 interview. "I went out to win every hole. I went out to murder my opponents just as badly as I could—I knew if I didn't get them first, they would get me."

Janssen, who moved to Charlottesville with her family when she was 15, didn't start playing golf until age 21. Fox hunting was her sport, until her favorite horse was injured and was put down.

Her father and two brothers were rabid enthusiasts of the game—both brothers played on the University of Virginia squad—and soon Mary Patton was taking lessons first from Farmington pro Art Doering, then from Pete Snead, brother of Sam Snead.

Anyone could see that she had the skill to be a great player. Anyone could see that she had the proper work ethic. She'd beat balls for hours, never quite satisfied with the result.

And that was a problem. It was equally apparent that she lacked self-confidence.

In 1954, she met legendary pro Tommy Armour at Boca Raton Country Club in Florida.

"Tommy told me I was one of the finest natural players he'd ever seen, and next to the Babe [Zaharias], I was the greatest," she recalled. "This began to help me psychologically after he told me this several times. I started to think I was better than I really was. It got so that when I was playing, I would think about what he told me, what he would do in my particular situation. It really helped."

She was no overnight sensation. Her first two trips to the State Amateur final were disasters—an 8-and-7 loss to Richmond's Betty Cralle in 1950, and a 10-and-8 defeat by Ann Pollard of Charlottesville in '51.

In 1956, Janssen put everything together. In the British Women's Amateur, she eliminated the defending champion and the French Amateur champion to advance to the final against fellow American and eventual champion Wiffi Smith.

As the years passed and she became more successful, Janssen also became more superstitious. Each day, she said, she would stand over the bathtub, wringing out a huge, water-soaked towel in order to build arm strength.

She always marked her ball with an Indian-head penny. She always played with a No. 4 ball.

"I'd play with a certain brand of ball, thinking I couldn't play badly," she said. "Then, all of a sudden, I'd have a terrible round and find it was me instead of the ball. It even got to the point where if I hit one bad shot, I'd change balls."

She began losing sleep, fretting the night away about one or two poorly played shots. People who didn't know said she should turn professional.

"I never turned pro because I didn't know whether I could take the strain from day to day," she said in '64. "After a while, I'd come home from a round and I'd immediately begin wondering why I'd missed this shot and what would have happened had I played that one a little differently.

"I began to worry about not getting enough practice. I couldn't sleep. I was always exhausted, and that came from only 14 tournaments a year. I knew the pros were making 30 to 40 annually, and that was just too many for me. I wouldn't have been able to take it."

Having felt that way for more than a decade, Janssen knew exactly when to say goodbye. She also knew how to console her vanquished opponent.

In the final of the 1962 State Amateur at the Cascades, Janssen was paired with Robbye King, then a college student and already the District of Columbia champion. King was 4-up through 27 holes, but Janssen prevailed 1-up, when King three-putted the final hole.

As the two walked up the hill separating the 18th green from the clubhouse, King suddenly stopped. There were tears in her eyes. She seemed overcome with disappointment.

Janssen stopped, too, and put both arms around King.

"Just take a deep breath and remember that I'm twice as old as you are," Janssen told her calmly. "Your day is coming."

King won the amateur title the next year, her first of six. Meanwhile, Janssen retired. In just 12 years, she had won 21 tournaments and finished second in another seven. She had nothing left to prove.

Mary Patton Janssen hoists the 1960 Virginia Women's State Open Championship trophy at the Cascades Course at The Homestead in Hot Springs, after being presented the trophy by VSGA executive director H.M. Blankinship.

four aces

Jane Mack, right, with Sam Snead and Donna Andrews at
the 1987 Virginia Women's State Amateur Championship at
the Cascades Course in Hot Springs.

JANE MACK

Whether it is golf or painting, Jane Mack has always displayed brilliant strokes.

Mack, who retired as an art teacher at Richmond's Hermitage High School in 1999 after 30 years in the classroom, won the Women's State Amateur four times during the 1970s, '80s, and '90s. While others have won it more often, no player in history has walked off with Virginia's biggest women's prize in three different decades.

"I've been a viable champion and a pretty good player for a long time," said Mack, who will talk about her life, but must be prodded into revealing much about her achievements. "I'm pretty proud of that. I never set out to set any records. I just set out to play. It just so happens that I practiced hard enough to develop a pretty decent game."

Mack also has been recognized for her talents as a painter. She was named Richmond's "Undiscovered Artist of the Year" in 1971. She's even had a couple of one-artist shows around the state capital.

"Having a love for art always helped with my golf," Mack said. "I'd find that after a day in school, I could go to Willow Oaks Country Club, go down by the river, and get totally lost. I see golf courses as beautiful places, places I gravitate to."

Mack was the happy recipient of lessons from Willow Oaks pro George Bird, who had a profound impact on Mack's career long after he retired to Florida. He was a former baseball player, tall as a reed at 6-feet-5. From their first time together, Bird sent a clear message to Mack that golf should not be divided by gender.

"One of the things I'm most thankful for regarding him is that he didn't teach me how to play *women's golf*," Mack said. "He taught me how to play *golf*. He never once allowed me to believe that I couldn't hit the shots that he hit, even though he was so much taller than I was and swung so much differently than I did."

Indeed, for years, Mack's game seemed to be defined by its raw power. Few, if any, in her circle of competition could stripe the ball as far as Mack. Fewer still attacked the ball with as much obvious relish.

"Back then, I had a 'draw-back-and-fire' approach to the game," she once said. "The problem was, I was never quite sure where the ball was going to go."

Mack didn't win the State Am for the first time until 1977, her 15th appearance. When she finally broke through, she took down one of Virginia's giants, six-time champion Robbye King-Youel of Charlottesville.

The largest lead for either player in the scheduled 36-hole final at the Cascades Course in Hot Springs was two. Mack prevailed with a par on the first hole of a sudden-death playoff.

"The first time I played in the State Amateur was 1962, the last time Mary Patton Janssen won," Mack said. "She beat Robbye in a match that went right to the very end. I've always remembered that because our situations were so much alike. Robbye was clearly the up-and-coming player when she lost to Mary Pat. I was the up-and-comer when I won for the first time. Plus, as I've told Robbye before, I admired her not only for how she was a champion, but also for how she lived her life."

Mack won on one of the Cascades' toughest holes, No. 1, a 394-yard par 4 that is anything but a gentle introduction to the course.

The following year, Mack won again in a performance she characterized as one of the incomparable days of her career.

Mack throttled 1976 and '79 champion Kay Schiefelbein of Alexandria 5 and 4 by playing the final 20 holes under par.

"There are few days in my competitive career that stand out the way that one does," Mack said. "There are days when you get to the course and you know you've 'got it.' That was one of those days."

Even before she had success in Virginia, Mack showed she had a game that was good beyond state borders. After competing in the U.S. Women's Open at Hot Springs in 1967, Mack came back six years later and qualified for the Open at Country Club of Rochester in 1973 and at La Grange (Ill.) Country Club the following year.

She also qualified for the women's U.S. Amateur in Atlanta in 1971 and in Seattle three years later.

In 1982, Mack again put together a masterful final performance in the State Amateur in whipping Robin Andrews of Galax 6 and 5. The title match was far and away the easiest for Mack. She had to win the preceding matches 1-up to get to Andrews, who was an All-American at Longwood College.

Andrews took the first two holes before completely falling apart. Mack drew even by making pars on Nos. 3 and 4, then captured the fifth, sixth, and seventh when Andrews made double-bogey, triple-bogey, and bogey in succession.

"I really lost my confidence after that," Andrews said. "I wanted so badly to win, and while what happened to me today is a good lesson, it's also a hard lesson."

Mack was medalist in 1985, the year Donna Andrews won her first of five in a row, and was one of Andrews' victims, 3 and 2, in the 1987 final.

Her history-making victory came in 1992. By then, Mack had undergone abdominal surgery, three surgeries on her knees, and back surgery. She may have been the only person in Hot Springs who thought she could win, and she did it in often-spectacular fashion.

In a sudden-death semifinal victory over Amy Ellertson, Mack aced the 149-yard 11th hole with a 7-iron. The following day against Sara Cole of Roanoke, Mack nearly repeated it. The ball stopped tap-in distance away, one of the crucial shots in a taut 2-and-1 triumph.

It was also the last step in Mack's three-decade marathon into Virginia golf history.

Jane Mack, a four-time Women's State Amateur champion.

they ruled the game

Harry Easterly Jr. used his experience as VSGA president as
training for his stint as USGA president in 1976 and '77.
Here, he presents Bobby Mitchell with a trophy for
winning the 1965 State Open.

THEY RULED THE GAME
HARRY EASTERLY

Harry Easterly once said that the "complete golfer" played the game, administrated it, and was involved in building and maintaining a golf course.

Even by those ambitious standards, Easterly reached "complete" status years ago.

Although never a player of national repute, the Richmond native was good enough to win a couple of Richmond City titles, advance to the final of the 1965 State Amateur, be low amateur at a State Open, and qualify for numerous U.S. Amateur Championships.

As an administrator, Easterly helped found the Richmond Golf Association and served as president. He was president of the Virginia State Golf Association from 1965 to 1966. After working through a maze of U.S. Golf Association committees, Easterly became the first Virginian elected president in 1976 and '77.

While his climb up the USGA ladder included course preparations for various USGA events—a task that often drew complaints from players as being too penal—Easterly also has played an integral role in the organization of the

Virginia State Golf Center, set to open outside Richmond in 2001.

It was Easterly who captured a commitment from renowned course architect Tom Fazio to design the course. Easterly has been in the thick of preparations for what will be a center unrivaled in the U.S.

"Not that Virginia needs any kind of boost when it comes to golf, but this will give us a tremendous one," Easterly said. "It'll focus people in the state on the fact that we're providing everyone with a place where they can play golf. It'll do tremendous things. It opens up the idea of having tournaments there. There will be a learning center, a nine-hole course for children, dormitories. It's going to be a tremendous addition to everything that's happening in the state."

Bringing golf to the people has been on Easterly's mind since he became interested in the administrative side of the game. Maybe subconsciously, it started when he was a young boy, and the great Bobby Jones came to Richmond for an exhibition at The Country Club of Virginia.

"Jones came to the course in a motorcade and I stood outside the front gates watching him go by," said Easterly, who guesses he was eight or nine years

Harry Easterly Jr. at The Country Club of Virginia—James River Course in Richmond.

old. "I have to admit that at that point in my life, I was more interested in the motorcycles that preceded Jones' car than anything else. But I got into that exhibition, and there was something about the way he responded to the gallery that I'll never forget."

Easterly, born Aug. 31, 1922, was chairman of the grounds committee when the USGA came to CCV for the 1955 U.S. Amateur. It was his first experience with the USGA, and he couldn't have enjoyed it more.

"I guess I was indoctrinated early by the USGA," Easterly said. "I read, learned, and digested about everything they could give me about amateur golf. I believe there ought to be a very clear line between amateur golf and professional golf -not that one is better than the other. The USGA has been very good about keeping that line. Professional golfers have one point of view. The USGA has another point of view. Both have their place in the world of golf."

In 1968, Easterly reached the USGA's fast track as an Executive Committee member, and he started pedaling hard.

Junior Committee. Public Information Committee. Chairman of the Championship Committee. Chairman of the Rules Committee. Treasurer.

On Nov. 15, 1975, Easterly was nominated for president of the USGA and was introduced on Jan. 31, 1976.

"I don't think the golfing world at large has the full appreciation of what the USGA means to golf," Easterly said at the time.

He set out to change that. The Associates Program had begun at Christmas of '75. Easterly prodded it along and nurtured it through its infancy.

"My theme was to bring the USGA out of the shadows, bring it to the people, make it more democratic," Easterly said. "I was lucky in that the climate was right for it. They've made tremendous progress since then in connecting with the people, but we made really good progress in that regard, too. I think everyone on the Executive Committee realized that it was a good thing to do."

As vice-president and chairman of the rules committee, Easterly took enormous criticism for being at the center of the move to change the U.S. Amateur from stroke play back to match play.

The Amateur had been contested at match play from its inception in 1895 until 1965, when it became stroke play. Easterly chafed for eight years as the event was played in the most odious manner possible, as far as he was concerned. It didn't matter that two of his closest friends, Lanny Wadkins and Vinny Giles, won the tournament under that format.

"That was the amateur game, the way it's played, and that's the best way I can answer the question of why I was so opposed to stroke play," Easterly said. "It's traditional, and I think it was a mistake to ever have departed from it. I'm extremely proud of having led the charge to get that changed."

In 1973, the Amateur returned to match play. In 1979, the format was altered to allow 36 holes of stroke-play qualifying, followed by match play, to determine the champion.

"It's funny, after all that was said back then, I don't hear anyone talking about how critical it is to have the Amateur return to stroke play," Easterly said.

Easterly learned to cope with criticism the way any true Virginian with a viselike grip on tradition would—by reading Thomas Jefferson.

"You can apply those lessons to anything you do," he said in 1975. "One of the lessons I've learned from him is about taking criticism. He could take it and just let it bounce off."

Easterly got a much closer look at that kind of grace under fire in the 1977 U.S. Open at Southern Hills Country Club in Tulsa. As president of the USGA, Easterly's job was to accompany leader Hubert Green for his final round.

As Green made the turn, Executive Committee members Sandy Tatum and Bill Williams approached Easterly with a problem unlike any the organization had faced before. A woman had phoned the FBI with information that three men planned to shoot Green on the 15th hole.

"Do you believe that?" Easterly asked.

"We have to believe it."

"I think we ought to forget it," Easterly said.

"You can't forget it. If they do shoot him, his blood will be on your hands."

Easterly and Tatum, who was chairman of the Championship Committee, pulled Green aside after he finished No. 14. They filled him in and presented three options: continue playing, take a 15-minute delay and play, or walk off the course and default.

Green started laughing.

"Oh, c'mon," he said. "It's probably one of my old girlfriends. Let's play golf."

Just when Easterly was starting to think Green had the right idea, the leader hit a terrible hook off the 15th tee.

"But he then hit a magnificent shot to the green," Easterly said. "The only question in my mind was, 'Should I walk close to him or away from him?' I decided to take the brave route and walk with him. Later I found out that this phone call, which had been represented to me as an urgent situation, had come in the night before. For some reason, someone decided to wait until we got on the golf course to bring it to my attention."

To this day, Easterly marvels at Green's poise. Walking onto the 15th green, an easy target for anyone so inclined, Green faced a 40-foot putt Easterly said most players would not have been able to stop five feet from the hole under normal circumstances.

Green, burdened by an unimaginable pressure, knocked it two feet from the cup.

"He was one cool guy," Easterly said.

When that Open was complete, Easterly treated himself to a flight to Dallas, where he met up with one of his idols for a fast 18.

"It was the perfect way to end a trying week," he said of his rendezvous with Ben Hogan.

In 1980, three years after his presidency ended, the USGA offered Easterly the post of senior executive director. He resigned from an executive position with Wheat, First Securities, to accept.

"P.J. Boatwright was president then, and no one wanted to do anything to undermine him," Easterly said, "but he was caught in a situation where the organization had grown tremendously. His area of expertise was in rules and competition. He kept that while I was overall chief operating officer."

Easterly resigned the position on Jan. 31, 1984, to enter family business. In his letter of resignation, he touched on a laundry list of accomplishments that were anything but glamorous, but vital to the USGA's growth and continued success:

- Determination of the location of Golf House
- Construction of a new building
- Immediate financing of a new building
- Launching of a capital campaign
- A major turf-grass research effort
- Implementation of the Golf Handicap and Information Network (GIN)
- Major computerization of USGA systems
- Consolidation and further expansion of the Associates Program

"I am proud to say that the above things and many others have already been accomplished under my administration, or will be well on their way by Jan. 31," Easterly wrote. "I therefore feel free to return to my family business . . . I plan to make whatever contributions I can to the programs of the USGA . . . I am full committed to the goals of the USGA."

Easterly continues to serve the USGA. Any former USGA president who also served as chairman of the rules committee remains an ex officio member of the rules committee. His friends in the Rules Section of USGA headquarters say Easterly is every bit as passionate about his duties now as he was the day he arrived.

Harry Easterly Jr. sits on a bench at the Country Club of Virginia's James River Course. The bench commemorates his contributions to the VSGA and the USGA.

they ruled the game

Bill Battle, show here with older brother John, was
U.S. Golf Association president in 1988 and 1989.

BILL BATTLE

By the time he became president of the U.S. Golf Association in 1988, Bill Battle's life already had been so extraordinary that presenting fellow Virginian Curtis Strange with two U.S. Open trophies may have been no more than a top 10 thrill.

Battle, of Charlottesville, was a World War II hero. He earned the Silver Star for gallantry when his PT boat helped rescue friend John F. Kennedy and his crew after Kennedy's PT 109 was rammed by the Japanese destroyer *Amagiri* during the Solomon Islands campaign in August of 1943.

Battle, the son of former Virginia Gov. John Stewart Battle, became a key ally to Kennedy during the 1960 presidential campaign. He helped conceive and implement the strategy in West Virginia and other predominantly Protestant southern states that Kennedy used to overcome his New England/Roman Catholic background and his image as the spoiled son of a millionaire.

Kennedy's victory in the West Virginia primary forced Hubert H. Humphrey out of the race for the Democratic Party's presidential nomination.

Following his election, Kennedy named Battle ambassador to Australia. It

was a post he held with distinction for three years until the emotional impact of Kennedy's assassination caused him to submit a resignation that President Lyndon Baines Johnson reluctantly accepted.

In 1969, Battle lost his own campaign to become governor of Virginia.

He served as president and CEO of Fieldcrest Mills in 1971. Nine years later, he was elected president of the American Textile Manufacturing Institute.

In his spare time, he headed a major capital-fund campaign for the University of Virginia, his alma mater. And he served on the State Council of Higher Education in Virginia.

Through it all, however, golf always held a prominent place in his life.

He had taken up the game under bizarre circumstances. One summer during his childhood, a polio epidemic swept through Central Virginia. The vaccine would not be discovered until the mid-1950s. No one knew what caused the disease, though there was a suspicion it was transmitted by tainted water.

Battle and his older brother John were forbidden to swim. Their parents refused to let them attend the movies.

Bill Battle, former USGA president, at the first tee of the South Course at Farmington Country Club in Charlottesville.

"My brother already played a lot of golf," Battle said with a smile and a shrug. "I started joining him every day."

It wasn't long before fellow members at Farmington Country Club nicknamed them "The Long Driving Battle Boys." Both participated in the State Amateur. Both played in the Kenridge Invitational, an annual amateur event at Farmington that featured the best players in the state. Both competed for the University of Virginia.

Although that was as far as he extended his playing career, Bill Battle was one of the founders of the annual Virginias-Carolinas matches that began in 1955.

It was at the 1957 matches, held in April at Pinehurst and in August at the Cascades in Hot Springs, that the seeds were sown that would make Strange's Open victories more emotional for Battle than anyone knew.

Battle's partner in four-ball matches was Tom Strange of Norfolk, whose twin sons, Curtis and Allan, were two years old at the time.

Battle and Strange were a formidable pair, winning both of their matches in the spring competition. Strange would beat P.J. Boatwright Jr. 3-0 in the summer singles matches, though he and Battle would lose their four-ball encounter with Boatwright and Bobby Chapman.

More important to Battle, he and Tom became good friends, a relationship that was cut short when Strange died of cancer in 1969.

Almost two decades later, as he watched Curtis approach the presentation stand at The Country Club in Brookline, Massachusetts, after beating Nick Faldo in an 18-hole playoff, Battle had trouble maintaining his composure.

"Both times Curtis won the Open, I gave him the trophy," Battle said. "Both times I got choked up. We were both very excited, but there wasn't but so much I could show. I heard that he told someone, 'Bill was pretty reserved, but I knew how he felt.'"

Even though Battle struggled to restrain his emotions that day, his tenure as USGA president was characterized by the calm, objective manner in which he guided the organization through an ugly legal ordeal that, handled differently, could have ruined it.

Battle's association with the USGA began in a curious place—a meeting of the Virginia Bar Association at The Homestead in Hot Springs. Battle knew Bill Campbell, USGA president in 1982-83, as a teammate in the Virginias-Carolinas matches and from the days when Battle practiced law in West Virginia.

Campbell was attending the conference and approached Battle about joining the USGA's executive committee.

"I said, 'Geez, Bill, I'm one of the guys who think you all are pretty silly,'" Battle recalled. "I said, 'I mean, wearing a tie and a blue coat when it's 110 in the shade! I respect you, but I'm not sure you want me.'"

Campbell replied that that was exactly why he wanted Battle. He wanted someone who had the courage to tackle the organization's rigid, pretentious reputation.

Battle agreed. When he was chairman of the championship committee, the USGA went to the white short-sleeved shirts and khaki slacks they wear today.

"The more you get to know what the USGA does, the more you respect it," Battle said. "I found there was a real acceptance of the view that we should soften our image a little bit. The game was getting to be popular, public courses were becoming prevalent, a lot of people were playing golf. To get their support and understanding, we had to relate to them."

Battle's presidency was marked by a problem that extended far beyond a dress code.

In the mid-1980s, the Karsten Manufacturing Corp. began making the Ping Eye 2 using the investment casting process. The process was limited. It could only make clubs with U-shaped grooves—square grooves they were called—not the traditional V-shaped grooves.

However, the square grooves scarred the golf ball on certain shots, prompting Karsten to round them at the edges.

The USGA contended that Karsten grooves were wider and closer together than those allowed by the rules of golf. Under what was called the "30-degree" method of measurement, the Ping Eye 2 grooves were five-thousandths of an inch too wide.

Battle now says, "They were wrong—and we were wrong.

"We had put in specs we couldn't measure," he said. "We didn't have an instrument . . . We had to adopt an arbitrary method. If we had taken 29, it wouldn't have affected Ping. If we had taken 31, it wouldn't have affected them. But we took 30, and it did affect them."

In January 1988, the USGA Executive Committee reaffirmed the organization's position that, starting in 1990, it would not permit the use of Ping Eye 2 irons in its competitions because it considered the clubs to be illegal. The Royal and Ancient Golf Club of Saint Andrews, Scotland, joined in that opinion.

In August 1999, Karsten Manufacturing fired back with a $100 million lawsuit charging both organizations with violating antitrust laws, slander, and interfering with Ping's current and future business.

"The interesting thing was there was no way we'd ever determined that this variation affected in any way the play of the game," Battle said. "It was so insignificant; it was a technical thing. When I looked into it, I said, 'Number one, we could easily lose this suit. Number two, it's going to cost millions of dollars.'"

Battle made it a point to get to know Karsten Solheim, the founder, and his son John Solheim. Battle found them to be honorable people. Rightfully concerned about the strength of his side's case and the possible erosion of the USGA's power should Karsten Manufacturing win, Battle argued that the two sides should settle.

The Solheims were ready. Many members of the USGA were not.

"There were still people bound and determined to go through with it," Battle said. "We had a heck of a fight in the Executive Committee. One of them made the strange statement, 'We have the right to be wrong.' And I said, 'My friend, there's no way that will fly.' "

In late January 1990, with Battle overseeing the final annual meeting of his term, a settlement finally was struck. The USGA would drop its ban on Ping Eye 2 clubs. Karsten Manufacturing would drop the lawsuit and begin producing a club with grooves that conformed to USGA standards. The USGA agreed to a grandfather clause that anyone owning a set of Ping Eye 2s produced before March 31, 1990, would be allowed to use them in competition.

It also admitted that the dispute had been about technology, and that there was no evidence that playing Ping Eye 2 clubs gave anyone an unfair advantage.

"I was able to announce it on my last night as president," Battle said. "The most significant thing was that Karsten made the statement that the USGA and the R&A ought to be the rule-makers for the game of golf. It was the only way it should be. No manufacturers should be involved."

It had been an arduous, relentless struggle that threatened the authority structure of the game. Battle had loved every minute of it.

"Frankly, this controversy probably made my term more enjoyable," he said. "It kept my interest, where handicapping and things like that might not have."

At age 67, Battle returned to the law firm of McGuire, Woods, Battle and Boothe in Charlottesville. He's retired now, lives in Ivy, Virginia, and can still be seen hitting his long drives down the fairways of Farmington.

Bill Battle, former USGA president, in front of the pro shop at Farmington Country Club in Charlottesville.

they ruled the game

PGA Tour commissioner Tim Finchem, who grew up in Virginia Beach, sits in the pro shop of the TPC of Virginia Beach at the grand opening in 1999.

TIM FINCHEM

As a 14-year-old boy, Tim Finchem spent hours on the golf course at the Little Creek Amphibious Base in Norfolk, where you could play all day for $1.

As a student and member of the golf team at Virginia Beach High School, Finchem found a practice haven at the city's Bow Creek Golf Course. Tom Strange was the pro there, and his sons, Curtis and Allan, were far from the only young players welcomed there.

Such beginnings had an impact on Finchem, who succeeded Deane Beman as commissioner of the PGA Tour on June 1, 1994, at the age of 47.

Under his direction, professional golf has mushroomed into a billion-dollar business, with tentacles reaching everywhere, but Finchem manages to save some focus for the little guy and girl.

How else does one explain Finchem's whole-hearted endorsement and leadership role in The First Tee program? Under the supervision of the World Golf Foundation, and in conjunction with the PGA Tour, the U.S. Golf Association, the PGA of America, and Augusta National Golf Club, the program aims to attract children to the game by making it more affordable and accessible. Facilities designed for that purpose are being constructed across the U.S.

Finchem's goal was to have 100 facilities completed or under construction by the turn of the century, with many more to come. Sure, it's basic marketing to hook future customers while they're young, but Finchem seems to have an underlying motivation that is pure.

"When I became commissioner, I reflected on the things that had gotten the Tour this far," Finchem said. "They really are the image of the game and the players. It's the unique structure that we enjoy as a sport without owners, without unions. It stands to reason that the more people who learn about the game, enjoy the game, play the game, the more that are going to be fans.

"To help the game grow is also a recognition of how we got here. It's the right thing to do, given that it's golf that supports all of our success."

Any conversation with him about the health of the game he oversees includes at least a couple of references to getting more youngsters involved, of his commitment to do what he can to make golf a game of the people.

PGA Tour commissioner Tim Finchem in the lounge of TPC of Virginia Beach.

PGA Tour commissioner Tim Finchem unveils a portrait of Sam Snead, as Snead helps him show off the painting at PGA Tour headquarters.

Finchem was on hand to announce plans for Virginia's initial First Tee facilities: a three-hole course scheduled to open in Richmond in Spring 2000; and a second facility in Chesterfield County outside Richmond, scheduled to open in Summer 2000.

A third facility, located at TPC of Virginia Beach, can be expanded from three holes for pee-wee golfers to nine holes for juniors. Designed by Alice Dye, it is expected to open in 2001, and could become the prototype for First Tee facilities throughout the nation.

"In basketball, you can always find a hoop to shoot at," he said. "In baseball or soccer—increasingly with soccer—if you want to play street ball, you can do it. The same holds true for softball or baseball. You can find a place to do it. That's not the case with golf. Until we get to that point, we're not going to be able to maximize our potential. That's the real objective."

"We want to create a situation where any kid—*any* kid—who watches a Tiger Woods, a David Duval, a Justin Leonard, and wants to learn golf, can. Or a little girl who watches Juli Inkster win the Women's Open can have the same opportunity to learn the game as Juli did."

Finchem is almost providentially qualified to guide pro golf into its next golden era—emphasis on the gold. He attended the University of Richmond on a debate scholarship, then earned a law degree from the University of Virginia.

After moving back to Virginia Beach, he ran for Prosecuting Attorney in 1977, but lost. That sent him to Washington, D.C., where he first became a deputy advisor for economic affairs to President Jimmy Carter, then the national staff director for the Carter-Mondale presidential campaign in 1980.

"If the presidential election had gone differently, I would have stayed in government from 1980 to 1984, and I'm not sure what would have happened to my life after that," Finchem said. "Losing the election for prosecuting attorney in Virginia Beach, that was the major development. Had I won that race, everything else would have been different.

"I'm glad I lost."

In 1981, Finchem co-founded the National Strategies and Marketing Group. Three years later, the PGA Tour became a client. In 1988, Beman wooed Finchem away from his own company to become the Tour's vice-president for business affairs.

When Beman retired in 1994, Finchem was chosen over a formidable set of candidates that included Charlie Meachem, then commissioner of the LPGA; Virginian Vinny Giles, president of Pros, Inc.; and Jack Frazee, former chairman of Centel Corporation.

In addition to First Tee, Finchem negotiated a television deal that goosed rights fees to $100 million per year. He announced the World Golf championships, three annual events with purses of $5 million each.

He called for tournament sponsors to increase purses to about $3 million at each Tour stop by 2002 and agree to five-year contracts. The Tour will subsidize those who commit to such an undertaking.

Sensing that the buy.com Tour had become exactly the type of future proving ground it was intended to be when it was formed, Finchem committed to shuffling some of the Tour's increased revenues in that direction. The larger the purse, the more intense the competition, the more appealing the buy.com Tour might become to fans.

Finchem acknowledged his background in May 1999 when he presided over the opening of Virginia's first Tournament Players Club course, TPC of Virginia Beach. Pete Dye designed the course, with Curtis Strange serving as a consultant.

"Little did I know when I was practicing at Bow Creek all those years ago, and Curtis Strange was just a kid hanging around, that one day he'd be telling me what to do," Finchem joked to the several hundred invited guests.

Finchem isn't afraid to point out the differences between him and Beman. His predecessor, he said, was a better innovator, always coming up with a new way to sell golf.

"I might be a little bit stronger on the management and communications side, but I don't think anyone could have matched what Deane did for 20 years," Finchem said. "He took it from very little to something very strong. My job is to nurture it and take it to the next level.

"Knock on wood, I don't think I've had any huge disappointments. The problems we have are really good problems, relating to growth and how to get to the next level. We have a lot of work to do to take the buy.com Tour to another level, which we intend to do. The Senior Tour still has room for growth.

"We want to take the whole sport to the level where it can effectively compete with the big team sports. That's a huge challenge, but as long as we're making progress, I don't have any concerns about mistakes thus far."

PGA Tour commissioner Tim Finchem addresses the audience gathered at the grand opening of the TPC of Virginia Beach in June of 1999. Design consultant Curtis Strange is at bottom right.

virginians and the cup

The Wanamaker Cup, given to the winner of the PGA championship, and the exact replica silversmith Mark Frankel made for Davis Love III.

VIRGINIANS & THE CUP

If the United States retains the Ryder Cup in 2001 at The Belfry in England, the replica of the trophy captain Curtis Strange will receive will have been made by one of his Williamsburg neighbors.

Silversmith Mark Frankel has been handcrafting Ryder Cup replicas for the PGA of America and the British PGA since 1983. He was working for Colonial Williamsburg then and was hired to repair the original cup, which had been damaged in travel.

A graduate of the prestigious Sir John Cass School in England and a member of the Society of American Silversmiths, Frankel has had his hands on golf's most glamorous prize ever since.

The original Ryder Cup, donated to Great Britain's Professional Golfers Association by Samuel Ryder in 1927, the year of the first matches between the U.S. and Great Britain, stands 17 inches tall and is made of nine-carat gold.

Frankel's made-to-scale reproductions, which are presented to the captain of the winning team, are made of sterling silver with gold plating.

Working out of a cramped garage, Frankel creates his Ryder Cups in exactly the same fashion as the original 70 years ago.

"There really isn't anything high-tech you can go through to produce these trophies," Frankel said. "Everything we do is at the bench."

Most of the components are created during a process called "spinning." Frankel takes a piece of silver and holds it tight to a shaped piece of steel. Then he puts the two onto a lathe, and as the lathe is turning, he molds the silver into the desired form.

The lid has three different spinnings that are put together. The handles are made from six pieces that Frankel solders into one.

It takes Frankel more than 100 hours to make a Ryder Cup because many of the trophy's decorations must be hand-tooled. He is among select company. There are fewer than 10 silversmiths in the U.S. qualified to tackle such large "presentation" pieces.

Although they have no idea who Frankel is, or where these cups were

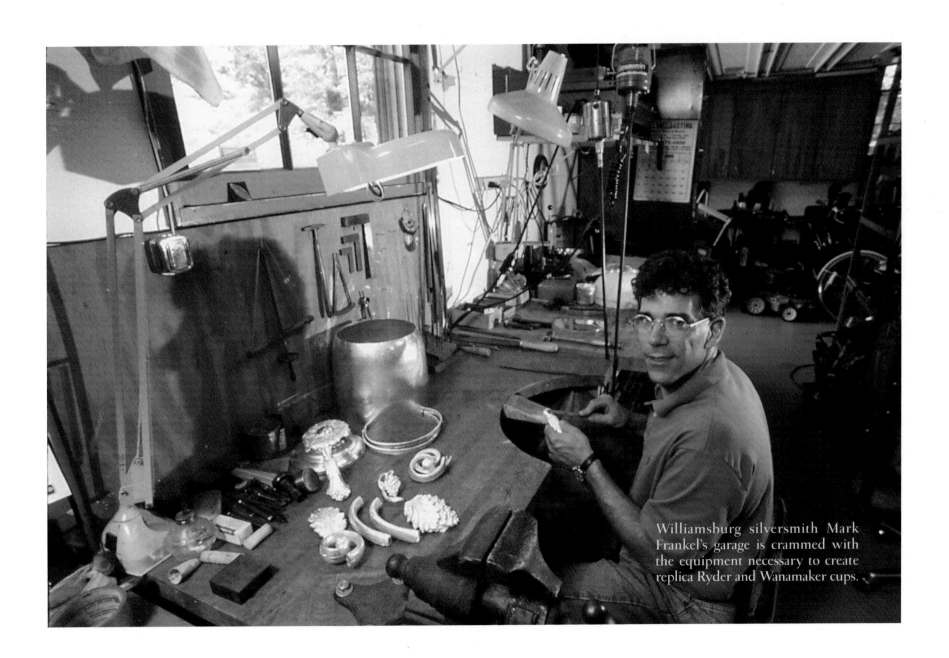

Williamsburg silversmith Mark Frankel's garage is crammed with the equipment necessary to create replica Ryder and Wanamaker cups.

Many of Virginia native Lanny Wadkins' Ryder Cup golf bags are on display at the Golden Horseshoe Golf Club in Williamsburg.

made, every winning Ryder Cup team captain takes more than a little bit of Frankel home with him.

His hallmark MJF, which appears in a cloverleaf on the base of every trophy, is a permanent reminder that without Mark Frankel, there might be no Ryder Cup.

Frankel's is one of a host of notable contributions to Cup competitions by Virginians. The most recent highlight was Strange's selection as 2001 Ryder Cup captain on Oct. 25, 1999.

"This is truly one of the most exciting days of my life," Strange said. "It was something I had always looked forward to, never thought it would happen maybe; dreamed about it.

"As a player, you qualify for the Ryder Cup team strictly on your ability to play the game. To captain, I feel you're chosen for your ability to lead, to prepare your players, and also win back the Cup. It's a daunting challenge, but I look forward to it very much."

Strange is the third Virginian to captain a Ryder Cup team. Sam Snead, who played on seven Ryder Cup teams, handled the task three times. Lanny Wadkins, who made eight playing appearances, was captain in 1995.

Wadkins and Strange have been on stage for a couple of the Ryder Cup's more memorable moments, pro and con.

Strange, a captain's choice by Wadkins, was 1-up against Nick Faldo with three holes to play at Oak Hill in Rochester in 1995. The U.S. started the final day with a 9-7 lead. Other players failed to win that day, too, in what became a 14-13 defeat.

But when Strange missed putts of four feet at 16, eight feet at 17 and seven feet at 18, any of which would have given him the match and the U.S. the Cup, he drew almost all of the attention.

"By the 15th hole, I knew it had all come down to my match," said Strange, who already had lost twice that weekend and was obviously struggling. "I was playing with Band-Aids all over my swing . . . . It's frightening to think what I'm going to feel like tomorrow."

On the day Strange was named Ryder Cup captain four years later, even Oak Hill in '95 had become a mostly pleasant memory.

"I had a wonderful week," Strange said. "I've always said win, lose, or draw, it's one of the greatest weeks of your life. It's a bit easier when you win, it's better when you play well, but my disappointment came because you want your play to justify your selection as a pick. Nick and I had a great match."

In 1983, Wadkins' 72-yard sand wedge to the final green at PGA National left him with a tap-in birdie that allowed the U.S. to escape with a one-point victory. But that's not the stroke he remembers from that year.

"The shot before the wedge, I've got to hit a 3-wood over water," Wadkins said, the corners of his mouth beginning to turn into a smile. "Curtis is standing six feet away from me when I hit it, and he's jumping up and down, yelling for it to 'Hurry' and 'Git.' And I just turned to him and said, 'Don't worry, Curtis, I hit it solid.'"

Wadkins said because the format of the Ryder Cup was so much different from what PGA Tour players face week in and week out, it energized him beyond other events each of the eight times he played.

"I always liked match play," he said. "I played so much of it as a kid that it was fun to come back and play it again. I think that one of the reasons I was so successful in Ryder Cup play is that I so looked forward to it. I like head-to-head stuff. I can be a little antagonistic with some of these guys sometimes. I thrived on it."

Despite 21 career victories on the PGA Tour, Wadkins lists his Ryder Cup experience as among his proudest accomplishments.

"What's special to me is that there are so many years involved," he said. "I missed one in '81 because of a surgery, so you're talking a span of about 20 years and I was in every other Ryder Cup. That's something not many players have been able to do."

LPGA star Donna Andrews was a member of the victorious U.S. team in the 1998 Solheim Cup matches at The Greenbrier in West Virginia.

"All I remember from the first day was standing there and the crowd cheering, 'Go USA' and 'Go Donna.' Betsy King was addressing her ball on the first tee and suddenly she says, 'Good Lord, please let me get this airborne.' It was a tremendous experience."

It's an experience Virginia amateurs have enjoyed as well.

Vinny Giles, along with friend and client Gary Koch, holds the Walker Cup record for largest winning margin in an 18-hole foursomes match. The two defeated Rodney Foster and Trevor Homer of Great Britain and Ireland 7 and 5 at The Country Club in Brookline, Massachusetts., in 1973.

Giles' 15 career Walker Cup matches is fourth highest all-time, after Jay Sigel (33), Bill Campbell (18), and Francis Ouimet (16). Giles' career record in singles and foursomes was 8-2-5.

His first Walker Cup appearance remains a treasured moment, although he chuckles at the clumsy way it began.

He and Steve Melnyk were partners in the opening match at Milwaukee Country Club in 1969. By the time the national anthem had been played and the opening ceremonies were finished, Giles was so emotionally wrought, he could barely lift the club.

"First shot, I hit the ugliest duck-hook you've ever seen, right under a tree," he remembered. "Melnyk came over to me and said something like, 'You sorry s.o.b.' For whatever reason, that kind of loosened us up and we went on to play well."

Strange had a 3-0-1 record in Walker Cup competition. In two appearances, Wadkins finished 3-4.

Kandi Kessler-Comer became the first Virginia woman to compete for the Curtis Cup when the U.S. Golf Association named her to the 1986 team that met Great Britain at Prairie Dunes CC in Kansas.

Robbye King-Youel had been an alternate 20 years before, but did not get into a match.

"Nothing will ever replace that feeling," Comer said. "Just having the opportunity to represent my country is something I'll never forget."

VIRGINIANS & THE CUP

RYDER CUP

Name	Year(s)
Sam Snead*	1937, '47, '49, '51, '53, '55, '59
Curtis Strange**	1983, '85, '87, '89, '95
Lanny Wadkins***	1977, '79, '83, '85, '87, '89, '91, '93
J.C. Snead	1971, '73, '75
Chandler Harper	1955
Lew Worsham	1947

* Captain in 1951, '59, and '69
** Captain in 2001
***Captain in 1995

SOLHEIM CUP

Name	Year
Donna Andrews	1994

WALKER CUP

Name	Year(s)
Vinny Giles	1969, '71, '73, '75
Curtis Strange	1975
Lanny Wadkins	1969, '71
Tom McKnight	1999

CURTIS CUP

Name	Year
Kandi Kessler-Comer	1986

the resorts

The first tee at The Homestead Course is the oldest in
continuous use in the United States.

THE HOMESTEAD

Since 1766, the world has come to The Homestead in Hot Springs seeking "the cure" for life's mental and physical aches and pains. While much about the grand old resort has changed, The Homestead's springs are no less warm today. Its mountain vistas are no less spectacular. Its emphasis on Southern hospitality is no less apparent.

The Homestead holds a unique place in American history. George Washington *really* slept there.

So did Thomas Jefferson, who is credited with designing the men's pool that opened in 1761. The Jefferson Pools, once known as the Warm Springs Pools, are located five miles north of The Homestead on U.S. 220.

Alexander Hamilton, Henry Ford, and John D. Rockefeller were frequent guests.

President Woodrow Wilson honeymooned there, as did Lord and Lady Astor. Mrs. Cornelius Vanderbilt, the queen of American high society, summered at The Homestead.

More than 350 Japanese diplomats were interned there for three months following the attack on Pearl Harbor in 1941.

The first historical accounts are from a diary by Dr. Thomas Walker, a medical missionary who, en route to Kentucky, traveled through the area, then part of the Ohio Territory.

In 1750, Dr. Walker wrote: "We went to Hot Springs and found six invalids there. The spring is warmer than new milk and there is a spring of cold water within 20 feet of the warm one."

Lt. Thomas Bullitt, one of Washington's officers at Fort Dinwiddie, built the first Homestead in 1766. After Bullitt's death in 1778, and until Dr. Thomas Goode acquired the property in 1832, there was absentee ownership.

Dr. Goode improved the bathhouses. By 1846, he was announcing the opening of a "modern hotel" and advocating that the waters in Hot Springs would cure gout, rheumatism, liver diseases, paralysis, neuralgia, enlarged glands, and spinal irritations.

The famous view of The Homestead tower, as seen from the 17th fairway of the Old Course. This Donald Ross masterpiece has existed since 1892.

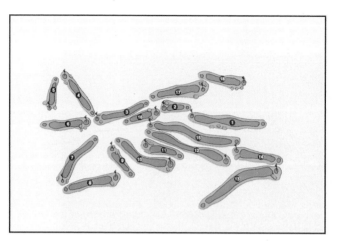

A routing map of the Old Course at The Homestead, designed by Donald Ross.

After Dr. Goode's death in 1858, the hotel passed through various hands. The Cascades Inn and The Homestead served as a hospital for Confederate officers during the Civil War. Later, General and Mrs. Robert E. Lee were frequent guests.

In 1891, Melvin E. Ingalls, president of the Chesapeake & Ohio Railway Company, formed a syndicate eventually known as the Virginia Hot Springs Company. Its purpose was to purchase the property from Col. J.A. August and W.S. Edmonds.

Ingalls was named president of Virginia Hot Springs Inc., and in 1914, his family bought controlling interest in the property.

Guided by the Ingalls—Melvin's son Fay and grandson Daniel also served as president—The Homestead quickly solidified its reputation as one of the world's premier resorts, one it easily maintains to this day.

In 1892, a branch of the Chesapeake and Ohio Railway was completed to Hot Springs. It enabled guests to travel to the resort by train. Thousands did until 1970, when the service was discontinued.

The Spa, the first of its kind in America, was erected in 1892 near the famous octagon pool, site of the 104-degree hot springs that feed the spa's indoor pool and mineral baths.

The year 1892 was significant for one other reason: Virginia's oldest golf course—The Homestead Course—opened for play.

Also that year, the Virginia Hotel was added, as were 11 cottages, known as Cottage Row. The Casino, now used as the pro shop for The Homestead Course, was built in 1893.

Donald Ross, the patron saint of American golf architects, was brought in from Pinehurst in North Carolina to design and expand The Homestead Course, now known as the Old Course. Ross turned the original six holes into 18, which opened in 1913.

While some of the legendary names in the design industry subsequently added their unique touches—Peter Lees, A.W. Tillinghast, and William Flynn—one thing has remained constant: The first tee is the oldest in continuous use in America.

That isn't all the history the Old Course has provided. One of the first member clubs of the United States Golf Association was the Virginia Hot Springs Golf Club, now 112 years old.

The Spa, Casino, and cottages remain from a fire that destroyed The Homestead in 1901.

In 1902, the main section of today's Homestead was built. A year later, the West Wing and the indoor pool were added. The Tower, trademark of The Homestead, was finished in Spring 1929.

In 1943, the Duke of Windsor and Wallis Warfield Simpson—the woman for whom he surrendered his throne—spent a month at The Homestead.

Sam Snead, who taught himself to play golf on The Homestead's "Goat Course," which was how the employees referred to an admittedly scrawny layout set aside for them, frequently accompanied the duke. Slammin' Sammy, the first pro at The Homestead's Cascades Course, was caught off guard the first time he learned that the Duke wasn't exactly concerned with strict adherence to the rules.

"He'd have a three-foot downhill putt and that thing would roll way past and he'd reach with his putter and drag that old ball right back into the hole," Snead remembered, laughing. "You'd have to ask him, 'What did you have there, sir?' because you never knew what he was going to come up with for a score."

Nonetheless, Snead enjoyed the Duke's company.

"He loved to laugh," Snead said. "Someone once came up to him with a camera and he said, 'No, no. Please. Move back. You're showing my wrinkles.' I told him a joke and he went, 'Heh, heh, heh.' Then I told him another one, and that must have really got to him. He started flapping his arms around and going, 'HA . . . HAHA . . . HAHAHA.' All of a sudden, you could have heard him laughing 500 yards away. And 'His Man' came up to me—he always had 'His Man' with him—and says, 'Mr. Snead, I have never heard him loff like that before.'

"I even told him one that was a little off-color once. He was the only one in the foursome laughing."

In 1952, Thomas Lennon joined The Homestead from the Carlton Hotel in Washington, D.C. Like Fay Ingalls, Lennon had a fervent interest in golf. A better-than-average player who worked diligently on his game, Lennon was medalist at the 1964 Virginia State Senior Championship won by William Smith of Charlottesville on the Old Course.

That was not a rare occurrence. From 1959 to

A lone golfer practices on the gigantic putting green next to the Old Course clubhouse at The Homestead.

1993, without interruption, The Homestead Course and the State Senior Championship were inseparable.

In September of 1959, Dan Ingalls announced that Robert Trent Jones had been hired to design a third course. The site would be the lower Cascades Gorge, about five miles from Hot Springs; hence, it would be called the Lower Cascades.

Ingalls was proud of the fact that Jones was implementing a relatively new design concept in creating the new course. Rather than spread two or three different tee areas on each hole, Jones was going to build one lengthy tee complex. The overall length of the course could be altered by nearly 1,100 yards just by the position of the tees.

That would be one of the many design nuances for which Jones would become famous. Today, it's known as the "runway" effect.

The Lower Cascades opened in 1963 and has been the ideal complement to the world-renowned Cascades Course.

In 1993, Dallas-based Club Resorts Inc. assumed management and co-ownership of The Homestead, adding it to an outstanding family of world-class resorts. Among them are Pinehurst in North Carolina; Barton Creek in Texas; Daufuskie Island in South Carolina; and Quail Hollow in Ohio.

In 1994, the Old Course received more than $1 million in upgrades, part of a multimillion dollar restoration for the entire resort. Rees Jones, one of the world's foremost designers, supervised the work, which included new bunkers and tees, as well as the relocation of the 18th hole.

1923
THE CASCADES
DESIGNED BY WILLIAM FLYNN

For the golf purist, this sign says it all: A fabulous
course, a brilliant designer and a legacy of excellence.

THE HOMESTEAD — CASCADES COURSE

No less an authority than famous golf author and historian Herbert Warren Wind called The Homestead's 6,659-yard Cascades Course "the world's finest mountain course." Nothing has changed since Wind's proclamation.

When *Golf Digest* released its rating of America's greatest 100 courses in May 1999, the par-70 Cascades was No. 53. That's high praise for a course that has been challenging players of all abilities since 1924, a layout born of necessity and conceived by inspiration.

One bucolic April day in 1923, a foursome that included three directors of the Virginia Hot Springs Company embarked on what they thought would be a peaceful, moderately paced round of golf at The Homestead Course.

They never anticipated the crush of players who had the same idea. They waited on every shot. It took an hour and a half to play the first five holes.

Then they arrived at a par 3 and discovered that there were 12 players ahead of them on the tee. If building a second golf course wasn't a priority before then, it became one that day.

Fay Ingalls, son of Homestead founder Melvin Ingalls and the president of Virginia Hot Springs Company from 1922 until his death in 1957, immediately tackled the problem. Ingalls, who was captain of the Harvard golf team as a senior, possessed an unabashed love for the game. The only greater passion he felt was for The Homestead. Ingalls wanted an architect who would design something worthy of national acclaim.

There was just one problem: None of the marquee designers of the era were available. Finally, a friend mentioned William Flynn.

Flynn had been part of the project at spectacular Pine Valley in New Jersey, but he did not have particularly glamorous credentials otherwise. He had worked on the construction crew that built Merion in Philadelphia, and he had briefly been the greenskeeper there.

Nonetheless, Ingalls invited Flynn to tour the Hot Springs area and gave

The seventh hole of The Cascades Course at The Homestead. "Seventh Heaven" (all the golf holes on the Cascades Course have names) is a 425-yard, par 4 with a pitched fairway like no other. This view is from the back of the eighth tee box.

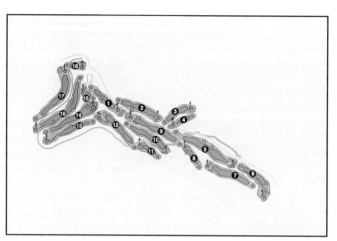

A routing map of the Cascades Course at The Homestead, designed by William Flynn in 1923.

him one day to put together a proposal. In his 1949 book *The Valley Road*, Ingalls recalled that Flynn arrived on a warm, sticky day, and the two immediately took off walking through dense brush and weeds, looking for the just the right spot.

"The hotter and more tired I got, the more I wanted to find out what Flynn thought," Ingalls wrote. "But he gave me not the slightest indication. At dusk we washed some of the dust and grime out of our throats with good scotch, and Flynn took a sheet of foolscap and made some figures.

"Studying these for a time he said, 'If you can get the piece [of property] on which the shack stands, I'll have twenty locations where I can put a putting green. I don't know how the holes will run but if I have two extra sites for greens I can build you a course.'"

Ultimately, Ingalls purchased the Rubino property, including the quarter acre on which the shack stood. Construction began later that year, and the first shot was struck in October of 1924.

"Flynn made his mark by the Cascades job," Flynn associate William Gordon told *The Richmond News Leader* in 1973.

Gordon was part of the Cascades project team and lived in Hot Springs during the year it took to carve out the course.

"The Homestead cleared the land—most of it was hacked right out of the forest," Gordon said. "And we did the grading. That was our policy. We wouldn't design unless we could build."

That doesn't mean everything was perfect right from the start. The engineer in charge of construction was not a golfer. Flynn's plans were not those of a construction engineer.

The Cascades' original greens were wildly sloped because of a miscommunication between the course engineer and Flynn, who in 1923 was also occupied with Cherry Hills in Denver. Ten

Cascades greens were eventually rebuilt. Other renovations were carried out over the years, the most breathtakingly curious coming on the 16th hole.

In the early 1950s, Ingalls himself redesigned and rebuilt the hole. The result was a gorgeous, gently curving par 5 of 525 yards from the championship markers, with a serpentine creek that runs down the right side before spilling into a pond in front of the green.

In 1951, Ingalls lured a famed architect to The Cascades: Robert Trent Jones Sr. He improved the seventh hole and built new 14th and 15th holes. Jones also designed a truly magnificent 17th hole. Like Ingalls' 16th, No. 17 is a par 5, but a dogleg left, with the creek running down the right side and a pond to the right of a well-bunkered green.

The Cascades proved to be a huge boost to Flynn's career. Ingalls later hired him to redesign the Homestead Course. He also built The River Course at the Country Club of Virginia, a third nine at The Country Club in Brookline, Massachusetts; the Spring Mill course at Philadelphia Country Club; and Shinnecock Hills in Southampton, New York.

Those courses alone have played host to 10 U.S. Opens.

As for The Cascades, it has been the scene of six USGA championships, making it one of only 17 courses in the United States with that distinction.

It is one of 10 Five-Star public access courses in the U.S. Virginia's best players have flocked there to decide tournaments of all consequence.

In fact, more than 240 Virginia State Golf Association championships have been contested there. From 1948 to 1973, the men's State Amateur was held annually at The Cascades—38 times in all. Since 1962, the women's State Amateur has been decided at William Flynn's little gem.

No one has enjoyed as much success at The

The entrance sign and the clubhouse for The Cascades Course at The Homestead in Hot Springs, Virginia, a short drive from the main resort complex.

Cascades as former U.S. and British Amateur champion Vinny Giles. The Richmond resident won six of his state-record seven State Amateurs at the Cascades. In 1968, when the tournament was contested at medal play, Giles won by 15 strokes.

It is fitting, then, that when The Homestead celebrated the 75th anniversary of The Cascades in 1998, Giles was chosen as honorary chairman.

The competition among America's best golf courses grows keener each year. Seventy-six years after its creation, The Cascades can still hold its own.

Here's a look at the most prestigious events staged at one of the nation's most prestigious addresses.

1928 U.S. WOMEN'S AMATEUR

A little history would have told you that Glenna Collett of Providence, Rhode Island, had a great chance to win the 1928 U.S. Women's Amateur at The Cascades.

Collett had defeated Margaret Gavin at Greenbrier Golf Club in West Virginia to win the 1922

Women's Amateur. She had beaten Alexa Stirling at St. Louis Country Club to win the same event in 1925. What chance did anyone in the '28 field have?

Not much, as it turned out.

In reaching the final against Virginia Van Wie of Illinois, Collett's most competitive matches were 4-and-3 victories in the quarterfinals and semifinals.

The final was scheduled for 36 holes. Although it didn't come close to going the distance, it was nonetheless a very long day for Van Wie.

Collett's smashing 13-and-12 verdict ignited her streak of three straight titles, forever establishing her as one of the greatest American amateurs and a pioneer in women's golf.

In 1952, LPGA founder, charter member and Hall of Fame member Betty Jameson donated the Vare Trophy to her organization. The award is named in honor of Glenna Collett-Vare and is given annually to the player with the lowest scoring average.

1966 CURTIS CUP

It was the 14th meeting between a women's amateur team representing the United States and one representing Great Britain and Ireland. Captained by Dorothy Germain Porter, the American women won easily, 13-5.

Competing in foursomes and singles, the U.S. led 2½ to ½ after the morning foursomes. By the end of the first day, the Americans had a comfortable 7-2 lead.

Barbara White Boddie and Carol Sorenson Flenniken captured the singles matches that capped off the U.S. victory.

Officially named "The Women's International Cup," the cup for the match was officially presented in 1932 by Harriot and Margaret Curtis, sisters who won the U.S. Women's Amateur four times between them.

The cup, a silver bowl of Paul Revere design, is inscribed, "To stimulate friendly rivalry among the women golfers of many lands." Although the Curtis sisters presented the cup in 1927, competition didn't begin until 1932, mostly for financial reasons.

1967 U.S. WOMEN'S OPEN

"There is little thought that this could be the year that an amateur would finally win the event,"

a reporter for the *Richmond Times-Dispatch* wrote on the eve of the tournament. "None has yet, and no one is given the chance this time out."

Indeed, the favorites for the $25,000 tournament—the largest purse in Women's Open history at the time—were Sandra Haynie, Mickey Wright, Carol Mann, Louise Suggs, and Kathy Whitworth.

Catherine Lacoste of Paris wasn't even an afterthought.

Yet the 22-year-old French Amateur champion had the perfect bloodlines to contend for the crown. Her mother was a former British Ladies champion. Her father had been a two-time Wimbledon tennis champion.

Lacoste trailed Haynie by one stroke after the opening round, then took over the tournament. Chipping and putting her way around a Cascades Course set up to play at 6,191 yards and to par 71, Lacoste became the first amateur to lead a Women's Open by firing a 1-under 70.

Her 141 total, which tied the 36-hole Open record, was five strokes better than Susie Maxwell and Margie Masters, six ahead of Shirley Englehorn, and eight up on Mann, Haynie, and Murle Lindstrom.

Still, no one figured it would last. The greatest women pros of the day weren't going to lose to an amateur. For half of Saturday's third round, Lacoste played into their hands.

She bogeyed the fourth hole from the rough, then made double-bogey 6 on the 349-yard sixth hole when she was short of the green with her second shot, hit a terrible chip, then three-putted.

Likewise, she missed the ninth green in regulation and could not get up and down for par. Her front-nine 40 had caused her five-shot lead to slip to three.

Then she righted herself, touring the back

nine in 1 under par, while the rest of the field retreated. As a gentle rain fell, Lacoste opened the final round with her five-stroke lead intact.

The rain would only get worse, as would Lacoste's play, though her 79 turned out to be good enough to capture the title by two shots over Maxwell and Beth Stone.

The cheery Frenchwoman, who became an instant favorite with a gallery that appreciated her constant charm and good humor, bogeyed five consecutive holes and six of seven on the back nine.

She hit over the first two greens, three-putted the 12th, couldn't get up and down out of a bunker at 13, and three-putted again on the 14th. A par on No. 15 did little to settle her. Lacoste immediately made bogey 6 on 16 when she nearly shanked her third shot into the water.

Suggs trailed by one shot after the 15th, then saw her chance for victory buried when her third shot to the par-5 16th became embedded in mud. She needed three more strokes to reach the green and took a double-bogey 7 to finish tied for fourth.

"I played like a clod," said Lacoste. "I was very lucky to have won shooting that score . . . a 79 . . . ugh. I didn't putt very well."

Nonetheless, there was much to celebrate. True to the Lacoste name, she did it in style. Moments after putting out on 18, she ran into the clubhouse, changed from shorts into a skirt and blue blazer, then came back for the trophy presentation.

The first amateur, first foreigner, and youngest contestant to win the Women's Open—a distinction she and Liselotte Neumann shared until 20-year-old Se Ri Pak came along in 1998—then called her father, Rene, to wish him a happy 63rd birthday.

"Bravo," he replied when informed of her victory. "Bravo."

The famous clubhouse of The Cascades Course with the 15th green in the foreground.

1980 U.S. SENIOR MEN'S CHAMPIONSHIP

The front field of Sam Snead's nearby farm was used as the practice range for this 26th annual championship. Bill Campbell may have been the only player in the field who already knew how to get there.

Campbell, an insurance executive from West Virginia who would become USGA president in 1982, had made the 30-mile trek from White Sulphur Springs to Hot Springs on several occasions. Campbell was an admirer of The Cascades, echoing Wind's declaration of the layout as "the best mountain course in the country."

In return, The Cascades treated Campbell like family.

Despite playing in just three previous events that year, Campbell won medalist honors in the stroke-play portion of the tournament. Campbell then cruised to a 5-and-4 victory over Minnesota's Gene Christensen in a first-round match.

The second round and quarterfinals, both played the next day, were more severe tests. Campbell was 2-down to both Joseph Simons of South Carolina and Robert Baker of Colorado before squeezing out 2-and-1 and 3-and-2 victories, respectively.

Against Dr. Ed Updegraff of Arizona in the semifinals, Campbell had to birdie four of the last five holes to earn a 5-and-4 decision.

In the other semifinal match, Keith Compton, a former Air Force lieutenant general from Texas and the 1978 U.S. Senior winner, moved out to a quick early lead and was never headed in beating fellow Texan Ed Hopkins 4 and 3.

As Compton was leaving The Cascades to prepare for the final, he stopped to congratulate Campbell and give him a gentle needle.

"At last, you're going to accept my invitation to play," Compton teased.

Campbell explained that Compton had been trying for years to get him to play practice rounds with him, invitations Campbell gave the impression he hadn't accepted.

"Everyone wants me in the practice rounds because I'm such a pigeon," Campbell joked.

Turns out that maybe Campbell was doing Compton a favor.

The slender West Virginian one-putted six times in winning the final, 3 and 2. Five of the putts saved par. Conversely, Compton's putting touch went AWOL. Prior to the final, he had three-putted twice in six rounds. Against Campbell, he did it twice on the front nine.

Campbell was 3-up at the turn and was never seriously challenged.

"He's just a great player," Compton said. "I had to play my best to beat him, and I couldn't do it."

Always gracious, Campbell claimed that there was another clear-cut winner that week: The Cascades. More than 140 players with a median handicap of 4 played two rounds of qualifying with average scores of 83 and 81, respectively.

"I think this golf course was pretty much the thing for this tournament," Campbell said. "It will not fade in the memory. The players will know it was played at the Cascades."

1988 U.S. AMATEUR

Eric Meeks rose from "good underdog" to top dog in one spectacular week.

A 23-year-old student at the University of Arizona, Meeks won the U.S. Amateur by jumping all over veteran Danny Yates of Atlanta 7-and-6 in the 36-hole final on a Cascades course playing to 6,568 yards and par 70.

Meeks, of Walnut, California, won the first four holes of the morning round and the first six holes of the afternoon session. Yates, 38, won eight holes, yet Meeks was 4-up at the lunch break, 10-up with 12 holes to play. For the day, he was 5 under par.

"That's as good a round as I've seen anybody play in the last round of a tournament that I've played in," Yates said. "He was in control, total control, of his game, from driving all the way down to his putting."

Although he had just been named a third-team All-American following his senior season at Arizona, Meeks admitted his college career had been less than he had hoped for.

"In my first three seasons, I didn't do anything," he explained bluntly. "Usually, I'm looked at as an underdog, a good underdog."

That certainly was the case in his third-round match. The opponent was Jay Sigel, two-time Amateur champion. Meeks wasn't intimidated, or if he was, he didn't let on. He beat Sigel on the third extra hole to advance.

Although he needed all 18 holes to do it, Meeks took care of two future PGA Tour players in the quarterfinals and semifinals: 2-up over Robert Gamez, 1-up over David Toms.

Yates, normally a steady, conservative player, went on a birdie binge to oust Jack Larkin of Atlanta 5 and 4 and University of Oklahoma player Doug Martin 4 and 3.

Although there was no real turning point in the final match, there was an unusual development that typified Yates' fortunes that day.

On the third hole of the afternoon 18, with both players in line to make birdie, Yates mistakenly lifted and marked Meeks' ball instead of his own. He assessed himself a one-stroke penalty.

"We both hit good shots to the green and I was sure mine was the closer of the two," he explained. "Like a dummy, I went right to Eric's ball and picked it up. In stroke play, that's not a penalty, but rules are rules and I should be smart enough not to mark someone else's ball."

In the end, it was an embarrassing mistake, but of little consequence to the outcome. Yates didn't know it at the time, but fate was at work as well.

"I had been playing real well before I came up here," Meeks said. "I just had the feeling that I was ready to do something great."

1994 U.S. WOMEN'S AMATEUR

From the beginning, it promised to be a crazy tournament. The medalists in the stroke-play qualifying were Leta Lindley, Erika Wicoff and Lori Teague.

Lindley had just finished a college career at the University of Arizona in which she was a four-time All-American and co-champion of the PAC-10 tournament.

Wicoff, a junior at Indiana, had been the Big Ten freshman of the year and the conference's player of the year as a sophomore.

Teague? She was a former college tennis player who had taken up golf four years earlier. She and her husband owned and operated a driving range, a nine-hole course, and a couple of pro shops in Hickory, North Carolina.

By the end of the first day of match play, seven of the eight members of the British Curtis Cup team had been eliminated. So had three of the four former U.S. Amateur champions in the field.

The only former champion left standing was the defending champion, 22-year-old Jill McGill of the University of Southern California, who had announced that she was turning professional after this tournament. McGill reached the final by coming from two holes down to oust 1994 NCAA champion Emilee Klein 1-up.

Her opponent would be 21-year-old Wendy Ward, a rising senior from Arizona State, who had finished second to Klein in the NCAA tournament.

While McGill had struggled to make the final and admitted that she was unhappy with her game, Ward had momentum. She zoomed into the match with McGill with a 7-and-5 blasting of 19-year-old Stanford sophomore Andrea Baxter.

McGill and Ward were more than a little familiar with each other's game from PAC-10 Conference battles.

"She's a super player," McGill said, shaking her head at the prospect. "It'll be a tough match."

She was right. Tied after 33 holes, Ward scratched out a 2-and-1 victory when she birdied the toughest par 5 on the course—No. 16—and McGill bogeyed what many considered the easiest, the 17th.

A crazy end to a crazy championship.

In 1998, the USGA announced that the Cascades would be host to the 2000 U.S. Mid-Amateur Championship.

The Cascades still wows them. Among the 20 or so international honors accorded The Cascades, perhaps one says it all. In 1998, readers of *Conde Nast Traveler* rated the Cascades 12th among the 50 best golf resorts in the world.

The famous checkerboard flag of the Cascades Course, designed by William Flynn in 1923.

Colonial Williamsburg is famous for its reenactors. Here, they
show off some traditional dance steps from the early 1700s
during an exhibition in 1999.

THE LEGEND OF THE GOLDEN HORSESHOE

It sounds like a fraternity celebration: 63 young men drinking champagne, wine, brandy, and rum while standing at the crest of the Blue Ridge Mountains.

Instead, it is the climactic moment in one of the most important expeditions in Virginia history.

In an attempt to encourage westward settlement, Gov. Alexander Spotswood organized a party of 63 men to explore the colony's western frontier in 1716. It was a journey that would take them over the Blue Ridge Mountains and into the Shenandoah Valley.

The journal of John Fontaine, a participant in the expedition, describes the explorers' celebration as they traversed the crest of the Blue Ridge:

"We drunk the King's health in Champagne, and fired a volley; the Prince's health in Burgundy, and fired a volley; and all the rest of the Royal Family in Claret, and fired a volley. We had several sorts of Liquors, namely Virginia Red Wine and White Wine, Irish Usquebaugh, Brandy, Shrub, two sort [sic] of Rum, Champagne, Canary, Cherry punch, Cider, Water, etc."

Eight years later, in an account found in *The Present State of Virginia,* author Hugh Jones described the toll taken on the expedition party by the rocky terrain:

"For this expedition they were obliged to provide a great Quantity of Horse-Shoes (Things seldom used in the lower Parts of the Country, where there are few Stones) Upon which Account the Governor upon their Return presented each of his Companions with a Golden Horse-Shoe (some of which I have seen studded with valuable Stones resembling the Heads of Nails) with this Inscription on the one Side: 'Sic Juvat Transcendere Montes!' (How delightful it is to cross mountains!): And on the other is written 'Tramontane Order.'

Who knows if Gov. Spotswood actually performed as described? None of the small golden horseshoes were ever found. What we do know is that from 1699 to 1780, Williamsburg was the capital of England's oldest, largest, richest, and most populous colony and the seat of power in the new nation's most influential state.

The United States may have been born in Philadelphia, but she was sent into labor by the events that took place here:

• On May 30, 1765, Patrick Henry offered to the colonial assembly, called the House of Burgesses, his resolutions defying the Stamp Act. It became known as his "Caesar-Brutus" speech.

• On May 16, 1769, George Washington introduced the Virginia Resolves against the Townshend Acts. It was one of the colonies' first challenges to British authority.

• On May 15, 1776, the House of Burgesses unanimously adopted Virginia's "Resolution for Independence" and called for the other colonies to declare their independence. They did so when the Continental Congress met in Philadelphia that July.

• On June 12, 1776, George Mason produced the Virginia Declaration of Rights. It became the model for the federal Bill of Rights.

• In June 1779, Thomas Jefferson introduced his Statute for Religious Freedom, in which he outlined his doctrine of separation of church and state. It was the foundation for the First Amendment.

In 1781, Jefferson moved Virginia's government to Richmond. In 1926, the Rev. Dr. W.A.R. Goodwin, rector of Bruton Parish Church, approached John D. Rockefeller Jr. about restoring what had become a forgotten little village to its colonial past.

The reconstructed Raleigh Tavern opened as the first public exhibition building in September 1932. Today, the restored city sits on 173 acres and is composed of 88 original buildings and homes, shops, public buildings, and other structures.

The view of the 18th green from the second-floor clubhouse restaurant of the Gold Course at Golden Horseshoe in Colonial Williamsburg. The layout is complete with pond, ducks, footbridge, and gazebo.

Sunset at Golden Horseshoe's Gold Course. Pictured are the 12th green (foreground) and the 16th green.

GOLDEN HORSESHOE — GOLD COURSE

It was never intended to make history, but rather to offer a visitor to Colonial Williamsburg a brief respite from history.

The Gold Course is a Robert Trent Jones Sr. masterpiece, located on 125 rolling acres of densely forested land a minute's stroll from the Williamsburg Inn, the Williamsburg Lodge, and the star of the show, Colonial Williamsburg.

The nation's largest outdoor living history museum, Colonial Williamsburg includes the 173-acre Historic Area, the restored 18th-century capital of Virginia. There are also five hotels and 12 restaurants.

Jones created the Gold Course at a time when island greens, runway tees, and sophisticated irrigation were the architectural exception to the rule. John D. Rockefeller, the guiding light behind the restoration of Colonial Williamsburg, began considering the addition of a golf course adjacent to the Williamsburg Inn almost as soon as it opened in 1937. Before they could act, the U.S. entered World War II in 1941, and the plans were put on hold.

Fred Findlay, then the greenskeeper at the Country Club of Virginia's James River Course in Richmond, was hired in 1945 to design the nine-hole course at the Williamsburg Inn. Findlay's course opened June 15, 1947.

In 1962, five-time State Open champion Jack Isaacs shot a course-record 62 during the start of a "Beat the Pro" tournament sponsored by the Williamsburg-James City unit of the American Cancer Society.

Isaacs toured the nine-hole course in 31-31, one shot better than the previous record, set by Fred Aucamp in 1957 and Frank Boyington in 1960.

With nearly 100 people watching, Isaacs smashed a 325-yard drive on the 18th hole, then dropped his approach 25 feet short of the hole. Williamsburg Inn pro George Tinsley and amateurs Norman Hornsby and Ed Key watched as Isaacs' record-setting putt fell into the cup on its last revolution.

Two years later, Jones would finish reconfiguring Findlay's work, incorporating many of his original tees and greens, to create the executive Spotswood Course, which opened on Oct. 31, 1964.

The Gold Course is famous for its picturesque par 3s. This is the 160-yard 16th, one of the first holes to feature an island green.

The stately main entrance to the Williamsburg Inn, located in the restored colonial capital.

Thirteen months before that, on Sept. 11, 1963, Jones' Gold Course opened. From first blush, awe-struck golf writers from Virginia and beyond urged Colonial Williamsburg officials to bring the course into the national spotlight.

"The course is worthy of a championship such as the Masters—as a permanent attraction," Richmond newsman Mac McGrew wrote in 1963 after visiting the 6,817-yard, par-71 course on the day it opened. "However, officials . . . say only that the course is designed to provide recreation . . . The course deserves better than that."

Later, the *Richmond Times-Dispatch* called the Gold Course "A new masterpiece of architecture that compares favorably with any of the world's beautiful golf courses."

The *Norfolk Ledger-Star* chimed in, describing it as "fantastically beautiful."

And, finally, this from the *Richmond News Leader:* "Nothing was overlooked in the planning of this course."

In fact, Jones, who personally inspected the work every two weeks during the 18-month construction period, referred to it as "the equal of Augusta National and one that will not take second place to any in the world."

Jones said it with the natural enthusiasm of the home run hitter who stands at the plate admiring the ball he's just launched into the upper deck.

How's the expression go? It's not bragging if it's true. Jones backed his statement by implementing design features that may seem standard today, but were uniquely his at the time.

Standing on the seventh tee, the golfer can watch action at the 12th, second, sixth, and 16th greens. You feel like you're sitting on top of the world.

Gov. Alexander Spotswood (above) poses for "a rendering" behind the 18th green of the Gold Course with wooden clubs used for "a Scottish game." Dressed in the traditional uniforms of the colonial era, a fife and drum corps marches at sundown.

At the rear of several of his trademark runway tees, Jones built mini-putting greens so players could practice their short strokes if play slowed slightly.

Beneath the ground, he laid a 27,000-foot pipeline down the middle of each fairway, with sprinkler heads every 90 feet, each capable of shooting a 120-foot circle of water.

On what was once marshland, Jones created three lakes that provide water for irrigation and are part of venues spectacular enough to take a player's mind off his game.

The 497-yard par-5 second hole features a long, tree-lined fairway that descends into a lake measuring 85 yards across and guarding the green.

Jones saved his best work for the par 3s, which players of all abilities and backgrounds routinely say are the best they've ever seen. Former British Open champion and 1999 Ryder Cup hero Justin Leonard called them "on par with any I've seen."

"God has heaven and Virginia has the Golden Horseshoe," wrote Jim Pettit of the Fayetteville (N.C.) *Observer-Times* after his first look at the course. "God wants to renegotiate. If there are a stronger set of par-3s than those on the Gold Course, it's not on this planet."

The finest of the set—certainly the most photographed—is No. 16. It measures 165 yards and plays from an elevated tee to one of the first— maybe *the* first—island green.

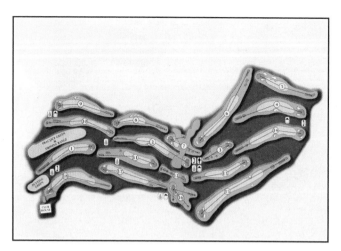

The layout map of Golden Horseshoe Gold Course.

Jones' decision to create an island green at 16 came after construction had started. Originally designing it to sit beside one of the lower lakes, Jones changed his mind and went for something daring. Workers used almost 6,000 yards of dirt in building the foundation on which Jones designed a green that is 180 feet long.

Coming off all that water on 16, Jones wanted a different look for the brilliant 17th hole, a 425-yard par 4 that winds slowly uphill to an elevated green. But a creek was already there.

Jones never flinched. He moved the stream underground, using 300 yards of pipe to do it.

Small wonder, then, that despite an explosion in world-class course construction in Williamsburg, the Gold Course remains the crown jewel.

"This is a wonderful golf course," Jack Nicklaus said during a 1967 exhibition at the course. "As fine a Trent Jones course as I've ever seen. Trent has done a beautiful job here; that is, he has made great strategic use of the terrain. There is plenty of trouble and it is not a course you can get careless with."

Nicklaus and fellow touring pro Mason Rudolph were paired against Vinny Giles, U.S. and British Amateur champion and seven-time State Amateur winner, and 1967 State Amateur champion Sam Wallace Sr.

Giles led Nicklaus by two shots with four holes to play, but Nicklaus birdied 15, 16, and 17 to shoot 67 and win by one. Thirty-three years later, Nicklaus still holds the competitive course record.

In 1997, Rees Jones was commissioned to do a restoration and renovation of his father's original work. It cost $4.5 million, but Jones succeeded in instituting new technology—such as a computerized double-row irrigation system that covers every conceivable corner of the course.

Challenged to make the course more difficult for the proficient player and more fun for the tourist golfer, Jones increased elevations in certain areas to provide better target definition and softened and gently sloped the course to help the high handicapper. He lengthened the course to its current 6,817 yards and rebuilt some of the perimeter areas of the greens to give the accomplished player more of a challenge.

Closed for a year, the course reopened on July 1, 1998. In November, former British Open champion Justin Leonard came to Williamsburg for an exhibition that was billed as the "Assault of the Gold Course."

As he had done with Nicklaus, Giles joined Leonard on the course. When they were done, Nicklaus' record 67 still stood, both men shooting 1-under-par 70s.

Giles' 68 was the amateur course record for 32 years. In September 1999, J.B. Lloyd of Wayzata, Minnesota, and Scott Masingill of Payete, Idaho, fired 67s during the opening round of the USGA Men's State Team Championship.

Played at the same time was the Women's State Team Championship, which was being contested at the Green Course. Texas claimed the title by one stroke over Virginia and Minnesota at 4-under-par 280.

Leading Texas in an event shortened from 54 to 36 holes because of storms was Bob Kearney of Houston. A 43-year-old computer programmer, Kearney shot back-to-back 68s.

The Virginia team of Keith Decker, Faber Jamerson, and Charlie Green made the strongest move after completing the first round tied for 13th. But the leading teams had just opened play when a long storm moved into the area and forced a decision to declare Texas the winner.

"You'd always prefer to have the players decide the outcome of a tournament," said Green, the '98 State Mid-Amateur champion and president of the Virginia State Golf Association. "We all had the same chances the first two rounds. Texas just did a little better job than the rest of us."

True to its original mission to remain a recreational haven for travelers and visitors, the Gold Course has played host to only a handful of state championships.

Allen Barber of Yorktown defeated Decker 5 and 4 in the 1992 State Amateur. Jim Alexander of Lynchburg beat Bob Moyers of New Market 4 and 3 in the 1993 State Seniors.

The picturesque seventh hole of the Gold Course, a 206-yard par 3 over water.

the resorts

The picturesque first hole at sunrise at the Golden Horseshoe
Green Course in Colonial Williamsburg.

GOLDEN HORSESHOE—
GREEN COURSE

Talk about precocious.

It took just seven years for architect Rees Jones' Green Course to move outside the orbit created by father Robert Trent Jones' renowned Gold Course.

In September of 1998, the Green Course became the first in Southeastern Virginia to host a United States Golf Association national championship, the Women's Senior Amateur.

The following year, the Green became just the second course since the USGA began in 1894 to host consecutive national championships when the U.S. Women's State Team Championship blew into town—almost literally, it turned out.

It's no coincidence that the USGA found the Green Course so appealing for women's championships. One of Jones' trademarks is the attention he pays to positioning women's tees.

"Rees didn't just design it from the championship tees," Colonial Williamsburg director of golf Glen Byrnes said. "He designed it to accommodate every player who would be on it, regardless of ability. The Green Course is capable of handling everything from a national championship to a group of inexperienced players."

Golf Digest thought so. The magazine designated the Green Course as one of the five best new resort courses of 1992. The course is part of a resort—America's first featuring father-and-son layouts—honored with six consecutive *Golf* magazine gold medals.

Rees Jones wasn't blessed with quite as gorgeous a piece of property as the spectacular land on which the Gold Course sits. There were design constraints brought on by the explosion in vacation and business golfers. Most don't play to single-digit handicaps. The line between challenging them and overwhelming them is fine.

Jones walked it like a tightrope artist. Multiple tee boxes and player-friendly fairway and green-side mounding were constructed to funnel errant shots back into play. Of course, there's always a price to pay, and Jones has 115 bunkers strategically placed, 16 of them on the par-5 fifth hole.

There are so many outstanding holes, it would be impossible to pick the best. But the 11th is a dramatic 195-yard par 3 that begins from an elevated tee and ends on a green set in an amphitheater. A pond guards the front of the putting surface. Pot bunkers fortify the rear, taking away anyone's ideas of playing it long and safe.

Jones saves the best, or at least his most stunningly beautiful creation, for last. The 18th is a 531-yard par 5 on which you must clear a substantial body of water to reach a fairway that is wider than it appears.

The closer you get to the green, however, the narrower the landscape becomes—Jones' playful way of making sure you remember who's in charge. It all ends at another amphitheater green, a natural place for those who preceded you to witness your final triumph or indignity.

Naturally, the USGA adored it, as did most of the 132 players who graced a stellar Senior Amateur field. Nine former Senior Women's Amateur champions were present, as well as a bevy of former Curtis Cup players and captains.

The only thing it didn't have were two Americans in the final. Instead, Gayle Borthwick of Canada met Valerie Hassett of County Clare, Ireland.

Borthwick, a member of the Canadian Golf Hall of Fame, had won the championship in 1996, when it was stroke play. The following year, the format was changed to match play, and Borthwick had fallen in the semifinals to Toni Wiesner, a lefty from Texas. Wiesner then lost to Nancy Fitzgerald of Carmel, Indiana, in the final.

Hassett, enshrined in the Ireland Golf Hall of Fame, was finishing a world tour of senior women's amateur championships with increasingly productive results.

She had tied for 10th at the International European Seniors-Amateur Championship Ladies and tied for sixth at the Canadian Senior Women's Amateur.

Before Borthwick could take on Hassett, she had to get past Fitzgerald, a frequent nemesis. The two had been paired in the final round of the Canadian Ladies National Senior Championship the past three years.

Fitzgerald had won on all three occasions.

This time, however, Borthwick kept their match close early with some nifty shot-making, then outlasted Fitzgerald down the stretch in posting a 2-and-1 victory.

Normally, she would have celebrated. But the semifinal and final were scheduled for the same day. It was beastly hot in Williamsburg that week, ideal conditions for losing composure and focus.

That's exactly what Borthwick's husband Bob told her during a phone call between matches.

"He said to forget what had gone on before and to get myself refocused," she said.

She did as advised, going 2-up after six holes, winning with a conceded birdie on No. 5 and a par on No. 6.

And while she was in danger of giving back that advantage, Borthwick scrambled for hole-saving pars from out of the woods at the 10th and from a green-side bunker on No. 13.

"Those two saves broke my heart," Hassett admitted later.

Meanwhile, the heat got to Hassett. She lost rhythm with her swing and found her putting touch ebb away. The match ended 4 and 3 for Borthwick after Hassett missed a four-foot par putt at 15.

"When you get tired, you can make those mistakes," Borthwick said graciously. "I love match play. I think it brings out a different side of you."

The 1999 U.S. Women's State Team Championship brought a different format to the Green Course. Forty-three states sent three-player teams to Williamsburg for a stroke-play event in which only the day's best two scores counted.

Tormented by thunderstorms, the tournament was shortened to 36 holes. The Florida team of Taffy Brower, Marla Jemsek-Weeks, and 1989 U.S. Women's Mid-Amateur champion Robin Weiss won with a 2-under-par 286.

Tennessee gave Florida its only real competi-

tion, finishing a shot behind its southern neighbor at 287. Pennsylvania, which won the inaugural championship in 1995, was third, nine behind the victors.

"We definitely had a strong team this year," said Weeks, a 1996 Curtis Cup team member.

"We got to hold the Judy Bell Trophy, that's the main thing," added Weiss, referring to the first woman president of the USGA. "To have our name on a trophy named for Judy Bell, who has done so much for golf, I think that's very special."

Golden Horseshoe had something else to celebrate in 1999: Venerable pro Del Snyder was selected "Teacher of the Year" by the Middle Atlantic PGA.

For the 66-year-old Snyder, who worked with Sam Snead at The Homestead before coming to Golden Horseshoe, it was his first MAPGA award, but his second special designation of the year. Earlier, in appreciation for 24 years of splendid service, Snyder was named Colonial Williamsburg's "Ambassador of Golf."

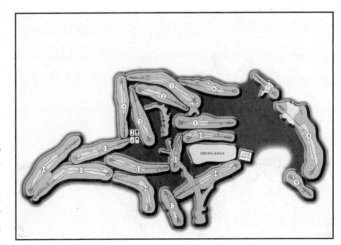

The layout of Golden Horseshoe's Green Course.

Two cannons set behind the 16th green of the River Course mark the site of an early American fortress situated along the James River, and is now incorporated into the layout of the Pete Dye-designed River Course at the Kingsmill Resort in Williamsburg.

KINGSMILL

Kingsmill owes its position in golf to its fabulously photogenic River Course, which has played host to the PGA Tour and the Michelob Championship since 1981. But that's hardly the whole story behind a premier resort that offers everything in golf and family entertainment.

It began in Williamsburg in 1969, when Anheuser-Busch purchased 3,600 acres of land where once sat the Kingsmill Plantation. Ironically, the property never belonged to the man for whom it was named.

In 1619, Richard Kingsmill was one of eight members of the Virginia Company of London who received a land grant in the Colony of Virginia.

Forty years later, Lewis Burwell III chose a parcel that is now the second fairway of the resort's Plantation Course to build his home. As construction began, Burwell sought a name to use that would convey the grandeur of his plantation and create a link to the early days of the colony.

Kingsmill, he decided, had the proper ring.

The plantation would be the scene of many battles with the native Pamunkey Indians. British troops and American patriots fought on the land during the Revolutionary War. In 1862, Union troops led by Gen. George McClellan engaged Robert E. Lee's Confederate soldiers at the Battle of Williamsburg, where 3,500 men were killed or wounded.

In 1950, the Colonial Williamsburg Foundation bought the land, then sold it to Anheuser-Busch almost 20 years later.

Busch Properties commissioned a series of archeological excavations at Kingsmill in 1971. Eight major digs and 35 minor sites were unearthed and fully and painstakingly examined before Busch Properties would allow construction to begin.

In 1977, August Busch III, president and chief operating officer of Anheuser-Busch Inc., attended a luncheon in Fairfield, California, to celebrate the opening of a new brewery. The mayor of Napa, California, pulled Busch and vice president of marketing Orion Burkhardt aside and confided in them his concern that the town might lose its men's professional golf tournament because of a lack of sponsorship.

Kingsmill's signature hole, the par-3 17th.

One of the entrances to the conference center at the Kingsmill Resort.

Busch asked Burkhardt to recommend whether Anheuser-Busch should take over sponsorship. What he didn't know—or maybe he did—was that Burkhardt had started caddying when he was seven years old and had been an avid golfer for more than 50 years.

In 1977, the Anheuser-Busch Golf Classic was born at Silverado Country Club in Napa. After the 1980 tournament, Silverado CC pulled out, leaving the event in the unusual position of having a sponsor but no home.

Enter, Kingsmill and the River Course, located less than a mile from one of the world's great family attractions, Busch Gardens. Designed by con-

troversial legend Pete Dye, the course sits barely three miles from the restored colonial capital. Dye often was brilliant in weaving the course over and around the original plantation.

"You can't design 300 years of history into a course," Dye said in 1973. "Here, it was just laid in naturally."

Nowhere is that more evident than on the 17th, a 180-yard par 3 bordered by the James River. It's where Burwell built a slip and ferry landing that served as a port for Williamsburg and the first customs house for the Virginia Colony.

The 17th green is a short distance below where Moody's Tavern once stood; ironic, given that the

property would eventually belong to Anheuser-Busch. When workers began building this frequently photographed signature hole, they uncovered a huge supply of wine and beer bottles dating back to the 18th century.

Historians have speculated that after crews were finished unloading their cargo, they walked up to the tavern for the colonial equivalent of happy hour. Often, they would carry a bottle or two down the hill to the ship, discarding their empties as they went.

The 17th hole was also where poa annua first appeared in the New World. That strain of grass, often a superintendent's worst nightmare, found its way here via a bale of hay aboard a Scottish ship that unloaded at Jamestown in the 1600s. It then floated down the James to the area of the 17th hole and, literally, took root.

The River Course was barely five years old when Busch ordered the first coast-to-coast transplantation of a golf tournament. Making history, as those who studied the colonies can attest, is never easy.

"The magnitude of everything, even shipping scoreboards from California to here, was amazing," said Harry Knight, retired vice president of Busch Properties. "Everything was a new experience. Those scoreboards were like giant jigsaw puzzles someone had to put together.

"It was a job of no small proportion, but what made it gratifying was the way that everyone wanted it—from the greenskeeper to the grass-cutters."

Vern Peak, who had been the tournament director at Silverado, agreed to serve in the same capacity at Kingsmill.

"The first time he saw the golf course, he turned to me and said, 'This is a John Mahaffey course,'" said Johnnie Bender, the tournament's current director. "He sounded so certain."

Peak had good reason. Although Mahaffey opened with a 1-over-par 72 that first year, he got the hang of the place as the week went on. His final-round 67 propelled him to a two-shot victory over Andy North.

Mahaffey, a congenial Texan whose 10 PGA Tour victories included the 1978 PGA and the 1986 Tournament Players Championship, almost won again in 1985. However, Mark Wiebe beat him with a birdie on the first hole of sudden death.

Kingsmill officials had already planned a facelift for the course following completion of the tournament in 1981, but even Peak couldn't have predicted how intensely the touring pros would dislike some of Dye's work. Or that they would take those complaints to the press.

"The reactions and criticisms of the pros were just one thing we considered," Knight said at the time. "I think what we'll have when we're done is a better golf course for everyone."

August Busch III made sure of that. During a meeting with his corporate lieutenants, Busch asked if the complaints he had heard were valid. When told that many of them had merit, Busch issued a two-word directive:

"Fix it."

Using plans by architect Ed Ault, with supervision from partner Tom Clark, the River Course underwent a substantial overhaul.

The green of the par-5 third hole was transported from the top of a hill to a valley next to a small pond. That eliminated a blind third shot and made it more possible to go for the green in two. It also left the golfers with a more dramatic, dangerous decision.

(The third green has since been moved nearer to where Dye originally positioned it, giving residents of Kingsmill an ongoing topic of discussion.)

The fourth tee was rebuilt and moved. The fairway was flattened, some trees were removed, and the green was enlarged.

Ault built a new green on No. 5 because the greenskeeper had difficulty keeping the original healthy. Ault also brought into play a creek that runs down the right side of this tough little par 3.

The eighth remains the most difficult hole on the course, and also one of the best places for fans to watch the action. Ault built a bigger, wider green, eliminated one of the original three tiers, and placed more mounds behind the green for spectators.

With the exception of Dye's breathtaking 17th hole, which runs along the James River, this may be the fans' favorite place to gather.

On the back nine, Ault added spectator mounds where bunkers had been on the par-4 11th hole. He moved the tee and built a new green on No. 12. He designed a new tee on the par-3 13th and the par-4 16th. The move at 16 made an already terrific hole even better.

Mahaffey, who as defending champion had more reasons than anyone to keep the course the same, loved the changes.

"So many times, when a course is changed to make it better for Tour players, the changes make it all but impossible for the average player," he said. "I think the reverse is true here. What they've done is make the course better for everyone."

Since then, the 6,853-yard course hasn't undergone any changes nearly as drastic. Whatever rift resulted between Dye and Kingsmill has long since been forgotten. Dye even supervised some work there a few years ago and happily used Kingsmill touring pro Curtis Strange as his consultant on the Tournament Players Club of Virginia Beach, which opened in 1999.

While Anheuser-Busch may have done the PGA Tour an enormous favor in the late 1970s by taking over the tournament in California, then moving it to Williamsburg, the Tour didn't always reciprocate.

For years, the Anheuser-Busch Golf Classic, as it was called until 1996, was victimized by its July date. Many top-name players were already in Great Britain preparing for the British Open. In addition, July in Williamsburg means blast-furnace temperatures and humidity unlike any the pros see, other than in Memphis.

The competition improved dramatically beginning in 1997, when the tournament date was moved to October. The course was in its best condition ever. The players came to town eager to per-

The fifth hole at Kingsmill's River Course.

form well in one of their last attempts to move into the top 30 money winners and qualify for the $5 million Tour Championship, held two weeks later.

That 1997 tournament, by then known as the Michelob Championship, turned out to have something else special going for it.

David Duval.

The slender Georgia Tech graduate was a four-time All-American in college, something only Gary Hallberg and Phil Mickelson had ever achieved. In his first three seasons on the Tour, Duval had done just about everything expected of him: won rookie of the year, set a money record for rookies with $881,000, then finished 10th on the money list in 1996 with $977,000.

Duval just hadn't won. Worse, or more dramatically at least, he had finished second seven times, causing some to wonder whether he'd ever get over the hump.

"I know I can play this game well and I know I can win golf tournaments out here," Duval said after finishing 36 holes one shot behind leader Duffy Waldorf. "Have I done it? No. Will I? Absolutely."

By the 15th hole Sunday, when Duval rolled in a 25-foot putt for eagle 3 to take a three-shot lead over Grant Waite and Waldorf, it seemed he would rout the field.

Then Waite and Waldorf combined to make seven birdies down the stretch. Coupled with Duval's bogey 5 at No. 16, the trio finished 72 holes tied.

Waldorf all but eliminated himself on the first playoff hole, the 18th, when he pushed his tee shot well right of the fairway. Waite, meanwhile, hit his down the middle, 175 yards from the pin, which was tucked on the top shelf of a multitiered green.

Duval slammed his drive 294 yards down the middle, leaving him with 141 yards to the flag. His 9-iron approach landed on the top shelf and stopped 10 feet from a birdie. The moment he struck it, it was headed for the bottom of the cup.

Much has been made about Duval's apparently stoic nature. It wasn't in evidence that day.

Tears welled in his eyes as he reminisced about a round he played with his grandfather when he was 10. He was ahead of his "grandpappy," as he called Harry Poole, but made a double-bogey on the last hole to lose by a shot.

When his grandfather died of cancer while Duval was attending Georgia Tech, he vowed that he would dedicate his first Tour victory to his memory. The moment became even more poignant when Duval mentioned that his paternal grandfather, Hap Duval, died the same week.

"All my grandfather wanted to do was see me play on the tour," Duval said quietly.

By the following October, the man who for three years couldn't win had become the guy who couldn't lose.

Duval became only the second player in the history of the tournament to successfully defend his title. His 16-under-par 268 was three shots better than Phil Tataurangi and capped off a remarkable 12-month period in which he had become the darling of the golf world.

In the 24 events he played between the Michelob championships of 1997 and 1998, Duval won seven times.

"I don't want to wake up," he joked. "It's a lot of fun, it really is. I look back at what's happened in the last 12 months, and it's certainly not something I would expect."

Crucial to Duval's romp in '97 was his ability to master Kingsmill's par 5s. He played them in 10-under-par for the week. He had his margin of victory by the time he made the turn on Sunday and coasted home.

"I think we all knew that when he did win it was going to be a landslide," said Tataurangi, a 27-year-old from New Zealand. "Winning is winning. It gives you a certain kind of confidence that you can't gain by finishing second."

Duval is hardly the only player to get his first Tour victory at Kingsmill. It's part of the tournament's tradition.

In 1994, Ronnie Black fired an 8-under 63 in the final round to overcome a seven-shot deficit and nip Willie Wood by one stroke.

In 1988, Tom Sieckmann outlasted Mark Wiebe on the second hole of their sudden-death playoff to win $117,000.

A year later, Mike Donald, Tim Simpson, and Hal Sutton started their sudden-death playoff on

Sunday. But after Sutton was eliminated, rain and darkness forced a continuation to the next day. In near solitude and with another storm threatening, Donald won with a birdie on the fourth extra hole.

And in 1995, Ted Tryba held off former U.S. Open champion Scott Simpson and third-round leader Jim Carter for his first victory.

In 1990, Virginians were treated to an all-Commonwealth final pairing: Richmond native Lanny Wadkins vs. Norfolk-born host pro Curtis Strange.

Wadkins, five years older, and Strange hadn't competed head-to-head since the semifinals of the 1970 State Amateur at The Cascades. Wadkins won 4 and 2, then whipped his younger brother Bobby the next day for the title.

"I was always just far enough behind Lanny that we never went head-to-head," Strange said after the third round. "When I was growing up, Lanny was the superstar, the next step ahead."

As was usually the case when Wadkins was hot, he was unbeatable. His final-round 68 gave him a five-shot victory over former Masters champion Larry Mize, the largest spread in tournament history.

In 1984, the King of Beers signed the King of Golf to build a second course at Kingsmill. Arnold Palmer and Ed Seay fashioned a 6,605-yard layout—known as the Plantation Course—that Palmer never pretended was in competition with the River Course.

"It wasn't intended to be extremely difficult," Palmer told a crowd of 2,500 during the opening ceremonies. "We wanted to build a golf course that families can go out and enjoy playing."

The strength of the Plantation Course is in its greens, which have clever undulations and contours and compensate for other areas where the course is generous.

The Plantation Course was the site of the 1995 VSGA Junior Championship, won by Cameron Yancey of Blackstone with a 54-hole total of 217.

Strange and architect Tom Clark combined in July 1995 to create the Woods Course. Immediately honored by *Golf Magazine* as one of the "Top 10 New Courses Available for Public Play," the Woods Course is 6,782 yards and plays to a par of 72.

Set on 200 acres of densely wooded land, the Woods Course is distinguished by a number of significant archeological sites that have been carefully preserved.

Deep ravines, large fairway bunkers, and a bunker located in the center of a double green are just some of the design features that make the Woods Course fun and special.

So do the amenities Kingsmill offers. There are 400 luxury guest rooms and suites overlooking the James River, golf courses, tennis courts, all within a short walk of an elegant, 6,000-square foot conference center and sports Club.

Kingsmill also offers one-, two-, and three-bedroom suites that feature complete kitchens, spacious living and dining areas, fireplaces and outdoor decks.

In addition to the three championship courses, golfers can test their skills on the par-3 Bray Links Course, where holes range from 58 to 109 yards.

The Kingsmill Golf Academy is a recent addition to the lineup. Golfers can opt for one-, two- or three-day schools.

Coming by boat? Kingsmill's marina has 91 slips for rental on an overnight basis. It's accessible to the James River, Chesapeake Bay, and the Intracoastal Waterway.

In January 1998, Kingsmill announced it had opened Williamsburg's first and only spa, featuring six massage studios, two facial rooms, a wet treatment room, manicure and pedicure stations, and a hair-care salon.

The spa, which offers everything from European skin-purifying facials to seaweed and paraffin body treatments, is part of the Kingsmill Sports Club.

SOME OF KINGSMILL RESORT'S AWARDS:

- *Mobil Travel Guide* Four-Star Award
- Member of Preferred Hotels and Resorts Worldwide
- *Golf* magazine's Top 10 New Courses You Can Play
- *Golf* magazine's Silver Medal Award
- *Golf Digest's* Best in State
- *GolfWeek* magazine's America's Best Courses
- *Links* magazine's Best of Golf
- *Petersen's Golfing Magazine's* Top Practice Ranges
- *Metro Golf* magazine's "The A List"
- *Meetings and Conventions* magazine's Gold Key Award
- Corporate Meetings and Incentives Golden Links Award

the resorts

A shaded walkway leads to the main building of the
Marriot Manor Club at Ford's Colony in Williamsburg.

FORD'S COLONY

Many recognized its enormous potential. Some tried to use it to their advantage.

Only Richard Ford Sr. and his family brought it to life.

In the early 1980s, Ford discovered a twice-bankrupt community in James City then known as Middle Plantation, just a few miles from Colonial Williamsburg.

The community included a golf course laid out by Ellis Maples. However, the course had never been played and the fairways were overgrown with trees 10 inches in diameter.

Ford, whose Realtec Inc. built several courses at developments in North and South Carolina, could not resist. He purchased the property, then decided to bring Maples' son Dan on board not only to resurrect his father's course, but also to design two additional courses.

While the community and Maples' wonderful course designs have flourished for more than 15 years, the Ford's Colony that Maples and Ford envisioned from the start still isn't quite completely finished.

But it is, oh, so close.

A giant step forward was taken in June 1999 when the 6,621-yard, par-71 Blackheath Course was dedicated, leaving Ford's Colony just nine holes shy of three distinct, separate 18-hole layouts.

The Blackheath name celebrates both the birth of golf in England and the settlement of nearby Jamestown by three shiploads of English explorers in 1607.

"Every day at Ford's Colony we feel a responsibility to respect the legacy of the land and history that is Williamsburg and Jamestown," Ford said during the dedication. "I think we've done that today with both the vintage architecture and the naming of the Blackheath Course. Dan has done a wonderful job with its graceful and challenging design."

What Maples also accomplished with aplomb was blending nine holes that opened in 1992, originally called the Gold, with nine new holes carved

From the tee box of the fourth hole (par 4, 402 yards), the signature hole of the White Nine at Ford's Colony in Williamsburg.

from his fertile imagination. Such tapestries are seldom so seamless.

Maples offers a sweet mixture of old and modern at Blackheath. There's an island tee on the par-3 third hole. There's a frightening island green on the par-4 18th.

If that sounds like a lot of water, consider this: There is wet stuff on 13 holes, although one never gets the sense of being overwhelmed.

By the time 2000 becomes 2001, Maples will combine another new nine with the Blue Nine, which opened under his supervision in September 1986. That will form the final 18-hole piece of the Ford's Colony puzzle.

While that sounds a little confusing, there is one thing crystal clear. Maples' first design, originally known as the Red/White and now called "Marsh Hawk," after the predominant symbol in the Ford's Colony logo, has earned its place among Virginia's finest courses.

Regularly ranked among the state's top five by virtually every major golf magazine, the Marsh Hawk played host to the 1998 and '99 State Open championships, jointly conducted by the Virginia State Golf Association and the Middle Atlantic section of the PGA.

The 1998 State Open allowed Leesburg pro Rick Schuller to complete a peculiar progression he had begun in 1995.

Schuller, an Old Dominion University product, had led the tournament after the first round. He had led it after the second round. He had led it after the third round, and he had led it after part of the fourth round.

All anyone remembered was that he hadn't led it at the end of the fourth round. He had tied for fourth in 1995, fifth in 1996, and sixth in 1997.

A 35-year-old teaching pro at River Creek Country Club in Northern Virginia, Schuller posted a 4-under-par 68 in the third round. That gave him a share of the lead with Ron Cooke, head pro at Kiskiack Golf Club in Croaker.

"It's been a pleasure to have led," Schuller said following his third round. "But I still want to be in this position at the end."

He didn't tell anyone at the time, but as a senior at Fairfax High School in 1981, he had written down some of his immediate goals. One of them was to win the State Open.

He finally made it happen by following his third-round 68 with another on Sunday to win by four shots over 23-year-old amateur Paul Scaletta of Richmond.

"I knew coming into this year I was peaking as a golfer," Schuller said. "I've learned a lot about the golf swing as a teacher. Being one of five kids, I'm very competitive. This is something I really wanted."

It was the biggest jewel in an opulent crown he had fashioned during the course of the year. Earlier, he and Bud Lintelman had captured the Middle Atlantic-PGA Pro-Assistants Championship. He had also taken the State Assistants tournament by shooting 69-65 at Kiskiack.

Speaking of Cooke, the third-round co-leader who struggled mightily on Sunday and finished 11th, rarely has a man suffering so exhibited such gallant sportsmanship.

Paired with Schuller, Cooke gave the winner all the support and encouragement he needed to finally break through.

"I've never played with someone who encouraged you, helped your shots along so much," Schuller said. "To hear that makes it a lot easier. He's gracious and was fun to play with. I was trying to do the same for him."

The following year, 22-year-old amateur Faber Jamerson of Appamattox shocked everyone but himself by routing the field by eight shots in the second-most lopsided Open in Commonwealth history.

Only Robert Wrenn's 12-shot triumph at the 1991 Open was larger. Jamerson's bulge tied the margin by which Woody Fitzhugh defeated Vinny Giles in the 1986 Open at Willow Oaks Country Club in Richmond.

Jamerson came to Ford's Colony with a one-dimensional wardrobe but a multifaceted game. It started in the 1998 Central Virginia Invitational in Lynchburg. Wearing a yellow golf shirt, Jamerson was 9 under par and won the tournament.

Later, in the final round of the Crown Royal Open at ultra-tough Royal New Kent, the yellow-clad Jamerson fired a 3-under-par 69.

At the State Amateur held at Boonsboro Country Club, Jamerson won the medal and crashed his way into the semifinals before losing 1-up to eventual champion Steve Marino. What made the closeness of the match all the more remarkable was that Marino began the round eagle-par-eagle and still only won by the narrowest of margins.

Suddenly, the light went on inside Jamerson's head. Not a soft-white light, but a mellow-yellow one.

"I'm just as superstitious as I can be," Jamerson said after 36 holes of the Open. "I've got four yellow shirts with me."

With an 11-under-par total of 277, eight strokes better than Vienna's Pat Tallent, 10 ahead of Fieldale's Keith Decker—the only other two players under par—Jamerson probably could have risked playing bare-chested and still won.

Rob McNamara of Farmington in Charlottesville, the 1995 champion after a playoff with Frank Ferguson of Falls Church, was fourth and the low pro in the field. He had some rather blunt advice for Jamerson, who confessed that he was uncertain whether he should try playing professionally.

"He's not sure he's good enough [for the Tour]," McNamara said. "He *is* good enough. He ought to give the circuit a go. He may be rising to the top right now."

McNamara also paid the new champion a compliment that his mother and father, both in the gallery, probably found more endearing.

"He's the nicest boy I've played with in years," McNamara said. "A real pleasure to be paired with."

Virginia's best seniors started the migration to Ford's Colony in 1995, when the Senior Stroke Play Championship was held there. Bob Moyers of New Market was four shots better than Claude Williamson of Waynesboro and C.H. Smith of Hampton at 3-under-par 141.

It's fitting that the seniors came first to Ford's Colony. They are a major part of the clientele Ford had in mind when he bought the property almost two decades ago.

In the 1980 census, Virginia ranked 11th among states drawing the largest number of people who moved after they turned 60 years old. With the history, climate, and family-style amenities Williamsburg and the rest of southeastern Virginia had to offer, Ford figured Williamsburg was a prime attraction.

"The retiree is no longer beholden to anybody," Ford said in a 1985 interview. "He's wealthy to the extent that he can take care of himself. That's the party we cater to."

As evidenced by the list of awards below, the Fords do that in spectacular fashion.

In addition, The Dining Room consistently earns the DiRoNa Award (Distinguished Restaurants of America) and the AAA Five Diamond Award. Only 35 dining establishments in the United States receive the latter.

In 1996, Ford's Colony took a lead position in the formation of the Williamsburg Area Golf Association. Eleven courses joined with local hotels to form an association whose purpose was to make Williamsburg a golf destination competitive with Pinehurst, North Carolina, or Myrtle Beach, South Carolina.

Mike Tiernan, vice president of golf operations for Ford's Colony, was elected the newly formed organization's first president.

"It's been our goal all along to make Ford's Colony and Williamsburg a major East Coast golf destination," Ford said proudly. "Williamsburg's mild climate and accessibility to major cities make it the ideal location.

"It is so gratifying to see Williamsburg become what I always knew it could be."

FORD'S COLONY AWARDS

• Voted No. 1 Master Plan in the continental United States by the American Resort Development Association

• Selected as one of the "Top 20 Retirement Communities in America" by *New Choices* magazine

• Voted one of the "Top 20 to semi-retire" by *Golf* magazine

• First Place and National Finalist, Take Pride in America, for outstanding effort on behalf of America's public lands and natural and cultural resources; awarded by the U.S. Department of the Interior and the Commonwealth of Virginia

• Featured in *The 50 Best Retirement Communities in America* by Fred and Alice Lee (published by St. Martin's Press, New York)

• Named one of the "100 Best Master-Planned Communities in America" by *Where to Retire* magazine

• Selected as one of the top 50 golf communities by *Luxury Golf Homes* magazine

The first hole of the new Blackheath Course at Ford's Colony in Williamsburg.

A national historic landmark, the *Miss Ann* has ferried resort guests to and from the inn and lodge and other points along the river and bay for years.

THE TIDES

Six thousand experts can't be wrong.

In 1999, *Conde Nast Traveler* asked its 6,000 readers to evaluate and rate 225 golf resorts from around the world. They were to consider the design of the course, the speed of play, the pro staff, the accommodations, the food, and the other activities available.

The Tides Resort in Irvington, a tranquil oasis 50 minutes north of Colonial Williamsburg near the Rappahannock River in Virginia's Northern Neck, finished 25th. Readers voted the food at The Tides third best—in the world—while the pace of play at the resort's Golden Eagle and Tartan courses was ranked ninth.

"It is a great honor for The Tides to be included on such a list of distinguished golf resorts," said Lee Stephens, president of The Tides. "*Conde Nast Traveler* is an internationally known publication that stays on the cutting edge of travel trends and hot spots."

They are hardly the only ones so impressed.

The American Automobile Association (AAA) has rated The Tides a four-diamond resort.

Lanier's Directory declared The Tides the 1999 "Family Resort of the Year."

Gourmet named The Tides one of America's "Rooms at The Top."

Golf Digest gives The Tides' Golden Eagle course four stars and consistently places it among Virginia's top 10 courses.

It's hard to believe that such charm and grace had such humble origins.

E.A. and Ann Stephens, both natives of the Northern Neck, purchased an overgrown, neglected piece of property known as the Ashburn Farm in the early 1940s, never intending to turn it into the popular location it has become today. They simply liked the look of the land.

Before long, however, a friend suggested that they build a hotel. Once they stopped laughing, what had seemed such a "silly idea" at first blush became an intriguing possibility.

The Golden Eagle's charming eighth hole, a 175-yard par 3.

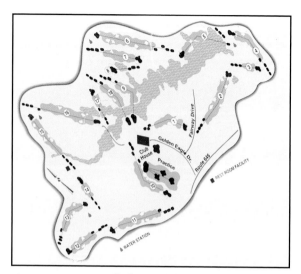

A routing map of The Golden Eagle Course at The Tides Resort in Irvington.

With E.A.—or Big Steve, as he was called—serving as the contractor and Ann as the decorator, the Tides Inn became a reality on July 15, 1947.

"Mother fortunately had the taste of a Virginia lady to match the enthusiasm of Dad," owner Robert L. Stephens once said. "It was her distinct touches and decrees in the early going which set the tone for the Inn."

The staff at The Tides operates under one simple, all-encompassing credo: "Treat our guests as if they were welcome friends in our home."

They take it seriously. Repeat guests at The Tides are called "old friends." One Virginia travel expert wrote, "Visiting The Tides Inn is like dropping in on the longest-running family house party in Virginia."

While the accommodations at The Tides are

uniformly spectacular, and the food and the golf experiences of a lifetime, the centerpiece of the resort is 72-year-old *Miss Ann.*

To say the least, she has a fascinating past.

Launched on April 10, 1926, as a private yacht named *Siele,* then *Sea Wolf,* she was commissioned by the United States government in spring 1941 as the USS *Aquamarine* and assigned to the Navy throughout World War II to conduct experimental work with radar, mines, and underwater communications. In addition, the 127-foot yacht served as tender to the presidential yachts *Potomac* and *Williamsburg* from 1945 to 1946.

Although she was in desperate need of repair, E.A. Stephens purchased her in 1951. She has been refurbished. In 1991, she was rebuilt, and as Tides general manager Randy Stephens said, "She is as much a part of the resort as we are."

Miss Ann is a busy lady. On Sundays she makes a moonlight cruise. On Mondays and Fridays she takes guests on a cruise down the Chesapeake Bay for a fried-chicken luncheon. On Saturdays she makes what is affectionately called a "whiskey run" to nearby Urbana, a tiny town on the south bank of the Rappahannock River.

On Nov. 12, 1998, *Miss Ann* was listed in the National Register of Historic Places. Only places that are considered to have been significant to American history, architecture, archeology, engineering, or culture receive such high honor.

After 30 years of friendly competition, the Stephens-owned-and-operated Tides Inn merged with the Stephens-owned-and-operated Tides Lodge in 1998. The Tides Resort then became the largest family-owned resort in the Mid-Atlantic.

The Stephens family spared no expense when building a golf course. They hired George Cobb of Greenville, South Carolina, at the time, the consult-

ing architect for the Augusta National Golf Club, home of the Masters.

It was Cobb who designed the famous bunker located on the left side of the 18th fairway at Augusta National. It's been the stage for some of the Masters' most memorable shots, including Sandy Lyle's towering 7-iron in 1988.

Tied with Mark Calcavecchia, Lyle hit a blind shot on the green, and the ball took a bounce forward, then rolled back to 10 feet of the hole.

Lyle then drained the putt to become the first player to win the Masters with a birdie on 18 since Arnold Palmer in 1960.

The Tides' Tartan Course, designed by Scottish architect Sir Guy Campbell (with help later from Cobb), opened in 1957. The 6,587-yard par 72 is a solid test of golf set in the shadows of the Tides Lodge.

Twenty years later, Cobb returned to Irvington to design a sweetheart of a course, The Golden Eagle. It is one that would receive considerably more national exposure if it were located in a more metropolitan portion of the Commonwealth.

"You couldn't have a big tournament here because the Northern Neck is too thinly populated," Cobb said in a 1977 interview. "But I'd love to see a U.S. Seniors Championship here. The seniors would love the golf course and the accommodations."

Visitors to The Golden Eagle conduct their business in a two-story clubhouse that was adapted from Madame John's Legacy in New Orleans, said to be the oldest private clubhouse in the Mississippi Valley.

The first time Virginia's pros took a whack at Golden Eagle's 6,950-yard layout, only two of 30 players broke par 72. That should be all one needs to know about its toughness.

The entrance to The Golden Eagle Course, a short drive from The Tides Resort in Irvington.

Cobb called Golden Eagle one of the largest clearing projects of his distinguished career. Thousands of slender hardwoods were removed, though more than enough thick forestation remains. Just ask the players.

Cobb offers at least three truly spectacular holes. The 450-yard fifth hole, a menacing dogleg left, is guarded down the left side by a lake that offers the ultimate risk-reward challenge.

The finishing holes on the front and back nines are kissing cousins featuring the same tricky characteristic. Both require lake-carrying approach shots to elevated greens that slope dangerously downward.

The Golden Eagle has just begun to receive its just due, hosting three Virginia State Amateur championships since 1987.

That year became a historic occasion, as Richmond's Vinny Giles won the title for a record seventh time. Make no mistake, however; The Golden Eagle more than held its own.

"There were a lot of delays with guys looking for their balls," said Harry Rutter. A transplanted North Carolinian who had recently moved to Virginia, Rutter joined Giles as the only two players to beat or match par during the first round of 36-hole qualifying. "It's a golf course that makes you think on almost every shot. You can't just stand up there

and whack it. It's tough, but it's probably the best course I've played in Virginia."

Scores might have been even higher if management at The Tides hadn't just reconstructed severely sloped greens on Nos. 17 and 18.

"I figure Vinny saved us from spending that money for 10 years," said Bob Lee Stephens, son of E.A., and the resort's second owner. "Before it opened in 1976, Vinny came up here to play it and critique it and he told us not to change a thing about the 17th hole. I found out later he had birdied the darn thing."

Giles wasn't quite as sharp the next day, finishing one shot out of the playoff for medalist between Rutter and J.P. Leigh of Portsmouth. Leigh, 39, won with a chip-and-putt par on the third hole.

"Maybe when I was younger, getting a win here would have been a bigger thing," said Leigh, a popular perennial contender who had never claimed victory. "But I've been beaten every which way you can get beat over the years and that keeps you from getting too keyed up.

"It's not like it was in the early 1970s, when you'd have Curtis Strange, Vinny Giles, and the Wadkins brothers winning all the time and 2,000 people coming out to see it. It's still a great title to have, and without a superstar in the field, it's wide open."

The only thing wrong with Leigh's logic was his implied dismissal of Giles. Then again, it had been 16 years since Giles had last won the State Am.

"Teenagers don't even know who Jack Nicklaus is," Giles, then 44, had said earlier in the week. "To them, I'm just another old guy who's playing better than he knows how."

Giles marched through the quarterfinals match with another Richmonder, 1980 State Am winner Mark Lawrence, winning 4 and 3. Then came the marquee pairing of the tournament, Giles vs. Tom McKnight of Galax.

McKnight had won the 1984 Amateur over Mike Pratt of Richmond at the Country Club of Petersburg. The following year he squeaked by Leigh in the final at Fairfax CC. He had also captured the 1985 State Open at Farmington in Charlottesville. He was not someone you took lightly.

Giles didn't. He took a 2-up lead with a birdie on the eighth hole, then began lasering his approach shots closer and closer to the cup.

He birdied the 10th from eight feet, the 11th from three feet, and the par-4 12th from two inches. The 5-up lead held, and Giles found himself in the

final against 25-year-old Steve Douglass of Virginia Beach after an easier-than-expected 5-and-4 triumph.

"He was my idol when I was a teenager," McKnight said, "and he's even more my idol now than he was three hours ago. I just wonder if some of these younger guys realize exactly what Vinny's done and how much he's meant for amateur golf in Virginia."

Douglass knew, and despite finishing the morning segment of the 36-hole final 3-down, he refused to fold. With a couple of birdies on the front nine after lunch, Douglass closed to 1-down. There they remained until the 18th.

Both men drove down the center, and both easily navigated their shots over Lake Irvington—though neither stopped his shot on the green.

Douglas was in a bunker behind and left of the green. Giles was in a bunker below and to the right of the green. Douglass, away, nearly holed his sand shot, the ball coming to rest two feet beneath the hole.

Giles blasted out, but didn't have enough oomph on the ball to get it up the hill to the cup. It stopped 20 feet beneath the hole, and he missed the par-saving putt by two feet.

Douglass conceded Giles' bogey, then prepared to tap in the two-footer that would force sudden death.

He missed, pulling the putt off line to give Giles a stunning 1-up victory.

"I was comfortable from the first swing of the match until just about the last," said Douglass. "To be honest, I just got nervous and pulled it. I had one foot on the first tee [for the playoff]."

Giles was classy in victory, calling the unprecedented seventh win "a matter of timing." Slightly better putting, he allowed, would have given him more breathing room and eliminated the need for the late drama.

"I hit the ball as well today as I had all week," Giles said. "I was 1-over for 36 holes, and that's good playing on a golf course like this. But the putting just wasn't there."

At the State Amateur at Golden Eagle 11 years later, clutch putting carried Jay Fisher of Suffolk to the most prestigious victory of his young career.

"This is the biggest thing I've ever done in golf and, hopefully, just the beginning," he said. "Considering it's the State Amateur, this is the best I've ever played."

A 21-year-old rising senior at Furman University, Fisher advanced to the final against Pat Tallent of Vienna by beating not one Giles, but two.

Conlin Giles of Norfolk was a close friend of Fisher's, and they played a quarterfinals match indicative of players who were well familiar with each other's game. Fisher ran out to an early lead, sagged a bit in the middle, then closed fast for a 3-and-2 victory.

Later that day, Fisher took on the "other" Giles—Vinny—in the semifinals. By the time Fisher and Giles reached the 18th hole all even, Tallent had already eliminated Norfolk's Troy Thorne and was in the gallery watching play.

Giles drove into the fairway of the par-4 dogleg right, 125 yards from the hole. Fisher, who had pulled into a tie by making par at the 17th, drove into a fairway bunker and was 133 yards away, and the lake to carry.

Fisher clipped his 9-iron shot cleanly, easily carrying the water, stopping the ball 15 feet from the hole. Giles hit an indifferent approach into the right fringe, pitched to four feet, and then watched Fisher drain the winning putt.

In the 36-hole final against Tallent, a 44-year-old former basketball star at George Washington University, Fisher didn't take the lead until the 10th hole of the afternoon session, the 28th of the day.

The Golden Eagle's 411-yard, par-4 ninth hole, photographed from behind the green.

He immediately lost it, then didn't regain it until the 17th, a wicked 202-yard uphill par 3 that had bedeviled Tallent all week. Tallent, a low-ball hitter, almost never found a way to keep his tee shots on the green. In eight attempts, he had made par just twice.

Against Fisher, he hit what he called his best tee shot of the week, but the ball rolled through the green and into the rear fringe. Fisher, who hit his shots considerably higher, was on the green, 45 feet away.

Tallent, unaccustomed to chipping out of Bermuda rough, fluffed his second shot, leaving it 12 feet from the hole. Fisher, facing a speedy down-hill putt, rolled it 10 feet past, but made the par-saver coming back. Tallent missed.

At 18, both drove into the left rough, but Tallent's shot settled behind a small grove of trees. From there, he hit his approach into the water guarding the green, while Fisher hit his ball over the green, then chipped past the hole.

When Tallent missed a 15-footer for bogey, he conceded the match.

"The kid just made some incredible putts," Tallent said. "He was unflappable. He never hit any nervous shots. It all came down to his putter. He made three huge putts on the last five holes, the shortest of which was 10 feet."

The one that did the most damage, however, came on the par-4 13th hole. Tallent, 1-up, had a 14-foot putt for birdie after a spectacular approach

from a fairway bunker. Fisher had what seemed like a tough 25-footer for birdie.

Fisher made his, Tallent didn't.

Two holes later, Fisher holed a 15-footer for birdie to take a lead. Tallent was 20 feet away, but needed two putts.

"I felt like anything that was in reasonable range had a good chance of going in," Fisher said. "What was reasonable? Fifteen, maybe 20 feet. I didn't make any huge, long putts, but anything that was close was going in."

If the Stephens family could, they'd fix it so that every guest at The Tides Resort could make the same boast. They'd consider it the least they could do for old friends.

With mountain wildflowers in bloom, golfers take aim at the
fourth hole, a 146-yard par 3, at the Devil's Knob Course.

WINTERGREEN

Wintergreen's 11,000 acres, 43 miles southwest of Charlottesville, extend from the Blue Ridge Mountains to the valley below. There couldn't be a more spectacular venue for a first-class, family-oriented getaway.

Once thought to be inaccessible wasteland, today Wintergreen plays host to thousands of guests each year and is considered one of the premier resorts in the United States.

It offers a wide variety of activities: tennis, skiing, hiking, horseback riding, and swimming. Uncommonly sensitive to nature since its beginning, in 1998 The Wintergreen Nature Foundation introduced The Field Studies Institute, a weekend series of programs led by noted scholars who examine the rich natural history of the Blue Ridge.

Two-day symposiums are offered in everything from Trout Stream Ecology to Butterfly Gardening to Native American History.

"Wintergreen is the rarest of creatures—a resort that embraces conservation as the guiding light of its growth and development," wrote the author of a story in *Best Golf Resorts in the World* in 1993. "Rarer still is a resort that offers players two fine courses completely dissimilar in style and climate."

Wintergreen's original course, Devils Knob was designed by Ellis Maples, former president of the American Association of Golf Course Architects. It opened in June 1976.

At 3,851 feet, it is the highest course in the state and offers 40- to 50-mile views of the Shenandoah and Rockfish Valleys.

The fairways are narrow, tree-lined, and accented by natural rock and ponds that offer the player far more to observe than the slope of the fairway or the grain of the green.

In the valley is Stoney Creek. A $4 million design by Rees Jones, Stoney Creek opened in 1988 and has since been one of the top-ranked courses in the state.

Noted designer Rees Jones has added the new Tuckahoe Nine course at Stoney Creek, giving the course 27 holes. From this vantage point behind the green, the first hole can be seen 457 yards away, with plenty of water hazards to avoid.

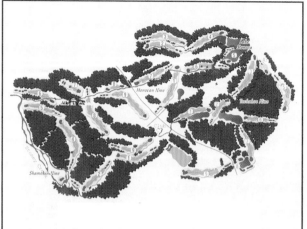

A map of the 27 holes at Stoney Creek at Wintergreen shows the Tuckahoe Nine, the Shamokin Nine, and the Monocan Nine. A large sand bunker (right photo) protects the green at the par-4, 349-yard sixth hole on the Tuckahoe course.

The layout features all of Jones' trademarks: bold mounding designed to give the less-skilled player as many friendly bounces into the fairway as possible; multiple tee boxes for players of all skill levels; and generous greens.

With play at an all-time high, Jones was asked to return to Wintergreen to expand Stoney Creek to 27 holes.

He created a playable and visual masterpiece.

Taking advantage of natural elevation changes, the Tuckahoe Nine opened in May 1998 and immediately drew praise for the challenge its terrain and water hazards offered.

Stoney Creek has played host to two of the Virginia State Golf Association's premier events: the 1989 Mid-Amateur championship won by Frank Moore of Virginia Beach and the rain-soaked 1995 Men's Amateur.

The tournament was supposed to start on Wednesday, June 28, with two rounds of stroke-play qualifying. But the week before, the golf course and surrounding Nelson County received seven inches of rain. Streams were dangerously high. Several roads were washed out. The course was sodden. Only continuous work by course superintendent Bob Ruff kept Stoney Creek from joining that portion of the state under water.

The night before the start of qualifying, four more inches of rain fell. When it continued drizzling Wednesday morning, the course was deemed unplayable. VSGA officials cut qualifying from 36 holes to 18. It was the first of a daily postponement, cancellation, or reduction in play caused by the weather.

"Everything was underwater," former VSGA executive director Wallace McDowell said, "even our hazard stakes."

"We need at least two to six hours of dry weather to get the course playable again," Stoney Creek pro Chris Warring added. "Right now, there's so much water in the fairways, there's no place to take relief."

The tournament finally got the break it needed Thursday afternoon. Jimmy Flippen Jr. of Danville won the qualifying medal. The son of the 1958 State Amateur champion, Flippen shot a remarkable 5-under-par 67, one shot better than Chesapeake's Billy Judah and two ahead of Richmond's David Partridge. They were the only players in the field to break 70.

"It was sopping wet out there, but everyone had to play the same course," said Flippen, a former member of the University of Virginia golf team.

Another member of the University of Virginia family, renowned sports psychologist Bob Rotella, may have been the most surprising qualifier. Rotella, a popular Svengali with professional athletes from all sports, crafted a 1-over-par 73 that, considering the circumstances, may have been the most remarkable round of the tournament.

"I just played real solidly," said Rotella, who made 10-foot putts to save par on his first three holes and had one-putt pars on Nos. 17 and 18. "I missed some greens, but I got it up and down most of the time. I played a good, solid round, just what you need to do in this qualifying."

Rotella, who had precious little previous experience playing at this level, gave first-round opponent Mike Finsterle of Gainesville all he could handle before losing 1-down.

"He kept telling me in the cart, 'I'm a really good competitor,'" Rotella said.

Finsterle proved it late in the match. After Rotella climbed from 3-down to a tie with a birdie-2 at 16, Finsterle answered with a birdie on 17 and closed out the match with a par on the finishing hole.

"My feeling was, 'I'm coming. I got him. And I'm going to get him,'" Rotella said. "He was feeling it, but he hung in there. Right when I thought I had him, he got away."

Finsterle couldn't escape rain or tournament sensation Jeremy Paulson of Front Royal in the afternoon round. Paulson, 18, shocked Flippen 5 and 3 in the morning, then edged Finsterle 1-up with a birdie on the 18th hole in one of several afternoon matches twice interrupted by showers.

Three of the eight quarterfinalists were former champions: Partridge, who had won in 1993; Keith Decker of Fieldale, winner in 1998 and 1991; and Scott Inman of Springfield, the defending champion.

Of those, Partridge may have had the most momentum coming in. The week before, he had captured his second successive Richmond City title. Not long before that, he had taken the Kenridge Invitational at Charlottesville's Farmington Country Club for the fifth time in his career.

Saturday's quarterfinals were haunted by rain again, bringing the total rainfall at the course to 14 inches in 10 days. The last quarterfinal match, Decker against Partridge, was the one most affected by the untimely downpours.

The players came to the 18th hole all square. Decker hit his approach shot into a greenside waste area, after which an intense storm began. Decker wedged his next shot to 10 feet, but by the time he got to his ball, puddles had formed where moments before there had been no trace of water.

Decker waited for 10 minutes while maintenance workers used squeegees to dry the area between his ball and the hole. Finally, as he stood over the putt, thunder boomed and a bolt of lightning was spotted in the distance.

If it bothered Decker, he didn't show it. After backing off and collecting his thoughts, he made the putt, after which Partridge missed an eight-footer for birdie that would have ended the suspense.

As it happened, after a three-hour rain delay, Partridge won the match on the first hole with a par to set up a semifinal encounter with fellow Hermitage Country Club member Simon Cooke.

That would have to wait a day. In an unprecedented move forced by the weather, the VSGA moved the semifinals to Sunday and reduced the final to 18 holes instead of the usual 36.

Partridge, 40, was taking on the 22-year-old Cooke, a second-team All-American at Virginia, and his final opponent in the 1993 State Amateur at James River Country Club in Newport News. Partridge had won that meeting 5 and 4.

"Secretly, I think he's wanted to play me again," Partridge said. "He's got a score to settle with me.

"Clearly, he's a superior player, and I had to play my very best against him to win in '93. I'll be up all night trying to figure out how to play better than I'm capable."

In the other bracket, Inman would meet fellow Springfield Golf and Country Club member and friend Dan Derisio.

Inman and Derisio had been teammates on the West Springfield High School golf team, after which the two had faced each other in Southeastern Conference competition between LSU and Alabama, respectively.

Since returning to Northern Virginia, they had dominated the competition at Springfield G&CC. Inman had won four club championships. Derisio had won two.

"He's the sheriff, I'm the deputy," is how Derisio described their relationship before the match. "But sometimes the deputy wins."

Not this time. Inman ousted Derisio 3 and 2, while Partridge turned back Cooke 4 and 3. Then Partridge defeated Inman 3-and-2 with some remarkable iron play.

Inman and Partridge traded three-putt bogeys before Inman went 1-up with a 10-foot birdie on the par-3 eighth.

Golfers practice putting in front of the club-house at Devil's Knob Golf Course at Wintergreen Resort. Guest suites in the background are perched high atop the Blue Ridge Mountains.

"I was a little indifferent at the beginning," Partridge said. "I gave myself a little talking-to and said, 'You're not going to back into this thing. You're going to have to play better.'"

He did, winning the next four holes. Laser-like iron shots on nine and 11 left him with one- and two-foot birdie putts. He won the 10th and 12th holes with par after Inman got into trouble off the tee.

"I didn't putt that well today," said Partridge, who admitted that was the weakest part of his game. "But then I started hitting it so close, a chimpanzee could have putted them in."

Inman, who holed a serpentine 40-foot birdie putt on 14 for a halve to stay in the competition, thought Partridge should have taken more credit for his outstanding play.

"He was a tough man to beat," Inman said. "He had those irons working again. David does get into trouble when his putter lets him down, but he hit it so darn close, he didn't have to worry about it. From the ninth hole on, he was flawless."

The same is said for Wintergreen. Among the resort's countless awards:

• Gold Tee Award from *Meeting and Conventions* magazine, which called it "One of the best golf and meeting properties in the U.S."

• Silver Medal from *Golf* magazine, as one of the country's "Top Golf Resorts"

• Named one of the "Top 100 Golf Resorts in the World" by *The Golfer* magazine

• Stoney Creek ranked as the No. 2 course in Virginia and the No. 34 resort course in the United States by *Golf Digest*

• Devils Knob selected as one of the top "women-friendly courses in the country" by *Golf for Women* magazine

• 1976 selection as one of the "Top 50 Best Golf Resorts" in the U.S. by *Conde Nast Traveler*

A rock outcropping is a certain distraction when teeing off from high atop the par-4, 408-yard 16th hole of the Devil's Knob Course at Wintergreen Resort.

classy designs

A sea of tulips beautifies the clubhouse of the
Robert Trent Jones Golf Club in Gainesville.

ROBERT TRENT JONES
GOLF CLUB

Throughout his career, Robert Trent Jones Sr. loved to put on a good show, selling his work and revolutionary changes in golf-course design with an unmatched flair.

When some members of Baltusrol's Lower Course were viciously critical of the work Jones did in redesigning the par-3 fourth hole in 1952, Jones grabbed them and a club and brought them to the tee of the 194-yard hole.

Jones, a pro-caliber player as a young man, hit the ball into the hole on one hop. As he walked away, he reportedly turned back and said, "Gentlemen, I think that hole is eminently fair."

Jones made what his friends would consider an amazing endorsement, and what his critics could consider more evidence of unabashed showmanship in 1991.

After surveying his work on a 200-acre course in Gainesville, Jones told club president Robert Russell that he had just completed the best design of a career that included more than 400 courses throughout the world.

"Well," said Russell, "if it's the best course you have ever built, why don't we just name it after you?"

Jones, then 89, had purchased the 200-acre property around 1975 because it was "so beautiful and so near Washington." He did not object to Russell's suggestion.

That conversation eliminated any identity crisis the new club in Prince William County might have. The Robert Trent Jones Golf Club immediately took its place next to capital-area institutions such as Congressional Country Club and Burning Tree.

In no time, Robert Trent Jones—or RTJ as it's called—became a playground for the fabulously wealthy and powerful. Former president George Bush and former vice president Dan Quayle enjoyed membership. Vernon Jordan, friend and advisor to President Bill Clinton, is a member, too.

Judy Bell, the first woman president of the U.S. Golf Association, holds a membership. So does Supreme Court justice Sandra Day O'Connor.

Picture perfect: the 185-yard, par-3 11th hole at the Robert Trent Jones Golf Club in the early morning.

Jones' remarkable background is woven into each of his creations. The first person to use college expressly to study for a career in course design, Jones developed his personal curriculum at Cornell. He mixed class work in landscape architecture, economics, public speaking, surveying, horticulture, agronomy, and hydraulics.

"A great course," Jones said in 1993, "is one that combines lots of natural beauty with fair shot values. As the player stands on the tee, he should be able to weigh risk against benefits. If he decides to bite off a slice of pond on a par-5, for example, so that he has a chance of being on in two, he assumes the responsibility of perhaps a 230-yard carry dead straight, and a terrible penalty if he doesn't make it.

"One thing to remember: Great courses may be beaten, but they are never defeated."

The courses Jones designed and remodeled are proof of that.

He worked with Bobby Jones on Peachtree in Atlanta in the late 1940s. That's when he added the name "Trent" to avoid possible confusion with his co-worker. He also worked on Augusta National's 11th and 16th holes, giving them a personality of their own instead of living as the prelude and postscript to Augusta's famed 12-15 stretch.

After seeing how Jones toughened Donald Ross' relatively benign Oakland Hills in Michigan before the 1951 U.S. Open, Ben Hogan labeled the course "a monster."

Suddenly, it became fashionable for clubs playing host to the Open to have Jones give their course the once-over before opening the gates to the players. Baltusrol did it, as did Olympic in San Francisco; Southern Hills in Tulsa, Oklahoma; Oak Hill in Jones' hometown of Rochester, New York; and Congressional in Potomac, Maryland.

Jones' name is synonymous with many of the world's most revered layouts: Firestone-North in Ohio, Hazeltine in Minnesota, Spyglass Hill in California, Old Sotogrande in Spain, Dorado Beach in Puerto Rico.

Jones' commitment to nature is abundantly clear at RTJ.

Lake Manassas comes into play on half of the holes of the 7,258-yard, par-72 layout. The fairways are narrow, and Jones was again true to his philosophy in designing 18 large, wide greens that offer an infinite number of pin placements.

Jones' greens can confound even the most experienced player. That was one of many reasons RTJ was the perfect choice as the site for the first Presidents Cup competition between the United States team and non-European Internationals in 1994.

More than 15,000 fans turned out on the final day to see the American team pull out a 20-12 victory that was much closer than the final score indicated. (See U.S. Hoists First Presidents Cup in Making Memories.)

There was little doubt the 1996 event would return to RTJ. The players raved about the golf course. The fans were warm and appreciative. Although it had been criticized as being a Ryder Cup knockoff—and in many ways it was—a strong foundation had been laid two years before at RTJ. This was the time and the place to continue building.

There would be differences from the inaugural event, which was characterized by great sportsmanship and camaraderie among the players, coaches, and captains. Eight weeks before Presidents Cup II, a player rebellion by the International team led to the removal of David Graham as captain. Australian Peter Thomson, a five-time British Open winner, was Graham's replacement.

Guiding the U.S. team would be Arnold Palmer, celebrating his 67th birthday that September week.

Palmer, who flew his new plane in on Monday, immediately went to the course to confer with his team and play some practice holes with them, five days before the competition started.

"I haven't shown up for a tournament on a Monday in 40 years," Palmer joked. "I just want to watch the guys, get their feelings on some of the pairings. . . I don't want them to take this too lightly, because I know the International team is after us."

Palmer had good reason to believe that.

In 1994, Greg Norman withdrew from the International team because of health problems. Japan's Jumbo Ozaki and South Africa's Ernie Els declined invitations because they had previous commitments. This time, all three were present, giving the International team the first-, third- and sixth-ranked players in the world.

The Internationals also had tremendous depth in Nick Price, Steve Elkington, Vijay Singh, Frank Nobilo, David Frost, and Craig Parry.

Although the United States was typically strong with Fred Couples, David Duval, Davis Love III, Mark O'Meara, Phil Mickelson, Cory Pavin, and Scott Hoch, the International team seemed to have the edge in talent and motivation.

"This is probably more important for us than it is for the U.S. team," Thomson said. "It's the first time we've had an event where we can show that the best golfers in the world don't reside on the Atlantic Rim—the U.S. and Europe is what I mean."

The opening ceremonies were attended by former president George Bush; Bob Hawke, former prime minister of Australia; F.W. de Klerk, former president of South Africa; Canaan Banana, former president of Zimbabwe; Sitivenie Rabuka, prime minister of Fiji; and Virginia Gov. George Allen.

The next day, with President Clinton watch-

A lone golfer tees off on the picturesque ninth
hole—a 200-yard par 3 from the championship
tees at the Robert Trent Jones Golf Club.

ing, the U.S. team raced to a 7-2 lead. The highlights of the day were morning and afternoon matches between Americans Couples and Love and Internationals Norman and Robert Allenby, described by Thomson prior to the competition as "invincible."

That's how Norman started, holing a 35-foot birdie putt on No. 1. But Couples answered with a five-footer to halve the hole. From there, neither team enjoyed more than a one-hole advantage until the 383-yard 17th.

Couples was three feet from the Americans' ninth birdie of the match when Norman missed a six-footer for par. He conceded the putt and the U.S. 2-and-1 four-ball victory.

The afternoon match, using an alternate-shot format, was even more taut. Allenby had a five-foot par putt on the 18th hole that would have given the Internationals a halve in the match. But it slipped by the edge, the final shot in a 1-up triumph for Couples and Love.

"Peter [Thomson] laid down the gauntlet to us by saying if they could stop us, they'd stop the whole team," Love said. "We knew this morning that it might be a boost to their team if they got a point. We didn't want that to happen."

The five-point margin was identical to the one enjoyed by the Americans after the first day of the '94 Presidents Cup. That year, the Internationals charged back to trim their deficit to 12-8 entering the final day.

This time, they'd do better than that, winning three of four best-ball matches in the morning and four of five alternate-shot matches in the afternoon to finish the day down by only 9-10.

The Americans needed to win six of the 12 singles matches to retain possession of the cup. That didn't look to be a problem after Hoch's 1-up victory over Zimbabwe's Mark McNulty gave the U.S. 15 points with four matches still going.

Then the Internationals made one more charge. Elkington beat Justin Leonard 1-up; Nobilo defeated Tom Lehman 3 and 2; and Norman took out Pavin 3 and 1. That left everything riding on the Couples-Singh match.

Couples led 1-up through 16 holes. As thousands of fans raced back to meet the two players, Couples hit his approach to the par-4 17th 40 feet from the hole. Singh's shot stopped 25 feet away.

Then Couples sent his ball diving into the heart of the hole, an amazing birdie that Singh had to duplicate or lose the match. First, though, Americans came running onto the 17th green to celebrate Couples' shot. Later, there would be whispers that someone may have run through Singh's line, inadvertently kicked up a spike mark that made a difficult situation worse.

When the crowd was finally quiet, Singh rolled his putt towards the hole. About halfway there, it hit a spike mark, bounced a hair to the right, and rolled by.

"It had a 50-50 chance if it went straight over

it," Singh said. "But it went right. I thought if I had gone down to 18, I would have had a good chance."

In addition to Couples, other American heroes included Mark O'Meara, who was undefeated in five matches, and, of course, Palmer.

"Every time it got tight, I asked myself, 'What would A.P. do?'" said O'Meara. "He'd hitch up his pants and go forward. I thought about that often."

Emotions aside, Palmer made a brilliant captain's choice in his selection of David Duval, then winless on the PGA Tour. Duval responded to Palmer's faith in him by posting a 4-0 record.

"Mr. Palmer motivates everyone," Duval said. "I looked at him and told myself, 'I'm not going to get beat.'"

The Presidents Cup was staged at Royal Melbourne Golf Club in Australia in 1998. The International team defeated the U.S. team, captained by Jack Nicklaus, 20-11.

The next match is in September 2000 at Robert Trent Jones.

AWARDS FOR ROBERT TRENT JONES

No. 2 by *Golf Digest*, America's top state golf courses, 1997-98.

No. 3 by *Golf Digest*, America's top state golf courses, 1995-96.

No. 33 by *GolfWeek*, America's top 100 best modern courses, 1997.

No. 92 by *Golf Digest*, America's 100 greatest golf courses, 1997-98.

The rear of the gigantic brick clubhouse at the Robert Trent Jones Golf Club in Gainesville.

classy designs

The famous octagonal room in the Main House at Farmington CC
in Charlottesville. It was designed by Thomas Jefferson in 1803 and
has been restored to its original glory.

FARMINGTON COUNTRY CLUB

The land on which Farmington Country Club in Charlottesville sits is as much a part of American history as it is golf history in Virginia.

Ownership dates back to 1744 and a royal grant to Michael Holland by George II. In 1758, Francis Jerdone acquired the land. He built the original section of the Farmington mansion around 1760, and might have had a long, happy life there if not for his politics.

Jerdone was an old-guard Tory. In 1779, at the height of the American Revolution, the U.S. government confiscated 3,000 acres of property and 52 slaves.

Somehow, Jerdone made peace with the fledgling government long enough to have his property returned, which he then deeded to George Divers of Philadelphia in 1785.

Divers and Thomas Jefferson were close friends, so much so that Divers named a son Thomas Jefferson Divers. In 1802, Divers asked Jefferson to favor him by drawing some plans for the main house. Out of that conversation was born the famous octagonal room that has become Farmington's historical foundation.

Divers evidently didn't believe the fact that Jefferson was president of the United States at the time would keep his friend from helping on the project. Jefferson apparently didn't think so, either, for he plunged head first into the project in 1803.

Unfortunately, Divers became ill before the work was completed and was forced to leave his home. Jefferson promised to keep an eye on the project. On one of those visits to Farmington, he became so frustrated by what he considered shoddy workmanship that he fired the construction crew. Divers died before work was completed, and it wasn't until Gen. Bernard Peyton acquired the property in 1852 that the interior was finished.

Jefferson's original plans called for two rooms. The nine round windows of the Jefferson Room are said to have been ordered by Jefferson for use

The sun sets on a Farmington Country Club member and the final hole of the club's North Nine.

The Main House at Farmington CC in Charlottesville—the pillared entrance leads into the octagonal room, designed by Thomas Jefferson in 1803. The actual entrance to the building is just to the left of the pillars.

at nearby Monticello, but they arrived too late. Jefferson is said to have then offered them to Divers for inclusion in the Farmington mansion.

Peyton turned Jefferson's original plan into four small rooms with a central hallway. Today, the Jefferson Room is one huge chamber. Edward S. Campbell, professor of architecture at the University of Virginia, supervised the adaptation in the mid-1900s.

Farmington was lucky to have emerged unscathed by the Civil War, although one of the club's legendary stories involves a poacher from Union Gen. Phillip Sheridan's march through Charlottesville in 1865.

The lady of the house at the time was Mary Ann Miller Wood Harper. When one of Sheridan's foraging parties stopped at the plantation, the widow Harper offered them rare French wines and even raised the British flag out front in an effort to keep them from ransacking her property.

One member of the party broke away and sneaked upstairs into Mrs. Harper's bedroom, now Room 21. Mrs. Harper, holding a sword that had belonged to General Peyton, quietly approached behind him, then whacked him on the rump with the flat blade of the sword.

The stunned soldier flew out an open bedroom window and onto the roof of the front porch.

Mrs. Harper, the story goes, ran to the window and yelled at the offending soldier, "No damn Yankee can come into my house without a proper introduction."

In 1927, 50 prominent Charlottesville-area businessmen known as Farmington, Inc., purchased the property. Their intention from the start was to transform Farmington into a country club.

Hired to design the course was Fred Findlay, a brilliant Scotsman who would eventually live in a cottage on the Farmington grounds with his daughter and his son-in-law, R.F. Loving.

Findlay had a fascinating background. Enlisted in the British Army when he was 13 by his father, Findlay became an expert bugler who sounded the call for the Charge of the Light Brigade at Bal Aklava in 1855.

Findlay was very much into nature, letting the terrain take him where it wanted. His design of Farmington reflects that. The course extends on all sides of the clubhouse, with the magnificent 14th hole laid out in the virtual shadow of the Jefferson Room.

"My life has always been coupled up with nature," said Findlay, who often shot his age, even in his 80s. "I am sure there is nothing that keeps one closer to God."

There's a pond inhabited by Canadian geese on No. 4. At No. 7, a creek bisects the fairway in two places. The green at No. 9 is shrouded in trees.

The 10th is a 255-yard par 3 that is characterized by flat, open terrain. The 13th measures just 310 yards, but all of it is uphill, with a creek that bisects the fairway.

Statistically, the 17th is the easiest hole on the course, 188 yards from an elevated tee to a green positioned deep in a valley. What it may lack in difficulty it makes up for in aesthetics.

In a 1959 interview, Findlay acknowledged that Farmington and the River Course at the Country Club of Virginia in Richmond were his two finest works.

Farmington was a place that attracted the rich, famous, and powerful.

During a visit there on July 4, 1936, President Franklin D. Roosevelt and First Lady Eleanor Roosevelt watched part of the State Amateur.

Less than two weeks later, Lady Nancy Astor, First Woman of the British Parliament, came to Charlottesville. She was visiting her brother, Col. W.H. Langhorne, who was ill at the Blue Ridge Sanitarium.

During her stay, Lady Astor played what a member described as a "brisk" round of golf at Farmington before seeing to her brother.

Actress Greer Garson stopped at Farmington during a whirlwind tour to sell war bonds during World War II. The movie *Mrs. Miniver*, in which she portrayed a British housewife trying to keep her family alive during the German bombing of England, had just been released. Later, she would win the Academy Award for her performance.

"I was born overseas, and little did I think when I studied about Virginia and Sir Walter Raleigh, that I would ever come to Virginia," Garson told an adoring audience. "I feel as much at home here in Virginia as if I had been born here. You have been so loyal, and I bless you for it."

Robert F. Kennedy played golf there with Bill Battle, shortly after President Kennedy had named Battle U.S. Ambassador to Australia.

Advice columnist Anne Landers spent a July afternoon in 1967 telling Farmington members "what a total square" she was.

Others who have immersed themselves in the charm of Farmington include Adlai Stevenson, Thomas Dewey, Barry Goldwater, Norman Vincent Peale, and actress Anne Baxter.

THE GOLF

Farmington has provided the backdrop for some of the state's most memorable tournaments. Chandler Harper won the 1933 State Amateur by a whopping 10 and 9 over Lansing Eubank of Richmond. That's the second-most lopsided final in the history of a tournament that started in 1911.

Bobby Cruickshank won his fifth consecutive State Open in 1937 at Farmington, beating Ernie Ball of Charlottesville by two shots in an 18-hole playoff.

Twenty-two years later, Joe Cannon of Charlottesville beat Clare Emery of Arlington for

An aerial photograph of Farmington CC in Charlottesville, showing the Main House, with pillars, the pool, tennis courts, extensive guest wings, and the 10th green (foreground left), the 13th green (foreground right), and the 18th green.

the State Open on the first hole of a sudden-death playoff.

Appropriately enough, Farmington was chosen as the site for Virginia's most historic State Open, the one that ended a unique civil war found nowhere else in the United States.

Beginning in 1958 and continuing through 1984, Virginia was the only state to have two State Opens.

The older of the two began in 1924 and was sponsored by the Virginia chapter of the Mid-Atlantic PGA. The other, which was begun in 1958, was sponsored by the Virginia State Golf Association.

After years of negotiations, the two sides finally settled their differences in the summer of 1984 and turned to Farmington to host the first merged event. It was a natural choice. The cup awarded to the winner of the Virginia PGA State Open was, and remains, known as the Farmington Trophy. It was donated to the VSGA in the early stages of the event's history, before the VSGA dropped its sponsorship of the tournament in the mid-1930s.

"We wanted to come to one of the finest golf courses in Virginia for our first merged State Open, and we're delighted that Farmington accepted the tournament," said Vinny Giles.

Giles, who was long an advocate for a single Open, represented the VSGA in negotiations, along with Harry Lea of Danville and Tommy Kidd of Petersburg. Representing the Virginia PGA were Peter Hodson of Willow Oaks CC in Richmond, Leo Steinbrecher of Richmond CC, and Bill Smith of the Country Club of Virginia.

"We wanted to be the host club, for our roots here go back to the original trophy for this championship," Al Garrett, general chairman of the event said. "We members are anxious to see what the big

boys will do when they come to Farmington this summer."

The "big boys" did OK—but reinstated amateur Tom McKnight did better. He defeated professional Mark Carnevale by two shots to win the title.

Since 1932, Farmington has played host to one of the state's most prestigious amateur tournaments, the Kenridge Invitational. The tournament was originally intended for Charlottesville residents who were not Farmington members, the University of Virginia golf team, and other invited clubs in the state.

The trophy was donated by Hollis Rhinehart Sr., and named "Kenridge" after his home on Ivy Road in Charlottesville.

Wynsol Spencer of Newport News won in 1939, the same year he captured the first of five State Amateur championships.

Other notables in the state who won it include Ray "Buddy" Loving Jr., the maternal grandson of Fred Findlay, and a 10-time club champion. Loving captured the cup and the champion's bright blue blazer in 1951, '52, '55, '59, '61, and '62.

Former U.S. Golf Association president Harry Easterly won in 1956. Another former USGA president, Bill Campbell of West Virginia, won in 1963.

Vinny Giles and Keith Decker are among two-time winners. David Partridge of Richmond has won the Kenridge five times since 1986.

In 1993, the U.S. Golf Association brought its men's Senior Amateur to Farmington. A record 2,275 players entered, with Joe Ungvary defeating Jerry Nelson 7 and 6 in the final.

THE PEOPLE

While Farmington had a way of attracting colorful characters who enriched the history of the

place, perhaps no one was more flamboyant than the tall, reed-thin Ms. Sydney Elliott.

An accomplished pianist and composer who liked to belt out bawdy tunes on the clubhouse piano, Elliott was the state tennis champion before taking up golf.

Elliott, who was 5-feet-8 and wore a 10AAAA shoe, was an immediate sensation, winning the State Amateur in 1949, 1952, and 1953.

Nicknamed "Slug-Nutty" by Farmington pro Joe Cannon, Elliott left her mark on Farmington golf in more ways than one. Before the 1951 Women's State Amateur at Farmington, Elliott had some friends build an outhouse near the 10th green. If other members protested, there is no record of it, and soon the other women at the club playfully dubbed the makeshift rest stop "Sydney's Springs."

Farmington member Anne Pollard won the tournament in '51, then hit a dry spell that lasted until 1964.

Popping raisins from first tee shot until final putt, Pollard defeated Robbye King, a future Farmington member then living in Norfolk, 3 and 2 at the Cascades Course in Hot Springs.

Somehow, the California Raisin Advisory Board found out about Pollard's nutritional strategy. An opportunistic public-relations department put out a national press release extolling the ability of their favorite fruit to provide a quick energy boost—and pointed to Pollard's triumph as a perfect example.

In 1964, Elliott became the first woman golf pro in Virginia, and joined the Farmington staff. She was 39 at the time, and she died in 1977 at age 52.

Findlay, the course architect responsible for what makes Farmington golf special, continued to shoot his age well into his 80s. He died in 1965 at the age of 93.

The stone facade pro shop at Farmington CC has an extensive selection of carts in front of the building that leads directly to the South Nine part of the course.

classy designs

The clubhouse of the James River Course at the
Country Club of Virginia in Richmond.

THE COUNTRY CLUB OF VIRGINIA

No club has done as much to popularize golf in the Old Dominion as the Country Club of Virginia.

Formed in 1908 by members of Hermitage Country Club after a disagreement over expansion plans there, CCV today boasts three beautiful and distinctive courses.

The Westhampton Course, with its elegant Jeffersonian-style clubhouse, is a 5,800-yard, par-69 layout that opened in 1910.

Eighteen years later, the James River Course opened. Designed by William Flynn, with revision work by Robert Trent Jones Sr. in 1954 and Rees Jones in 1993, it is a 7,022-yard par 72 that has the respect and admiration of golf's elite players and administrators.

Rounding out the 54-hole complex is the 6,933-yard Tuckahoe Course. The first nine holes were designed by Ed Ault, after which Joe Lee blended Ault's nine with plans of his own to form the final 18.

The club became a landmark address in the evolution of the game in the Commonwealth when a Scottish immigrant named Bobby Cruickshank went there as head golf professional in 1932.

Cruickshank stayed for 15 years, during which time his magnetic personality and brilliant game drew people to the sport as never before.

"Wee Bobby" as he was known, won 20 professional tournaments and was golf's leading money winner in 1927. He captured the Virginia State Open six times in seven years. (See a profile of Bobby Cruickshank in Champions II.)

Cruickshank proved to be a prophet in 1935 when he was asked about renovations made to the James River Course by Chicago-based architect G.A. O'Neill that added 400 yards to the overall length.

"I've played courses all over the world, and this remodeled course will compare favorably with any of them," Cruickshank said. "It doesn't go in for

Golfers must navigate the overhanging trees on the 176-yard, par-3 14th hole of the James River Course at the Country Club of Virginia in Richmond.

excessive length, but it lacks a lot of being easy. You could play any tournament at James River, including the National Open."

In 1955, following more renovations in which six tees were lengthened, traps were added to the sixth and 18th holes, and three new greens were built after consultation with Robert Trent Jones, the U.S. Golf Association brought the National Amateur to CCV.

Maybe the tournament should have been called "The Harvie Ward Show."

The handsome 29-year-old North Carolinian was an overwhelming favorite to win the event, especially after three members of the nine-man Walker Cup team failed to qualify. The U.S. Amateur was just about the only tournament to elude him.

In 1948, he beat Frank Stranahan and Dick Chapman in the prestigious North and South. The following year, he won the NCAA title. He won the 1952 British Amateur, the '54 Canadian Amateur and had starred for the victorious '55 Walker Cup team. He was nearing the end of a brilliant season in which he already had been low amateur at that year's Masters and U.S. Open.

There were 12 Virginians in the field, but state hopes rested primarily on three players—Wynsol Spencer of Newport News, Wayne Jackson of Hampton, and George Fulton Jr. of Roanoke.

Spencer was a four-time State Amateur champion who had won four matches in the '54 Amateur before bowing out.

Fulton, another former State Amateur king, had shot a course-record 66 at the James River Course when it played to par 72 (it had been changed to a par-70 for the Amateur).

Jackson was a 20-year-old student at Randolph Macon College. He would go on to win

State Amateurs in 1956 and '65 and the State Mid-Amateur in 1977.

Also in the field was a 15-year-old high school junior from Columbus, Ohio, named Jack Nicklaus, whose even-par 70 in the final practice round was one of the low scores of the day.

Ward, who drew a first-round bye, gained an easier path to the final after a slew of upsets the first day. The biggest to fall was Billy Joe Patton, the gregarious North Carolina native and crowd favorite. He lost 1-up to unheralded George McCallister of Los Angeles in 23 holes.

When Ward finally got to play, he needed all of his skills to post a 1-up, 19-hole victory over Ray Palmer.

Although a long and accurate hitter, Ward had a game that was built around the extraordinary putting he exhibited using a putter he had found in a locker at a Tarboro, North Carolina, golf course two decades earlier. He had put it out where the original owner could claim it, but the club's wooden shaft was broken and no one came forward.

Ward replaced the broken shaft and a second wooden shaft years later when it warped.

"I've deserted it for other putters," he said. "But I always keep coming back to this one."

Ward gained momentum by beating Gordon Scott 5 and 3, Robert O. McCall 3 and 2, and 19-year-old University of Florida junior Jim McCoy 6 and 4 and advanced to the 36-hole semifinals against 29-year-old Bill Booe of Connecticut.

In the other bracket, 39-year-old insurance broker William Hyndman played the role of giant-killer in making a surprising run into the semis. He beat Frank Souchak, 19-year-old Purdue star Joe Campbell, and former Walker Cup member Jimmy McHale to meet 135-pound Hillman Robbins.

Neither semifinal was particularly close. Ward took a 2-up lead after Booe, a former placekicker for Yale's football team, bogeyed the first two holes. When Booe started the back nine the same way, Ward had all the advantage he needed to move on.

Hyndman was 6-up after 23 holes. Robbins rallied to win four of the next five, but could get no closer.

Ward was at his competitive best the following day. With his tee shots long and true and his rusty old putter never more deadly, Ward broke Cruickshank's nine-hole course-record 32 by one stroke and led 5-up at the turn.

He was only slightly less spectacular on the back nine, firing a 35 that allowed his bulge to grow to 8.

There was no letting up in the afternoon, as Ward cruised to a 9-and-8 triumph.

Showing a wonderful flair for the dramatic, Ward then presented the ball to Ben Baird of Richmond, the pro shop employee who had sold it to him that morning.

"I don't remember all of the matches," Ward said years later. "In the finals, I guess I was just really ready to go."

Twenty years later, the U.S. Amateur returned to CCV and the James River Course. Virginia's competitors in the '55 event may have been considered longshots, but the Commonwealth's entries in 1975 were at the top of everyone's list of favorites.

Vinny Giles, the 1972 Amateur winner, was the closest thing to a defending champion since the '73 and '74 champions had turned pro.

Then there was Curtis Strange of Virginia Beach, the North and South and Eastern Amateur titlist that year.

However, neither lasted nearly as long as hoped or anticipated. Giles, suffering from back spasms, hit only four of 15 fairways in losing to Stan Price of Pittsburgh in 19 holes.

"I knew I was supposed to lose, but I didn't want to embarrass myself by losing 8 and 6 or something like that," Price said. "I just figured I'd watch him and see what I had to do to become a better player. I can't believe I actually beat him!"

Strange, picked by Giles to win the title, lasted until the fifth round before falling 2 and 1 to Fred Ridley, a 23-year-old law student from Florida.

Ridley advanced to the final against 21-year-old University of Houston star Keith Fergus, who had made short work of his matches to that point. For seven consecutive matches, Fergus was done before playing the 17th and 18th holes.

Much to his chagrin, he would have to face both of them in the final.

Six-up after 19 holes, Ridley lost the next four holes. Four-up with five to play, he lost three in a row to Fergus' par, birdie, and par.

"I think my mind might have strayed a little bit," Ridley said. "But Keith was playing real good. I wasn't just giving away those holes."

Then came the 17th, a 206-yard par 3. Just 1-down, Fergus made bogey on the hole when he missed the green with his tee shot. That should have been enough for Ridley to win, especially after he hit his tee shot on the green. But the Winter Haven, Florida, resident left the door ajar when he needed three putts to get in the hole from 40 feet.

Both players found the fairway with their tee shots on the climactic hole. Fergus, away, hit a 4-wood he called "the best shot I hit all day." It didn't finish that way. The ball bounced hard about 10 feet short of the hole on the 457-yard par 4, then wound up off the green in a forklift holding an ABC-TV camera.

"I thought I was back in it on 18," Fergus said. "I was really pleased with my second shot,

but it rolled right off the green and into a very bad spot."

A pitch that stayed in the rough behind the green led to a double-bogey, giving Ridley a 2-up victory.

"It's been an unbelievable week for me," Ridley said. "I'm still waiting for someone to knock me on the head and wake me up."

In addition to the U.S. Amateurs, other major events held at CCV include the Southern Amateur and four State Opens won by some of Virginia's brightest stars.

Cruickshank won his first Open in 1933. Danville pro Al Smith, a former tour player, won in 1958. Smith's protégé, former touring pro Bobby Mitchell, won in 1965. Finally, Lanny Wadkins took care of brother Bobby by one shot and the rest of the field by more than that to capture the 1971 VSGA Open.

A lone tree looms over the first tee of the James River Course at the Country Club of Virginia in Richmond. This opening hole is a 424-yard par-4 that gently slopes down to the green and has plenty of water along the right side of the fairway and around the green.

classy designs

The impressive clubhouse at The Virginian Golf Club can
be seen from most of the holes on the back nine.

THE VIRGINIAN
GOLF CLUB

One look at The Virginian Golf Club will have you questioning who really designed this strikingly picturesque layout in the border town of Bristol—Tom Fazio or Tom Swift?

Named the second-best new private course in America by *Golf Digest* in 1994 and No. 53 among the Top 100 Modern Courses by *Golf Week*, The Virginian is a marvel of imagination, design and technology.

In 1997, it made history by becoming the only American course ever to host the State Amateur championships for two states, Virginia and Tennessee. While that may seem odd, Bristol spills over into both states, giving each a reason to consider the course for its most prestigious annual event.

Why not? Located deep in the highlands of Southwestern Virginia, just 95 miles north of Asheville, North Carolina, The Virginian has graced the covers of seven national publications, including *Golf Digest, Links, and Golf.*

"I had the pick of the land and the freedom and flexibility to do what I wanted with it," said Fazio. One of the world's great modern course design-

ers, Fazio collaborated with Larry Best of Land Design Inc., his partner on such beauties as Champion Hills and the Old North State Club at Uwharrie Point, both in North Carolina, and Thornblade in South Carolina.

"I had so much fun working on it," he joked, "I'm almost disappointed it's finished."

Actually, the people fortunate enough to live in Virginia's gorgeous Southern Highlands couldn't wait for Fazio to put the finishing touches on a course that doesn't have to take a backseat to any in the state. Those who visit often sound more than a touch jealous.

"I loved it the moment I saw it," said John Rollins, who won his second of back-to-back Virginia State Amateur championships at The Virginian in 1997. "Every hole was a fun hole to play. When you get a golf course like that, you have such a good feeling, it helps you play better. It was one of the best uses of land I've ever seen."

The 7,005-yard par 72 remains lush and pristine, in part, because of a

The par-3, 13th green (foreground) and the short par-4 12th green are close neighbors in the hilly terrain of the back nine at The Virginian Golf Club in Bristol.

The Virginian Golf Club's signature hole is the lovely 210-yard eighth titled "The Virginian." The hole features a dramatic elevation change from tee to green; the green is fronted by an imposing stream with a patio and gazebo that has a waterfall running under it.

computer-controlled irrigation and fertilization system called Network 8000, designed and engineered by Toro Corporation.

The system is based on an evapotranspiration system that is calculated by a weather station located on the course. The station monitors and measures a number of factors and calculates the course's need for irrigation. Part of the system delivers liquid fertilizer as the course is irrigated, maintaining a constant moisture level in the soil, as well as the proper amount of nutrients.

But that's just the beginning of the story.

There are ecological considerations galore at The Virginian, making it one of the country's most environmentally conscious communities.

There are 10,371 trees, shrubs, and flowers at the front entrance of the club, seven miles off Interstate 81.

The Virginian's fairways are sodded with 40 acres of Zoysia grass, which requires 60 percent less water and 35 percent fewer chemicals to maintain.

The artesian well located on the stunning, downhill par-3 eighth hole pumps five million gallons of water daily.

There are more than 19 miles of drainage pipe underground, enabling The Virginian to recycle 27.3 million gallons of water per year.

The Virginian contains more than 700 miles of communication cable underground, which serves 1,427 sprinkler heads and 37 satellite controllers.

While Fazio did his best to create his own weather, he realized he could not control the real thing. The cart path between the 13th green and 14th tee passes through a tunnel that also serves as a storm shelter in which as many as 16 carts can take refuge. It is wired and grounded for lightning protection.

Fazio's 13th green may be his finest work in Bristol. It sits below slopes that are covered with tall grasses, the main stage of a brilliant amphitheater peaceful enough for a pastor to preach a sermon in.

It would also be the ideal setting for a cluster of houses, but everyone involved in the planning and design of The Virginian rejected anything that might take away from the aesthetic grandeur of this magnificent hole.

"The greens were perfect," Rollins recalled. "If you hit it on the green, all you had to do was get your putt on line. They rolled true from start to finish.

"It was my first time playing on Zoysia fairways. They were unbelievable. It gave me such a good feeling because I knew the fairways were going to be good. We play good golf courses in the State Amateurs. Some of them are even great. To me, everything about The Virginian made you feel special, like this was more than an amateur event."

The Virginian played host to the 1994 Virginias vs. Carolinas team matches, won 148-68 by the Carolinas. In 1995, it played host to the Tennessee State Four-Ball championship. In 2003, it will play host to the U.S. Senior Amateur Championship, its first U.S. Golf Association event.

Meanwhile, the accolades keep pouring in.

The Robb Report named The Virginian the third-best golf community in America. It also called it one of the best 18 places in America to live.

It's little wonder Fazio said, "I like the way the whole place feels. From the country drive to get there, through the stone entrance walls, you know something special is going on out there."

The par-3 13th could be an unlucky undertaking for many who play this mammoth golf hole. Measuring 235 yards from the back tees, it's all carry over a gorge up to an elevated green with daunting tall native grasses whispering in the wind.

classy designs
The James River Country Club clubhouse in Newport News
viewed from the circular drive in front of the building.
The museum is located in the wing to the left.

JAMES RIVER
COUNTRY CLUB

Jim McMenamin's name won't be found on any list of the world's great golf-course architects. The Hampton native designed one course, James River Country Club in Newport News, then quit while he was ahead.

McMenamin's narrow, tree-lined 6,400-yard layout, a par-70, can be a friend to those who play the game with accurate, precise shots off the tee, though they still must navigate cozy greens surrounded by rough and sand. It is an exercise in futility for the big boomer who can't keep his hands off the driver.

James River's greens were rebuilt and design modifications made by Lester George in a 1994 modernization. Nonetheless, James River is a fine example of classic work done by someone who had a complete understanding of the game's nuances.

McMenamin obviously learned a considerable amount from Donald Ross, who was hired in 1926 by officials of Norfolk Country Club to design their new course. McMenamin, a much-admired amateur and local pro, was hired a year later as club professional, but was also instrumental in aiding in the construction of Ross's plan.

McMenamin, so beloved by the members of the defunct Norfolk CC that they erected a monument to him at what is now known as Sewell's Point GC, then turned his attention to James River, which opened on July 4, 1932. James River's famous golf museum, located in the left wing of the clubhouse, opened the same day.

When the *Daily Press* of Newport News compiled a fanciful list of the Virginia Peninsula's toughest 18 holes, an area that stretched the 50 miles from Williamsburg to Norfolk, James River was well represented.

The first hole is a 445-yard par 4 that has been made only slightly less daunting in recent years by the removal of a huge tree on the right side that blocked the players' view of about half of the green.

The other James River contribution to the "toughest 18" is No. 3, a 216-yard par 3 that plays slightly uphill. There is water to carry from tee to green,

The short par-3 17th hole at James River Country Club in Newport News is only 155 yards from the back tees, but looks much longer because it demands a forced carry over the water.

The mammoth 482-yard, par-4 18th hole at the James River Country Club in Newport News finishes up at a clubhouse that nudges the James River.

and an enormous trap left of the putting surface that swallows shots hit even a smidgen off line.

James River has twice played host to the State Open, won by Claude King of Virginia Beach in 1961 and Rick Bendall of Danville in 1970.

It also played host to the State Amateur in 1978, when Sam Wallace of Williamsburg defeated John Cuomo of Roanoke, and in 1993, when David Partridge of Richmond won.

Mid-Amateurs Dicky Linkous of Roanoke and Allen Barber of Yorktown captured the state title in that age category in 1987 and '97, respectively.

Finally, one year before he turned pro, Davis Love III won the 1984 Mid-Atlantic Golf Association crown at James River.

However, no one would argue that the club's main contribution to the game lies in its wondrous museum, which was likely the first of its kind in the world.

Ironically, the man responsible for bringing the museum into being neither played the game nor knew much about it.

Archer M. Huntington, principal owner of the Newport News Shipbuilding and Drydock Company, had a passion for collecting that is evidenced by the 10 museums he is credited with founding throughout the United States.

In 1931, Huntington not only offered to fund the wing at James River CC in which the museum is housed, he dispatched an assistant plant engineer to Scotland with a simple, yet overwhelming, assignment.

John Campbell was instructed to buy everything—clubs, balls, books—he could find about golf that he considered of value or of museum quality.

Campbell, a native of Glasgow and an avid student of the game, spent Huntington's money with relish. He returned with treasures that even today are the envy of golf organizations throughout the world.

Officially opened on July 4, 1932—predating the U.S. Golf Association's museum by almost two decades—the Golf Museum and Library houses close to 2,000 artifacts that demonstrate how the game was played from its birth to today.

It is the home of the world's oldest identifiable club, a Simon Cossar putter dating back to 1790-1800.

How do they know? Cossar, a celebrated club-maker in his day, rubbed the putter with a red keel that gave the wood a sparkling finish. Red keel was used on clubs made prior to 1820, before resin varnish was invented.

There also are nine clubs made by Hugh Philip, the first official club-maker to the Royal & Ancient Golf Club of St. Andrews.

One Philip-made spoon is stamped with the initials "R.T.B," for Major Robert T. Boothby. He was the primary person responsible for bringing Old Tom Morris back to St. Andrews from Prestwick in 1865. Morris is credited with helping to set up the first British Open in 1860. He finished second to Willie Park that year, but won the tournament on four other occasions.

Just a few feet from Philip's club is the putter Horace Rawlins struck at the Newport Golf Club in Rhode Island in 1895 to win the first U.S. Open. Not far from there is the bag and complete set of clubs Great Britain's Harry Vardon used in capturing the 1900 U.S. Open at the Chicago Golf Club.

Although many American players of the day used British-crafted equipment, the clubs Vardon swung were American-made and were some of Spalding's earliest productions.

In a case just to the left of the front entrance are three clubs donated by Bobby Jones, including the George Duncan-crafted brassie that Jones used in winning the 1930 Grand Slam.

Jones obviously had a sense of the historical significance of his gift, and sent along with it the following note:

"This is the brassie I used continuously from May, 1926, until after the amateur championship at Merion in 1930. It therefore had a part in winning every championship which I won, beginning with the British Open qualifying rounds at Sunningdale in 1926 and ending with the amateur championship at Merion in 1930."

The world's oldest golf ball is also on display. It was made around 1790. There are 150 other items that demonstrate the evolution of the ball.

Curator Weymouth B. Crumpler presides over the book containing the world's first known reference to golf. *Black Acts*, the first printed collection of Scottish laws, was published in 1566 and covered the period from 1424 to 1566.

In addition, the museum is home to *Scots Lawes and Actes*, published by Johannes Skene of Edinburgh in 1597, an update of *Black Acts*.

The two books covered the reigns of James I, II, III, IV, V, and VI, and Mary, Queen of Scots; and they contain the records of laws prohibiting the playing of the game on the domains of King James. Concerned because His Majesty's forces were spending more time playing golf than practicing their archery, he issued a defense-of-the-realm act that removed the clubs from their hands.

One of the floor cases contains a scale model of St. Andrews, reproduced from the map belonging to Dr. Alister MacKenzie, for many years considered the most accurate map of the Old Course.

There's a small exhibit devoted to the course-record 62 that Norfolk-born Curtis Strange shot on the Old Course in the 1987 Dunhill Cup.

Although the club is private, the museum and library are open to the public. Mamie Eisenhower, Elizabeth Taylor, and Arnold Palmer are among the thousands who have visited.

Some treasures on display at the museum inside James River CC.

classy designs

A challenge at any distance, the par-3 11th hole at
Washington Golf & Country Club plays 196 yards
from the blue tees, 170 from the whites.

WASHINGTON GOLF & COUNTRY CLUB

The rolling, hilly fairways offer beautiful views of some of Washington's most famous attractions, a relentless test of golf and more than a little history.

Thousands of Union soldiers camped on the land on which the Washington Golf and Country Club in Arlington stands today. The club has been a favorite getaway for several U.S. presidents and has played an important role in the development of the game in and around Washington, D.C.

In 1894, members of a literary group called the Metropolitan Club founded the Washington Golf Club on the Virginia side of the Potomac River. The nine-hole layout was the second in the state after The Homestead Course in Hot Springs. It was an instant success and an immediate social attraction for Washingtonians and Northern Virginians.

In 1896, the Washington Golf Club was welcomed as a member of the U.S. Golf Association, then only one year old. For a time, the club played host to an annual tournament in December in which anyone who was a member of the USGA was invited to compete.

The nine holes measured 2,680 yards, formidable for those days. Alas, the members didn't have a long time to test their skills on it.

In 1907, the owners of the land on which the course sat decided not to renew their lease with the club because they wanted to build on the property. After a couple of aborted opportunities to find a new home, 75 acres of nearby farmland were purchased from Adm. Presley M. Rixey.

Rixey had been a close friend of and physician to President William McKinley. Loyal to the McKinley family after the president's assassination, Rixey was appointed surgeon general by President Theodore Roosevelt. After deeding the land to the club, Rixey designed and built the new course and played a primary role in the club's history.

Just two years later, Donald Ross was hired to develop a new course.

Washington's G&CC's par-3 ninth hole.

classy designs

Golfing great Walter Hagen tees off
at Cavalier.

THE CAVALIER
GOLF AND YACHT CLUB

Opened in 1927 and designed by New York architect Charles H. Banks, each hole at The Cavalier Golf and Yacht Club in Virginia Beach is a reproduction of a famous hole found on courses in the United States, England, Bermuda, and Scotland.

Of those, the 202-yard par-3, 18th is likely the most interesting. Fashioned after the famous Redan hole in North Berwick, Scotland, a saucer-shaped green is surrounded on three sides by water, and contoured to deflect errant shots into Birdneck Point.

The first time he saw it, Gene Sarazen called it "the toughest finishing hole in the country."

Cavalier's 11th hole is a 180-yard par 3 over water, to an elevated green. It was patterned after No. 12 at Augusta National.

Cavalier has played host to a variety of professional events, perhaps more than any course in the state. Certainly, it has been the venue for the greatest variety of events in Virginia.

In 1932, the first Cavalier Open was staged. Paul Runyan won and made history by becoming the first pro player to shoot four consecutive rounds under par.

Sidney Banks, president of the nearby Cavalier Hotel and no relation to the course's architect, was always on the lookout for something extraordinary. In 1948, he found it in the Specialists Tournament.

It began when Banks read a syndicated column by Byron Nelson in which Nelson said he'd like to see a match in which the players hit only the shots for which they were most famous.

Banks contacted the Golf Writers Association of America, asking them to pick two teams manned by the players who were best at driving, long irons, short irons, trouble shots, and putting. The 18-hole event was held in April, as part of the 1948 Cavalier Open.

Sarazen and Walter Hagen, who was president of Cavalier G&YC that year, agreed to serve as captains. Ben Hogan and Sam Snead were obvious

The Bermuda grass is still dormant, but these two golfers enjoy a warm spring day at the Cavalier Golf & Yacht Club. These two are heading toward the peninsula green on the 18th hole, a difficult 205-yard, par 3 that is all carry over water.

The par-3, 11th at the Cavalier Golf & Yacht Club is another tricky hole, with more water to navigate. But the hole only measures 178 yards from the gold tees.

short irons. Dick Metz, runner-up in the 1938 U.S. Open and eventually Cavalier's touring pro, was the troubleshooter. Bobby Locke, just over from South Africa, was the designated putter. Sarazen's alternates were Ed Furgol and Chandler Harper, both of whom would go on to win major championships.

The golf cart had not been invented yet, so it was assumed that everyone would walk. Not Hagen. The Marine Corps finally provided jeeps for both captains, who rode down the middle of the fairway, followed by 14 players, 14 caddies, a referee, and thousands of spectators.

The captains arrived at the ball first, surveyed the situation and huddled with their teams. Even the gallery shouted out who they wanted to see hit the next shot and, gradually, a decision was reached.

The event was broadcast by NBC, with Walter Hagen Jr. and John Derr providing commentary.

Sarazen's team won 5 and 3 in a match that was generally viewed as anticlimactic. Thomson and Harbert were erratic off the tee, and the captains wasted no time deviating from the format and substituting other players on the tee.

Worsham won the 54-hole Cavalier Open with a 9-under 198. Total prize money for the tournament was $10,000, but each of the 17 participants, including the referee, was guaranteed $500. The deal was sweetened when Banks offered to give the players and their wives free rooms at his swank hotel, which sat high atop one of the few hills in Virginia Beach, a few hundred yards from the Atlantic Ocean.

In the summer of 1947, George Payton of Newport News won the State Open at Cavalier, beating a field that included Snead, Bobby Cruickshank, and Harper. Payton received the trophy from famed actor Joseph Cotten, a Petersburg native.

choices for the teams, but neither could compete. Hogan was ill and declined an invitation. Snead had a schedule conflict.

Even so, both teams had plenty of marquee appeal.

Driving for Hagen's squad was Jimmy Thomson, runner-up in the U.S. Open and PGA. Johnny Palmer, Eastern Open champion and a former runner-up to Snead in the PGA Championship, was chosen to play long irons. Jimmy Demaret, famous at the time as the 1940 and '47

Masters champion, was chosen for his short-iron play. Lawson Little, the 1940 U.S. Open champion, was the designated troubleshooter. Jim Ferrier, the 1947 PGA winner, was the putter. Lew Worsham, the '47 Open champion, and Bob Hamilton, '44 PGA winner, were Hagen's alternates.

Driving for Sarazen's team was Chick Harbert, the '47 PGA winner and future Hall of Fame member. Byron Nelson, already a Masters, U.S., and British Open winner, was to play long-iron shots. Herman Keiser, winner of the '46 Masters, played

Payton joined the tour shortly thereafter, and in just six months, he had risen to eighth on the money list.

Ben Hogan watched him play and called him "one of the best young players in the country."

In October, the 24-year-old Payton died 15 days after a car in which he was a passenger struck a railroad viaduct abutment on Chicago's west side, just a few miles from a tournament in which he was playing. Also in the car was pro Ralph Guldahl, winner of two U.S. Opens and a Masters, who escaped unharmed.

"He was one of the really outstanding youngsters," PGA president Ed Dudley said. "I've been saying all along that Payton, Lew Worsham, and Johnny Palmer were the three outstanding men who might be classed as comparative newcomers. He was a great medal player with a fine competitive edge."

Forty-eight hours after Payton died, in a match already arranged, the Cavalier hosted what turned out to be a memorial exhibition.

Worsham, the reigning Open champion and a close friend of Payton's, was joined by Babe Didrikson Zaharias, Walter Hagen Jr., and State Amateur champion Jack Hamilton.

From that exhibition grew the Payton Memorial Tournament, which is still held annually at Cavalier and draws some of the best talent, 24 years and younger, from throughout the mid-Atlantic region.

In 1946, Snead and Harper squared off in what may have been the most exciting Virginia State Open ever. Harper, who was seeking his fifth Open crown, trailed Snead by nine strokes at the start of the final 18 holes.

He shaved seven strokes off his deficit in the first six holes, then picked up two more strokes on the back nine to fashion a course-record 63 and tie his rival.

The 18-hole playoff between the two was postponed for one week to Easter Sunday. With more than 2,000 spectators following step-by-step, Snead fell behind by three strokes on the front side before blazing back on 16-18 to win by three shots.

In 1957, the Cavalier played host to what Norfolk golf writer Tom Fergusson termed "the most fabulous tournament of the women's circuit."

The Triangle Round Robin Classic lasted just two years, but featured the greatest names in the game competing in one of the most creative formats ever devised.

Mickey Wright, Betsy Rawls, Louise Suggs, Patty Berg, Marilyn Smith, Betty Jameson, Marlene Hagge, and Fay Crocker were among the headliners. Babe Zaharias telephoned tournament director Jack McAuliffe daily from the Houston hospital where she was battling cancer.

The purse was $12,000, the highest ever offered the women pros. Sixteen players competed, divided into foursomes. Each received a point for every stroke by which she beat the other players in her group. She also lost a point for every stroke by which she was beaten.

All players were matched against each other at some point in the five days of competition. The sponsor was the Triangle Conduit and Cable Company of New Brunswick, New Jersey. The president was McAuliffe, an avid proponent of women's golf.

In 1954, the tournament was held at the Cascades in Hot Springs. A couple of weeks later, Norfolk golfer Tommy Whillock was in Hot Springs to play in the State Amateur.

Whillock, who later became pro at City Park in Portsmouth, was walking through the Cascades clubhouse when he spotted a program left over from the Round Robin. He brought it to Banks, who acted on it immediately.

"It went over big," Whillock said. "It was new and the people loved it. The Cavalier course was ideal for the ladies to play off the men's white tees. The layout of the course made it easy for the gallery to follow what was going on because they could easily cross from the front nine to the back nine."

Berg, who was among the first women inducted into the LPGA Hall of Fame, agreed with Whillock's assessment.

"This place is paradise," she said. "And this golf course is out of this world."

Hagge won the '57 Round Robin by 22 points over Joyce Ziske. Hagge shot what was then an LPGA 72-hole record 286, though when *The Virginian-Pilot* made note of that in a story that wire services moved across the country, a writer from Tampa, Florida, immediately challenged its accuracy. He claimed Jameson had shot 285 at the Sarasota Open the year before.

Ultimately, Hagge's record was allowed to stand when it was discovered that Jameson's score had been made under winter rules.

Crocker defeated Wright by five points the following year, after which the tournament moved elsewhere.

The last great event at Cavalier may have taken place on May 31, 1965. Jack Nicklaus and local amateur Billy Kellam played three-time State Open champion Claude King and local amateur Les Watson on "Claude King Day."

Nicklaus shot 35-32-67 to lead his team to a one-shot victory, 143-144.

classy designs

Virginia Beach native Curtis Strange addresses the crowd gathered at the grand reopening ceremonies of Bide-A-Wee in Portsmouth.

BIDE-A-WEE

Chandler Harper had already secured the land for his new $200,000 golf course. He had already signed a deal with able Fred Findlay, then 84 years old, to do the design.

What he didn't have was a name for his exciting new venture. Having sifted through dozens of suggestions, Harper wondered if Findlay might have an idea.

The Scot launched into a story. As a child, he had once told his mother that he was going to run away from home.

"She said to me, 'Son, you had better bide-a-wee,'" Findlay told Harper.

"Bide-a-wee?" Harper repeated. "What does it mean?"

"Stay a little longer," Findlay explained. "Linger awhile."

Wasn't that exactly the message Harper hoped his new course would convey? His goal was to build a private club where people of modest means could enjoy a top-flight test of golf and not have to work a second job to pay for it.

"Bide-A-wee," Harper kept repeating to himself.

It became the home of the Portsmouth City Amateur, one of the oldest events of its kind in the United States. Under Harper's direction, it also became the American home for the World Seniors championship in the late 1960s and '70s, perhaps the most exciting precursor to today's Senior PGA Tour.

Russell Breeden, living in Charlottesville at the time and hankering for a career in course design, came with Findlay to help with the project. He would stay on for four years as greenskeeper before embarking on a successful design career of his own.

Bide-A-Wee was difficult from birth. Ground was broken on Dec. 1, 1954. Immediately, millions of deep-rooted reeds were discovered embedded in the soil. Findlay's crew had to plow the earth three times before the roots were broken enough to put down a passable fairway. The earth was so sour that Findlay had to lay down half a million pounds of lime.

"Waterloo" is the perfect name for the hazardous par-3 12th hole at the newly redesigned Bide-A-Wee golf course in Portsmouth.

Despite the problems, the front nine opened in less than a year. The back nine was ready in April 1956 and was celebrated with an exhibition featuring Harper, baseball legend Dizzy Dean, Duke University All-American and Portsmouth native Clarence "Ace" Parker, and touring pro Tommy Bolt.

The course oozed personality. Harper appreciated the fact that every hole at Augusta National, The Homestead Course, and the Cascades had names. He decided to follow suit.

The fifth hole, a 607-yard par 5, is called the "George Bayer" because when it was built, George Bayer was the biggest hitter in the game.

The seventh, a 230-yard par 3 over water, was originally called "Loch Essie," after Harper's wife. That was changed to "Loch McCoy" in 1999, in honor of Portsmouth deputy city manager Luke McCoy. He was a prime mover in the restoration and massive renovation of the course by Tom Clark and Curtis Strange.

The 14th was originally called "Loch Findlay," but changed to "Pinehurst" for the '99 reopening.

In 1959, Bide-A-Wee played host to the Virginia PGA Open, won by Al Smith of Danville. That event would return in 1961, 1966, and 1980. When Elizabeth Manor Country Club was in renovation in 1999, Bide-A-Wee stepped in to host the Eastern Amateur.

Harper won the 1968 PGA Seniors Championship at Palm Beach Gardens. At the time, Teacher's Scotch sponsored a match between the British and American PGA Senior champions. Harper defeated Max Faulkner at Downfield Club in Dundee, Scotland.

The victory itself wasn't overly important to Harper's career because he had left the regular Tour in '55, and there was only a token senior schedule to play. However, when Teacher's pulled its sponsorship of the World Seniors Championship in '68, Harper arranged to have the match continued at Bide-A-Wee. After a three-year run, he persuaded the British and American PGAs to play the match in Great Britain in even years and at Bide-A-Wee in odd-numbered years.

The first of those scheduled 36-hole matches featured Bolt against 53-year-old John Panton of Scotland and turned out to be a classic.

Bolt, 51, finally won by holing a nine-foot putt on the third hole of sudden death, though that hardly tells the story. The match, which required nine hours to play, begun in bright sunshine and blistering heat, was interrupted by a sudden downpour after 27 holes and finished in more withering early-September heat.

Panton, 2-down with two holes to play, staved off elimination by sinking birdie putts of 27 and 23 feet on the 35th and 36th holes, respectively. He and Bolt halved the 37th hole with birdies, after which Panton lipped out a 15-footer for birdie on No. 38 that would have meant victory.

"John Panton is the finest competitor I've ever played," Bolt said graciously. "And I don't know if there are any better competitors around."

In '71, Sam Snead and Faulkner squared off. Once again, the temperature was in the low 90s. Faulkner, who had publicly questioned how much ability the 59-year-old Snead had left, dressed in heavy wool socks and plus-4s. Although he changed outfits during the lunch break, he didn't change into anything cooler.

Faulkner led 5-up through 15 holes, but melted down the stretch in losing 3 and 2.

The last match at Bide-A-Wee was in 1977, won by Christy O'Connor of Ireland 4 and 3 over Julius Boros.

In 1991, Portsmouth officials informed Harper they would not renew his lease on Bide-A-Wee when it expired the following year. There was an increasing public outcry over the fact that Bide-A-Wee was a private, tax-free club located on public property.

Like many private clubs throughout the United States, Bide-A-Wee had no black members. Critics charged that its membership and admission policies were designed to keep it that way, although blacks had played the course in 1988 after Harper opened it for limited public play.

In spring 1992, Harper offered to buy the property and course for $1.5 million, plus spend another $150,000 in improvements. His offer was rejected.

After being closed for 15 months for renovation guided by Clark and Strange, Bide-A-Wee reopened to the public on April 6, 1999. As many as 5,000 trees, planted by Findlay and Harper 40 years before, had been removed. Miles of drainage had been installed. Eight new ponds had been built. New tees, fairways, bunkers, and greens had been constructed, as well as concrete cart paths.

What Clark and Strange didn't alter significantly was Findlay's routing or the narrow greens that were a hallmark of the original course.

Harper attended the reopening ceremonies. He received public praise from Portsmouth mayor James Holley, once an adversary, for his past service to the city.

Harper surveyed the $8 million in improvements and professed approval.

"My God, it reminds me of Augusta National," he said following the ceremony, lingering with friends in the pro shop while a new generation of golfers prepared to do the same out on the course.

The 501-yard 10th hole is known as "Between the Ponds"
for reasons that become obvious once you play it.

classy designs

Birdwood's fourth hole is a 179-yard par-3
from an elevated tee to a well-protected
green below, surrounded by water.

BIRDWOOD GOLF CLUB

Birdwood Golf Club in Charlottesville was intended to be a stern challenge for the scratch college golfer who had his eye on the pro ranks, a pleasurable getaway for the high handicapper, an oasis for those wanting to drink in the beauty of the Blue Ridge.

Give professor/architect Lindsay Ervin an A-plus on all counts.

Opened in May 1984 just a few miles west of the heart of the University of Virginia, Birdwood is a 6,800-yard, par-72 treat that sits on 170 acres of historic university property.

Considered one of the finest college courses in the United States, Birdwood played host to the 1990 State Amateur won by Hank Klein of Richmond 1-up over Mike Grant of Radford.

It also played host to the 1987 VSGA Junior Championship in which Kevin South of Richmond defeated Jon Hurst of Woodbridge by four strokes in a 54-hole event.

The University of Virginia played its Cavalier Classic at Birdwood from 1986 to 1996 and again in 1999. As many as seven of the strongest college teams from the Atlantic Coast Conference, Southeast Conference, and regional and national powers compete each year.

David Duval, then attending Georgia Tech, won in 1992 and 1993. In 1994, Virginia student Simon Cooke of Richmond set a tournament record with an 8-under-par 208 to defeat Stewart Cink of Georgia Tech and Richard Johnson of Augusta College by two shots.

The U.S. Golf Association discovered Birdwood in 1991 and brought to town the Women's Amateur Public Links Championship. Tracy Hanson, a sophomore at San Jose State, fell 3-down after six holes, then charged back to defeat Carri Wood of Mississippi State 1-up in the final.

Two months later, Birdwood played host to state qualifying for the U.S. Men's Amateur held in August at The Honors Course near Chattanooga, Tennessee.

"You had to walk 36 holes," University of Virginia golf coach Mike Moraghan said. "If you've ever been to Charlottesville in July, you know that there are days it simply isn't physically possible to do that because it's so hot. The night before, a cold front moves into the area, and the next day the temperature is in the 70s.

"It was a miracle."

Miraculous, too, are Birdwood's views.

The glory of Virginia's rolling countryside is visible from the third, fourth, and ninth holes on the front side; the 11th, 12th, and 16th holes on the inward nine.

Once you venture from the clubhouse, Birdwood exists on pristine land unscathed by houses, a natural retreat to a distant time in America's history.

In 1819, owner William Garth began building the brick mansion that is the property's centerpiece. He employed laborers who were building Thomas Jefferson's famous Rotunda at the same time. Birdwood Pavilion, though now

vacant, still stands, and there are occasional rumors the university plans to restore it to its former glory or incorporate it as part of a "new" clubhouse.

In March 1865, Union soldiers under the command of Gen. George Armstrong Custer marched through Birdwood, headed for Lynchburg. According to an account by Ada Pyne Bankhead, a 20-year-old resident of Birdwood at the time, the soldiers raided the plantation, destroying parts of the property and stealing horses and cattle.

"*All the fowls on the place were stolen, all eatables of*

An aerial view of Birdwood.

every description taken, except one side of bacon and a small sack of meal, which was presented to the cook," Miss Bankhead wrote in a memoir excerpted in 1979 by *The Daily Progress* of Charlottesville. "*And I have to thank that raid for having taught me to eat corn bread and bacon.... After all the damage was done, there came a note from the Captain of Massachusetts Cavalry (camped in the woods) to my grandmother, saying he sent her two guards, with orders to allow no one to enter the house, and hoping that 'his men would no more disgrace the uniform they wore.*"

In 1967, the University of Virginia purchased its first 550 acres of the Birdwood estate. Seven years later, it had acquired the rest. Originally, dormitories were to be built there, but the project was never acted on.

"The university probably wanted a golf course for a long time," said then-Virginia athletic director Dick Schulz.

A $1 million gift from Mrs. W. Alton Jones of Charlottesville lifted the golf-course project off the ground. In 1999, Birdwood merged with the university's Boar's Head Inn, and the course was opened to the public.

strokes of genius

Fred Findlay designed more than 30 courses in Virginia,
including some of the most revered.

VIRGINIA'S DESIGNER

FRED FINDLAY

THE PATRIARCH OF VIRGINIA GOLF

Fred Findlay was a jack of all trades and a master of them all, particularly if they pertained to golf.

Although the exact number has never been ascertained, there is little doubt Findlay designed more golf courses in Virginia than anyone else. In a 1959 interview with the *Daily Progress* of Charlottesville, he estimated that his latest creation, Meadowbrook Country Club in Richmond, was his 33rd in Virginia.

If so, Findlay would have created 36 courses in the Commonwealth, and more than 100 throughout the world, by the time he died in 1966 at the age of 93. Yet in other interviews, Findlay admitted uncertainty about how many Virginia courses he had designed.

The debate is immaterial. Findlay's impact on the sport in Virginia extends to every corner.

He designed and built the Country Club of Virginia's River Course in Richmond, where he also served as greenskeeper and course superintendent from 1935 to 1945.

He designed Farmington Country Club in Charlottesville, where he lived with his daughter and son-in-law from 1945 until his death.

He designed the original course at Keswick. Boonsboro Country Club near Lynchburg is a Findlay creation. So was the original Bide-A-Wee near the sea in Portsmouth, Ole Monterey in mountainous Roanoke, and Falling River in Appomattox.

Findlay's layouts have played host to dozens of important Virginia tournaments and continue to do so.

"Before starting a course design, I just walk over the site for a couple of days and study Nature's own work," he said. "Nature herself gives me most of my ideas."

In so many ways, Findlay was a Renaissance man.

Born in Montrose, Scotland, in 1872, Findlay had an artistic bent that he concealed from his father, Alexander, a sergeant major in the British Army who thought his son should follow suit. Fred hid a sketch pad in his bedroom, showing his work to his mother only when they were alone.

The 567-yard par-5, seventh hole at Farmington CC, a wonderful Fred Findlay design opening in May 1929. Findlay designed the North and South nines.

FRED FINDLAY'S LEGACY

1. Augusta CC (1927)
2. Bide-A-Wee CC (with R.F. Loving Sr., 1955)
3. Boonsboro CC (1927)
4. Carper Valley GC (1934)
5. Crater CC (1934)
6. CC of Culpeper (with R.F. Loving Sr., 9 holes, 1960)
7. Falling River CC (with R.F. Loving Sr., 1928)
8. Farmington CC (1928)
9. Glenwood CC (1925)
10. Hopewell CC (1940)
11. Hunting Hills CC (with R.F. Loving Sr. and Buddy Loving, 1965)
12. Ingleside CC (1926)
13. Keswick CC of Virginia (1938)
14. Lakeview CC (with R.F. Loving Sr. and Buddy Loving, 1926)
15. Laurel GC (1926)
16. Lawrenceville GC (with R.F. Loving Sr., 1960)
17. Luray GC (1934)
18. McIntire Park GC (with R.F. Loving Sr., 9 holes, 1952)
19. Meadowbrook CC (with R.F. Loving Sr., 1959)
20. Ole Monterey CC (1925)
21. Shenandoah CC (1942)
22. South Boston CC (1942)
23. South Hill CC (1935)
24. Spotswood CC (1935)
25. Swannanoa GC (1926)
26. Tides Inn and CC (9 holes, 1950)
27. Waynesboro CC (1950)
28. Williamsburg CC (1935, no longer exists)
29. Williamsburg Inn GC (9 holes, 1960)
30. Winchester GC (with R.F. Loving Sr., 1960)
31. Wytheville CC (9 holes, 1931)

RENOVATED COURSES

1. CC of Virginia (James River Course, 1931)
2. CC of Virginia (Westhampton Course, 1931)
3. Washington G&CC
4. Woodberry Forest GC (with R.F. Loving Sr.)

Findlay was 13 years old when his mother died. Soon thereafter, his father enlisted him in the army as a trumpeter. During the next 21 years, Findlay developed into a solo cornetist for the Portsmouth Royal Artillery military band, performed several concerts before Queen Mary, and eventually was elevated to bandmaster.

Already a scratch golfer who had helped lay out some courses in Scotland, Findlay resigned from the British army while he was stationed in Australia. Although he hoped to become a music teacher, he instead worked 12 years as the head golf pro at the Metropolitan Club in Melbourne and began to dabble in course architecture.

Perhaps the greatest influence in his life was his older brother Alexander, who emigrated to Philadelphia years earlier and was one of the true pioneers of golf in the United States.

In addition to designing courses in 19 states, Alex Findlay was noted for playing a series of exhibitions with Harry Vardon that helped introduce golf to America. In 1926, Alex Findlay visited the Vatican, where he tried unsuccessfully to design a six-hole course.

The Findlay brothers were close-knit. "I remember the night when he left Scotland for America," Fred recalled in a 1951 interview. "I cried and wanted to come with him. He patted my head and said, 'Not yet, laddie, you're a bit too young. Let me go to America and get the game started. Then I'll call for you and you can carry on.'"

After the death of their only son in Australia, the Fred Findlays came to Virginia to visit their daughter in the early 1920s and stayed.

In 1945, having designed 20 courses in Virginia, Findlay moved to Charlottesville to live with his daughter and son-in-law.

"I came to retire," he once joked, "but it looks like the people won't let me."

Indeed, Findlay completed 10 courses in Virginia after '45.

Part of what made Findlay special was his disdain for artificiality. He didn't carve up the land and redistribute it to meet his needs. He took what the land offered and allowed it to guide his hand.

It isn't something one can see from his contour maps or elaborate design prints. Findlay didn't believe in them.

As someone who frequently shot his age during the last 20 years of his life, Findlay believed in giving a golfer a break. He specialized in the short par 4. Most of his designs feature at least one hole where the long hitter or even the average player on his "A" game can drive the green.

Findlay never surrendered his desire to create art. Although he refused to attempt portraits, his landscape paintings were so striking and richly detailed that the Virginia Museum of Fine Art and several other galleries exhibited them in the 1950s.

Virtually every course designer the world holds in high esteem has left his mark on Virginia: A.W. Tillinghast, Donald Ross, Robert Trent Jones, Rees Jones, George Cobb, William Flynn, and Tom Fazio.

Fred Findlay dwarfs them all.

Fred Findlay surveys his work at Bide-a-Wee.

THE SLAMMER'S MAGIC WAND

SNEAD WINS 1949 PGA

The 1949 PGA Championship at Hermitage Country Club in Richmond ended with the most popular winner possible and an unsolved mystery.

Who loaned native son Sam Snead the putter he used to defeat Jackie Burke, Henry Ransom, Dave Douglas, Jimmy Demaret, Jim Ferrier, and, finally, Johnny Palmer in the May match-play marathon?

Snead, who could start a story at dusk and still enjoy everyone's rapt attention at dawn, wasn't saying.

"The fellow probably has forgotten I have it," a giddy Snead explained after taking Palmer 3 and 2 in the 36-hole final. "If I mention his name, he'll come and get it."

Snead borrowed the putter from a friend during a Winter Tour event. He had used it in Greensboro and won. He had used it at Augusta National and come away with the first green jacket ever awarded.

Now that blade had helped him achieve something unique at Hermitage, a narrow 6,677-yard par 71 that was created by famed architect A.W. Tillinghast and is known today as Belmont Golf Course.

Not only was Snead the first to win Masters and PGA titles in the same season, but by clinching the championship four days after his 37th birthday, he also had become the oldest man ever to win a major.

Snead had needed just 60 putts in the 34 holes it took to beat Palmer. Friends and foes alike agreed during the seven-day tournament that they had never seen Snead stroke the ball so purely.

"The first time I read a story saying Sam Snead can't putt, I'm going to look up the author of that piece and prove it to him," Demaret fumed after Snead beat him 4 and 3. "Sam is a great putter."

Snead played into their curiosity by carrying the putter with him everywhere he went. He guarded it like a piece of Dresden china. During the awards ceremony, someone in the gallery reached for it.

Sam Snead hits out of the dusty rough on his way to the 1949 PGA Championship at the old Hermitage Country Club, now the Belmont Golf Course, in Richmond.

The Louisiana pro had quit a job in Shreveport the month before when club officials tried to cut his salary.

Hill, a protégé of Craig Wood, had been a pro for 19 years. He and Claude Harmon had served as Wood's assistants at Winged Foot in New York. While the famed club provided the ideal stage from which to launch a career, Hill suffered from arthritis and rarely played in national events.

Nonetheless, with Hogan absent, the unemployed Hill was accorded the No. 1 seed after shooting 69-67-136 in qualifying for match play.

Then there was an incident in Snead's first-round match with Jack Burke Jr.

It happened on the 13th hole. Snead had just made birdie, after which both players took their drivers and headed for the 14th tee.

The pace of play was insufferably slow. Many contestants would finish a hole, then drop balls on the green to practice putting before moving to the next tee.

Finally, Snead and Burke hit. When Burke reached his ball, he could find neither his clubs nor caddie Rueben Epps.

PGA officials began a search. Eventually, both were found. Epps had snuck away from the action and was using the bag as a pillow as he napped under a shade tree.

Snead wound up winning 3 and 2.

The fans' dream final was Snead against Lloyd Mangrum, who had dominated the Winter Tour.

"Sure, you can have it," Snead told the man jokingly, "but you've got to take me with it."

That was the last of a long series of episodes involving Snead and an adoring public in Richmond that treated the event like a coronation.

In the middle of the final against Palmer, a fan reached through the gallery ropes, grabbed Snead's hand, and asked him to autograph a program.

"No . . . Not now . . . " a stunned Snead stammered. "I'm a little busy at the moment."

"It was easy to tell where Snead was playing," John Leard of the *Richmond News Leader* wrote. "Oohs and aaahs could be heard from the distant 14th all the way to the clubhouse."

There was no defending champion. Ben Hogan was still home in Texas, recuperating from the life-threatening injuries he had suffered when the car in which he and wife Valerie were riding crashed into a bus.

The medalist during qualifying rounds was Ray Hill, who came to Virginia looking for work.

Mangrum appeared well on his way to making the crowd happy. He whipped two-time PGA champion Denny Shute 6 and 5, Maryland pro Bob Hamilton 3 and 2, Herman Barron of New York 4 and 3 and Ray Hill 7 and 6.

In the semifinals, Mangrum faced Palmer, a 30-year-old North Carolinian, and fell apart, losing 6 and 5.

"I just gave out of gas," Mangrum said. "The grind got me . . . I was so tired, I didn't think I was going to make it."

After disposing of Burke, Snead dumped Henry Ransom of Illinois 3 and 1.

All matches the rest of the tournament were scheduled for 36 holes. Snead's next opponent was Dave Douglas, an unattached pro from Delaware who had beaten Sam by one stroke in the Texas Open earlier in the year.

Snead was visibly upset with his play early. After leaving a 50-foot putt eight feet short, Snead encouraged Douglas to "Shoot her in there, boy. I should lose this hole after that."

Walking off the 11th green during the afternoon round, Snead was heard mumbling to himself: "He can't do anything wrong. I can't do anything, period."

That changed almost immediately.

Three down through 30 holes, Snead won the 31st with a par 3, then ran off a pair of birdies on the 32nd and 33rd holes to draw even.

Douglas refused to fold. He birdied the 34th hole to go 1-up. Snead countered with a par on No. 35 to square the match again.

With a gallery of 5,000 watching, Snead laced a tee shot onto the green of the par-3 18th. Douglas's tee shot hit a tree and bounded down a hill. Snead won the hole and the match with a par.

"I admit I had begun to feel pretty good after the 30th hole," Douglas said. "But I was never really confident I'd win—not even that late and not even

with that advantage. I know Sam too well. He's liable to go crazy at any time."

Snead's quarterfinal match was against wise-cracking Jimmy Demaret, who had won the Masters in 1947.

"Nice going, Sam," Demaret had needled Snead moments after his victory over Douglas, "and good luck in next year's PGA."

Snead let his putter do the talking the next day. With another gallery of 5,000 looking on, Snead holed two putts of 25 feet, one 30-footer, a 15-footer, and one from 12 feet. He finished the morning round 3-up.

The afternoon was more of the same. Snead rolled in a 20-footer, a pair of 12-footers, and another 10-footer. Although the final score was just 4 and 3, there never was any question about who would win.

The beating didn't seem to dampen Demaret's sense of humor.

Snead was studying a 15-foot putt on the 10th green when a radio announcer positioned nearby boomed into his microphone, "Snead is putting now."

Sam backed away, muttering, "Quiet! Please!"

"Keep it up," Demaret shouted to the announcer. "Remember, I'm five down!"

In the semifinals against Jim Ferrier, Snead was 2-down after the morning round and 3-down after two holes of the afternoon 18. When he left a putt short of the hole during the afternoon round, Ferrier told him, "The object is to get the ball to the bottom of the cup."

Snead heard him. He holed a 70-yard wedge shot for eagle on the next hole, then one-putted nine times the rest of the way for a 3-and-2 victory.

Next up was Palmer, a former bomber pilot who had flown 21 missions in the Pacific during World War II. When he returned, he had studied Snead's power game and patterned his own play

with it in mind.

Palmer was 2-up after 16 holes of the morning round before Snead caught him with a birdie and a par on Nos. 17 and 18. Snead never trailed after that, winning the fourth, sixth, and seventh holes in the afternoon with birdies.

"I had my chance," Palmer said. "My irons were just no good. Just look at the score. Sam was six under par for the 34 holes."

That doesn't quite tell the story of just how dominant Snead was as the final match wore on. He made five birdies and just one bogey during the afternoon 18. That came on the ninth hole, the only one Palmer won.

With victories at the Masters and PGA in hand, Snead went to Medinah in Chicago for the U.S. Open. He lost to Cary Middlecoff by one stroke. Other than the fact that Snead never would have been saddled with his Open "jinx," who knows how different golf history would be today had Snead prevailed.

Maybe not as much as you'd think. The Grand Slam as we know it today did not exist.

Many American players skipped the British Open for financial reasons.

The Masters was less than 20 years old. While it was considered a significant event, it didn't hold nearly the status it enjoys today. During the PGA at Hermitage, one Virginia columnist referred to it as the "Little National Open."

The modern "Slam"—Masters, U.S., and British Opens and PGA Championship—didn't come into being until the early 1960s.

Snead, who was not fond of the British Open despite winning it in 1946, already had said he was skipping the '49 event at Royal St. George's.

Would he have changed his mind had he won the three most significant tournaments of the year?

He was one swing from having to decide.

Sam Snead makes a big putt in front of a huge gallery as he wins the 1949 PGA Championship.

making memories

Arnold Palmer easily handled the field at the 1988
Senior Crestar Classic.

LONG LIVE THE KING

PALMER WINS

They came to Hermitage Country Club hoping for a glimpse of the past. Arnold Palmer kept them wide-eyed for three days in a way that hasn't happened since and may never happen again.

He was bold. He was brilliant. He hit some shots where you never thought it possible a pro would go. He hit some recoveries his fans saw in their dreams that night.

He had not won a tournament in three years, but Palmer was in control of the 1988 Crestar Senior PGA Classic from his birdie on the first hole on Friday to his putt-out on the 54th, and final, hole Sunday.

It was Palmer as the conductor of a runaway train, pulling into the station with a final round of 2-under-par 70 to finish at 13-under 203 on Hermitage's Pine and Lake nines. Palmer was four strokes better than Lee Elder, Larry Mowry, and Jim Ferree and a star-studded field that included Bob Charles, Gene Littler, Gardner Dickinson, Bruce Crampton, and Chi Chi Rodriguez.

"When you haven't won in a couple of years, a lot of things go through your mind," Palmer said. "You wonder why you haven't won. You wonder if you're ever going to win again."

Palmer's 70th official PGA victory was fairly easy. Then 59, Palmer finished just a stroke shy of Rodriguez's 1986 tournament record 202. His 36-hole total of 11-under 133 was a 36-hole mark for the event and staked him to a three-shot lead over Walt Zembriski and Bobby Nichols.

"I felt confident, like I was playing well and felt physically well," Palmer said. "I wanted to win very badly, and I felt if I didn't make any bad mistakes, I could."

A crowd estimated at 15,000 was bunched mostly behind Palmer. Like everywhere he goes, he had always been one of the fans' favorites.

They had missed him in 1955 when the U.S. Amateur was staged at Richmond's Country Club of Virginia. Palmer was the defending champion, and there was the fervent hope he would decide to defend his title. He chose instead to turn professional.

By the time he pulled into Richmond to give a 1967 exhibition at Country Club of Virginia's James River Course, Palmer had won four Masters, two British Opens, and a U.S. Open. Such massive crowds were expected that November day that one local newspaper writer even gave "tips" on the best way to see as much of Palmer as possible.

"If you don't have binoculars and don't move briskly, you may not see anything," the writer advised. "You pay your money and you take your chances. It will be good exercise, anyway. And you can always tell your grandchildren that you 'saw' Palmer when he played in Richmond. Who's to know differently?"

The final-round crowd in '88 was more inclined to follow Arnie step-by-step. He did not disappoint.

After opening with a par, Palmer slashed a 1-iron second shot to 25 feet from the cup on the par-5 second hole and two-putted for birdie. Judging from the roar of the gallery, you'd have thought Palmer had done something supernatural.

On No. 3, he rolled in an eight-foot putt for birdie.

Then he received a major break.

His tee shot on the fifth hole looked like it was headed out of bounds. But when he got to the ball, he found it less than a yard inside the marker. While he cursed himself for not picking up what should have been an easy birdie, he thanked his lucky stars for coming away with par.

At No. 9, he finally made a mistake that cost him. Again, it came off the tee, where he drifted considerably left of the target area and into some trees. But Palmer made bogey exciting as only Palmer can, whipping a 4-iron through the trees to the green-side apron, when the safe play would have been sideways to the fairway.

"Hey, the worst thing that could have happened to me was that I hit a tree and made a 5," Palmer shrugged later.

He made 5 anyway, but in the most entertaining manner possible.

On the 10th hole, Palmer was eight feet off the green, 50 feet from the cup, when he elected to putt. Making a brazen stroke, Palmer sent the ball up a hill to four feet from the hole. He knocked it in for the momentum-saving par.

Meanwhile, no one even made a run at him.

Mowry, the defending champion, lost his competitive edge when he sent his second-shot approach to the par-5 16th into the water. It happened while Palmer was making a birdie 3 from 10 feet at the 14th.

Elder was in striking distance until a bogey late in the round. Ferree started strong with a 3-under 33 on the front, but could shoot no better than par on the back nine.

Southpaw George Lanning finished tied for fifth at 208, just five swings in back of Palmer. Lanning did all of his damage on Sunday, closing with a tournament-record 8-under 64.

Palmer would later say that he set a goal of shooting under par on the back nine. He knew he'd be almost impossible to catch if he did. True to his word, he came in at 1-under 35.

All of which made him the focus for an avalanche of affection from the gallery. Palmer did his best to return that emotion later.

"I enjoy the people so much," he said. "To see them out there gives me such a boost of power. The galleries have been so fantastic. Call it an army or gallery, they've been so good to me over the years, and it has meant so much to hear them cheering me on."

Arnold Palmer turned back the clock at the 1988 Crestar Senior PGA Classic.

making memories

Longtime LPGA great Kathy Whitworth flashes a big smile on the
18th green at Sleepy Hole in Portsmouth after winning her record
88th LPGA tournament at the United Virginia Bank Classic.

FIRST FOR THE LAST TIME

WHITWORTH WINS UVB CLASSIC

She had come to the 1984 United Virginia Bank Golf Classic road-weary and battle-fatigued.

Kathy Whitworth had been tied with Sam Snead for most official victories—84—for what seemed like an eternity, although it was barely 14 months.

Everywhere she went, people asked the same question, as though she could predict the future: How soon before you eclipse the great Slammer's mark?

Frankly, Whitworth was tired of it. She needed a rest, especially after a last-place finish at the UVB Classic.

"I was letting the pressures of the public and the press dictate how I was playing," she said. "I knew that if I didn't win my 85th, I could live with it. I couldn't allow myself to care if others couldn't."

Sweet elixir that vacation became. Whitworth ended the '84 season by winning the Rochester Classic, the Safeco Classic, and the Irish Ladies Open—career victories 85, 86, and 87.

When the 1985 season rolled around, Whitworth made a grudging concession to making that wish come true. She would enter just 22 events, her smallest workload in a decade.

There was little doubt that one of those entry forms was going to the Sleepy Hole Golf Course, a quirky little (6,196 yards) public course that had become a favorite stop on the circuit for reasons that had little to do with the golf.

The course represented just a tiny slice of Sleepy Hole Park, which offered a large campground and plenty of open fields. One year, a caddie organized a cookout and a softball game between the players and the caddies. It was such a huge success—Nancy Lopez once said she entered the tourna-

After finishing last at the 1984 UVB Classic Kathy Whitworth finished first in '85.

ment solely so she wouldn't miss the game—that it became a tradition.

None of that was on Whitworth's mind when she arrived at Sleepy Hole, where she had lost a sudden-death playoff to Sally Little three years earlier. Then there was that little matter of the previous year's last-place disaster.

Whitworth came out hot on Saturday, blistering the course for six birdies to take a two-shot lead over Spain's Marta Figueras-Dotti.

She even spun gold out of her one mistake, which came on the par-4 fifth hole.

Whitworth's drive on the 375-yard dogleg right landed in the right rough. Her approach wasn't much better, finishing in a green-side sand trap

that was 60 feet from the pin.

But she holed her explosion for a lucky birdie that got her to 2 under for the day. She finished 36 holes at 9 under.

"When I needed a break, I got one from the sand trap," Whitworth said later. "It is little things like that that give you momentum."

Still within striking distance entering the final round were some of the biggest names on the tour. Alcott, Coles, and Alice Miller were five shots behind. Juli Inkster and Pat Bradley were one stroke closer than that.

But it was Alcott who would put the most heat on the leader, rolling in four short birdie putts on the first 13 holes to pull even with Whitworth.

Even then, Alcott wasn't as steady with the putter as she would have liked, missing three straight 10-foot birdie putts.

When she made par at 18 to finish at 208, all Alcott could do was sit and wait for Whitworth to make a mistake. It certainly seemed possible.

Whitworth drove the ball poorly on the front side, playing it in 2-over 37. She confessed that she suddenly ran out of confidence in her putting.

"I had my chances (to make up strokes) on the front side," she fumed, "and I either over-read or under-read my putts. I was worried about that."

Whitworth opened the back nine by holing a 25-foot birdie putt. Even though she gave it back with a bogey at the par-4 11th, she had calmed herself—and proved it on one of the toughest holes on the LPGA circuit.

The 14th at Sleepy Hole was a 380-yard par 4 that the players had voted the seventh-most difficult hole of 1984. There were thick woods on the right, a ditch on the left that ran almost the entire length of the hole before bisecting the fairway just before the green. Two elevated bunkers had been strategically placed about 230 yards off the tee—prime landing range for the women.

Whitworth's tee shot was substandard, traveling just 205 yards. But she launched a 4-wood 175 yards, laying it to rest 8 feet from the cup., then holed the putt to keep a piece of the lead.

"I started to feel that if I hit it close I could make the putts," she said later.

On the par-4 17th, Whitworth was true to her word, knocking her approach shot to 7 feet from the hole, then dropping the putt that sealed her triumph.

"I really thought Whit would birdie something coming in," Alcott said. "Whitworth knows how to win. If I have to finish second, I like it to be behind her."

making memories

Fred Couples (left) is congratulated by team captain Hale Irwin, right, as the United States defeated the International Team during the inaugural President's Cup matches held at the Robert Trent Jones Golf Club in Gainesville in 1994. The U.S. won the competition 20-12.

U. S. HOISTS FIRST PRESIDENTS CUP

It had the hype and the heroics of a Ryder Cup without the hostility. The Presidents Cup was conceived in the fall of 1993, shortly after the United States defeated Europe in the Ryder Cup at the Belfry in England. The 15-13 U.S. victory convinced then-PGA Tour commissioner Deane Beman and deputy commissioner Tim Finchem that a second event would generate the same excitement.

They went about creating one that would mimic the Ryder Cup format, with several key differences.

Only European-born players are included on the Ryder Cup team that faces the United States. Beman and Finchem, with critical input from Australian Greg Norman and South Africans Nick Price and Ernie Els, decided the International team that would face the U.S. would come from players ineligible by birth from Ryder Cup consideration.

"I always felt that we could do about as well against the top European team with our next 12 guys who didn't make the American [Ryder Cup] team," Finchem said in 1994. "I don't believe they could say the same. I think our tour is that much deeper. I think we'll see that."

In September 1994, his hunch was proven correct.

As 15,000 spectators lined the lush fairways of the magnificent Robert Trent Jones Golf Club in Gainesville, not far from Bull Run, Fred Couples decided the inaugural Presidents Cup competition in America's favor with a shot worthy of the ages.

Couples and Price, then the world's No. 1 player, were locked in a taut duel on the final day. The Americans needed one more point to win.

Couples stood in a fairway bunker on 18, 147 yards from the flag, 9-iron in his hand. Moments later, he sent his ball soaring towards the green, spinning

U.S. captain Hale Irwin exchanges pleasantries
with former President Gerald R. Ford.

Fred Couples (right) accepts congratulations from Nick Price after the U.S. victory in the Presidents' Cup.

the Ryder Cup, organizers made certain that there were some significant differences.

Unlike the Ryder Cup, the Presidents Cup could not end in a tie. Before the competition began, each team captain placed the name of one of his players in an envelope. If the match was even after the regularly scheduled competition, the envelopes would be opened and the captains' choices would play sudden death to determine the winner.

None of the singles matches, the main event saved for the end of the three-day competition, could end in a tie. Players would continue until someone won.

There was no prize money. Net revenues were divided into equal shares that the players and captains designated for charities or golf-related projects of their choice. Contributions in their name were made through PGA Tour Charities, Inc.

Given the name chosen for the event, the PGA Tour wanted to stage the inaugural tournament in Washington. Officials of the Robert Trent Jones Golf Club, just four years old at the time, already had petitioned the PGA Tour, PGA of America, and the U.S. Golf Association about playing host to a major tournament.

Everyone agreed that the 7,238-yard, par-72 layout, which famed architect Robert Trent Jones had declared his finest work ever, was an ideal venue.

"The whole place is a magnificent facility," International team captain David Graham said. "The environment here is as good as this country has to offer."

In March 1994, the decision was made to go

right to left. It hit the rear slope, went into reverse, then started rolling purposefully towards the hole, stopping about 18 inches away.

The crowd erupted, mixing chants of "Freddie . . . Freddie . . . Freddie," with "USA . . . USA . . . USA."

Price smiled as he got to the green and viewed Couples' work. International team captain David Graham doffed his visor and bowed as Couples danced a light jig across the green on his way to the ball.

Price conceded the birdie, then nearly matched it with his chip shot. The ball stopped an inch from the lip.

Couples' 1-up triumph, in which he came from 3-down to win four of the final five holes, gave the U.S. its 17th, and decisive, point in a hard-fought 20-12 victory.

"Freddie's shot was a great one," Price conceded graciously. "It would have been great if I could have made the chip shot, too. But the way it turned out, Freddie deserved to win the match."

Sheepishly, Couples admitted that the Cup was clinched on what he called "a lucky shot."

"I'm not going to stand here and say I hit it right where I aimed it," he explained. "I was just trying to use the slope to my advantage."

Although the Presidents Cup was born out of

ahead with the tournament. Just seven months later, on Friday, Sept. 16, the match was on.

The American team featured Couples, Davis Love III, Corey Pavin, Tom Lehman, Phil Mickelson, Scott Hoch, and John Huston. While all were among the leading money winners on the Tour, at the time only co-captains Hale Irwin and Paul Azinger and Couples had won a major.

The International team began with the top two players on the Sony World Rankings, Price and Norman, though it soon lost Norman.

One of the driving forces behind the event, Norman had to withdraw before the start of play because of a severe abdominal condition that caused him to lose 11 pounds in two weeks. Replacing him was Bradley Hughes, an Australian Tour member who had played in six U.S. events that summer.

Leading the International team were David Frost, Steve Elkington, Frank Nobilo, Vijay Singh, Mark McNulty, and Craig Parry. Only Els, the reigning U.S. Open champion, and Japan's Jumbo Ozaki, who had previously scheduled commitments, turned down the chance to join the Internationals.

From the beginning, both sides went out of their way to exhibit sportsmanship, not gamesmanship. Both teams and their wives stayed in the same hotel. Players from both sides rode to the course together. They shared the same locker room.

"I don't want it to be war," Price said. "I want it to be played in the true spirit of the game. To me, that means play by the rules, applaud a person's good shot, a genuinely good feeling you have out there, and may the guy who plays the best golf win."

Early in opening matches delayed for nearly two hours by fog, the Americans took control.

The U.S. raced to a 7-0 start in four-ball competition, then settled for a 7-2 lead. Pacing the effort were Hoch and Jay Haas, a captains' choice selection. They went 2-0, defeating South Africans Frost and Fulton Allem 6 and 5 in the morning, then turning around to thump Parry and Japan's Tsukasa Watanabe 4 and 3 after lunch.

However, the match that had everyone buzzing was a morning game featuring Americans Couples and Love vs. Price and Hughes. The Americans won 1-up, with Couples and Love making birdie on seven of the first eight holes to take a 5-up lead.

But when Price, who earlier eagled the par-5 13th by holing a 192-yard 5-iron, made a 15-foot birdie two holes later, suddenly the match was even.

■　　　　　　　　　　　■

The Presidents Cup returned to Robert Trent Jones GC in 1996 and September 2000. In '96, Arnold Palmer was captain of the American squad, and Fred Couples again starred in a U.S. victory.
The complete story of that match is recounted in the chapter on the Robert Trent Jones GC in The Landscape of Virginia Golf.

■　　　　　　　　　　　■

After all four parred the 16th, Couples slid a 15-foot birdie putt in the side door on 17 to get the U.S. home.

"I remember the Ryder Cup [in '93]," Couple said later. "We had fog there, too, the first day. We sat and sat and sat, then got off to a bad start. This time, maybe it hurt them."

If so, the pain didn't last long.

In oppressively muggy conditions that sapped everyone's strength, the International team opened the second day by winning three of five best-ball matches, with Price-Elkington halving their match with Mickelson-Pavin.

When Frost and Australian Peter Senior opened play in the afternoon with a 6-and-5 victory over Irwin and Haas in alternate-shot competition, the U.S. lead was 9-6. The overall outcome suddenly was very much in doubt.

Love and Jim Gallagher Jr. gave the U.S. some breathing room with a 7-and-5 win over Nobilo and Robert Allenby, but Singh and Elkington countered with a victory to keep the deficit at two, 10-8.

Then Pavin and Loren Roberts squeaked out a 1-up win over Parry and Allem, and Mickelson and Lehman defeated Hughes and McNulty 3 and 2 to enable the U.S. to close out the second day at 12-8.

The Pavin-Roberts victory was huge. Three-down with six to play, they won four holes, guided by some pinpoint shots by Pavin.

Already a hero from the '93 Ryder Cup and the reigning World Match Play champion, Pavin holed out from a bunker at No. 15 to pull his team to 1-down. With the match even at 18, the diminutive Californian jammed his approach four feet from the cup to win a conceded birdie after Parry missed a six-foot par putt.

Sunday's singles matches may have been the best exhibition of golf the entire season. Eight of the 12 advanced to at least the 18th hole. When Couples hit his magnificent shot, four other matches were in the midst of sudden-death playoffs. They were halted after Price conceded, and each side was given one-half point.

In the end, it was great theater, including a surprise visit on Sunday morning from Norman. Looking gaunt and pale from his illness, he and his wife had flown to Washington to root for the International team. Though they lost, he was justifiably proud of what he had helped create.

"This baby's been born," he said. "It's out of the womb, here to stay. It's going to grow. It's going to get bigger and bigger."

PEETE AND RE-PEETE
AT KINGSMILL

Calvin Peete's career would have been one of the most refreshing in the history of pro golf had he never come to the Kingsmill Golf Club.

The uncommon events that occurred during his victories in the 1982 and 1983 Anheuser-Busch Classics in Williamsburg only enhanced an already unique story.

Peete might have been golf's most amazing two-time winner when he arrived in scalding Williamsburg in July of 1982. One of 19 children growing up in Detroit, Peete had been forced to quit school as a teenager. He sold goods to migrant farm workers out of the back of a station wagon.

He didn't take up golf until 1966, when he was 23, and he never figured to be much good. Peete couldn't fully extend his left arm, the result of a broken elbow he had suffered as a child.

But seven months later, he broke 80 for the first time in competition. By the spring of 1975, he was ready for the PGA Tour.

"I was like anyone else when I started playing the game," he said. "I whiffed 'em. I topped 'em. But I just kept playing because I liked the game. I guess I just got the bug."

Peete had some shortcomings. He wasn't one of the longest drivers on the Tour. He was only a fair long-range putter. He also had one uncanny plus.

He almost never missed the fairway off the tee. And he almost never missed the green once in the fairway. Peete led the Tour in driving accuracy and was second in getting the ball onto the green in regulation.

Peete had two victories, both in Milwaukee, including the tournament

Calvin Peete's forte was uncanny accuracy off the tee and from the fairway.

there two weeks before coming to Williamsburg. Even so, it didn't look promising that he would add victory No. 3 at Kingsmill.

Peete had a long history of severe back spasms, a condition he said was heightened by swinging a golf club. The pain had surfaced again the previous week at the Quad Cities Open, and he had considered withdrawing before the final round, even though he was close to the lead. He had played instead and finished a disappointing 16th.

On his way to Williamsburg, Peete stopped at Howard University Hospital in Washington, D.C., where a therapist he knew tried to relieve the stiffness in Peete's back. He had been successful enough that Peete decided to keep his commitment to tournament officials at the Anheuser-Busch.

What Peete didn't know was that once he got to Williamsburg, staying loose would be the least of his problems. The weather there during July was traditionally blast-furnace hot, with humidity so high it was possible to break into a sweat just closing a car door.

In heat that approached 100 degrees, Peete opened the tournament with a 5-under-par 66, one stroke off Bruce Lietzke's lead. Peete was in the middle of his swing on the third hole during Friday's second round when tournament officials sounded the storm siren. One of the players on a different part of the course had seen lightning.

"It almost scared the socks off of me," Peete said later.

Hours later, it was still raining too hard to play. Tournament officials were confronted by a major problem.

Only 66 of the 156 players in the field had finished 36 holes. Orion Burkhardt, the tournament's executive committee chairman, had two options.

One was to wipe out Friday's second-round scores, start over on Saturday and play 36 holes on

Sunday or the final round on Monday. The other was to allow Friday's early scores to stand, finish the second round on Saturday, and end what would become a 54-hole tournament on Sunday.

Both plans had flaws. Executives at NBC didn't want to televise the third round of a tournament on a Sunday, and they were against cutting into mid-afternoon programming on Monday.

Cutting the tournament to 54 holes left Burkhardt with another dilemma: how to handle the $350,000 purse. The contract between the Tour and its sponsors stated that any time a round was rained out, the sponsor could deduct 25 percent from the purse.

Burkhardt didn't want to do that. Since moving from California to Williamsburg in 1981, he had experienced a difficult time attracting top-quality fields. Kingsmill's reputation as one of the hottest stops on the tour drove some players away. So did the date, the week before the British Open. Many stars were already overseas.

Burkhardt huddled by phone with Anheuser-Busch executives in St. Louis. He then announced what no tournament director had ever uttered before. The tournament would be cut to 54 holes. The purse would remain intact.

"We wanted to give everyone a fair deal, both the players and TV," Burkhardt explained. "We want everyone to leave here happy on Sunday."

Burkhardt's decision was universally hailed. NBC, which was committed to televising just two hours of the final round, agreed to stay with the tournament until a winner was determined, even if it meant pre-empting other programming.

Peete returned to the course on Saturday and played the final 15 holes in 2 under par. His 68 and overall score of 134 put him two shots ahead of Bill Rogers and Rik Massengale, three up on rookie Hal Sutton and Payne Stewart.

"I thought our group of players got a much better break than those who finished Friday and sat out today's round," Peete said. "We'll have a little momentum going into the final round."

He didn't start play Sunday like a man with momentum. A bogey on No. 3—his first in 39 holes—dropped him one shot behind Massengale.

Peete pulled back into a tie with a 12-foot birdie putt on the sixth hole, then took the lead for good with a nine-foot putt for birdie-3 on No. 9.

"Cal had the ball so close to the hole all day that we really didn't have much of a chance," Massengale said. "He never left an opening."

Peete played the last eight holes in 2 under par. Included was a tricky 12-foot putt for birdie on No. 14 that kept him one shot better than Sutton, who was playing two groups ahead.

"I'm proud of the victory, and I'm glad I didn't have to go another 18 holes," Peete said. "My back was starting to ache."

BUCKING THE ODDS IN '83

Sutton, who finished third in 1982, came to Kingsmill the following year a more seasoned, confident player. He had closed out the '82 season with a rush, winning the Walt Disney Classic. His earnings—$237,424—were a rookie record at the time.

Sutton, 25, had opened the '83 season by winning the Tournament Players Championship in March. He was No. 1 on the money list and brimming with happy thoughts.

"This is where I got my start last year," Sutton said. "It's a good course for me."

Although he missed a 30-inch putt during the second round that would have given him a share of the course record, Sutton's 67-65-132 was good enough for a six-shot lead over Scott Simpson, Mark O'Meara, and Jodie Mudd. Seven shots back were Raymond Floyd and Tom Weiskopf. Peete trailed by nine.

Hal Sutton was a major contender in both of Calvin Peete's Anheuser-Busch Classic victories.

"I haven't had a bogey, and I don't think I've ever hit the ball as well for two straight days," Sutton said.

Sutton came back Saturday with a 2-under 69 to maintain his six-shot edge, this time over Peete and Payne Stewart, with just 18 to play.

While everyone conceded the fact that Sutton had a huge advantage, Peete insisted it wasn't insurmountable. The proof was his win in Atlanta earlier in the year, where he had come from seven shots down.

"I just can't count myself out," he said.

And the leader didn't talk like someone who had already won.

"Six shots seem like a lot, but if someone told me I could have par without playing tomorrow, I'd go out there and play," Sutton said. "I'll try to make birdies. I'm not going to shoot for the center of the greens. If I do that, I'll get beat."

He would have been better off taking the par.

Sutton, who hadn't shot higher than 1-under-par 70 in two years at Kingsmill, sprayed the ball all over the course Sunday.

He bogeyed the first. He bogeyed the third. He bogeyed the sixth after an errant tee shot that placed him in "the worst lie I have ever seen in my life."

He bogeyed the ninth, 11th, and 13th.

"I could tell right away that he was not as comfortable as he normally is," Peete said. "This is a course that lends itself to low scores, and he knew that.

"It might have been better for him if he had been leading by only two or three strokes. Then he probably would have won."

By the time he and Peete made the turn, Sutton had plummeted from six shots ahead to one shot behind. With four holes still to play, Sutton trailed by two and wasn't even in second place. That honor went to Tim Norris, playing in virtual solitude as most of the gallery followed Sutton with a macabre amazement.

Sutton, gracious despite his embarrassment, admitted he was consumed with negative thoughts practically from the first swing.

"They weren't there when I got to the first tee, but it might have happened as early as the second shot," he said. "I wasn't even thinking about what Calvin was doing. The only person I can do anything about is me. And I couldn't do anything about him today."

Sutton finished with a 6-over 77. Peete, after three birdies in the last five holes on the front nine, coasted home in par on the back nine. His total of 276 was one shot better than Norris, two strokes less than Sutton and Lanny Wadkins, who had fired a course-record 63 on Saturday to move into contention.

"It's not anybody's fault but my own," said Sutton, who admitted that he'd never played with that large a lead before. "It was a learning experience. I'll be in the lead some other time. Maybe I'll cope with it better next time."

Peete went on to complete one of the best seasons of his career. He was chosen to play on the '83 Ryder Cup squad. He also won the Ben Hogan Award from the Golf Writers Association. The honor goes to an individual who has achieved something significant in golf by overcoming a physical handicap or illness.

SCORE ONE FOR INKSTER'S GINTY

It was a tournament with many different names and many different locations, but only one choice for most-memorable shot.

Using a 4-wood she called "The Ginty," Juli Inkster nearly holed a 220-yard shot on the first hole of a sudden-death playoff with Nancy Lopez, Betsy King, and Rosie Jones in the 1988 Crestar Classic at Sleepy Hole Golf Course in Suffolk.

Inkster's subsequent eagle—secured with a putt of six feet—ended a personal drought of 20 months and made prophets of LPGA administrators.

Eight years earlier, when Crestar Bank was known as United Virginia Bank, and the tournament was staged at Elizabeth Manor Country Club in Portsmouth, officials had approached the LPGA about moving the event to Sleepy Hole.

The LPGA agreed, but on one condition. Change the 18th hole from a par 4 to a par 5.

Sleepy Hole's 18th was 451 yards, with a tight landing area off the tee, a narrow throat to the green and trouble everywhere else. On the left were woods and, nearer the green, a marsh with yards of tall reeds that led out into the Nansemond River. To the right were trees and the Obici House, a former country hospital that each year was converted to a locker room for the women.

The LPGA's rationale was simple. The 18th was the perfect tournament-decider. It had great risk. It had the potential for great reward.

Still, it wasn't until Sally Little beat Kathy Whitworth in a one-hole sudden-death playoff that started on No. 1 that LPGA officials decreed that future playoffs at Sleepy Hole would start at 18.

There were none until 1988, when Virginians witnessed one of the greatest showdowns in women's golf history.

Inkster, Lopez, Jones, and King each finished the 54 holes of regulation play at 7-under-par 209. They then traipsed to the 18th to begin a playoff that was inches from never happening and inches from involving an unprecedented seven participants.

Amy Alcott, Sherri Turner, and Missie Berteotti all had chances to join the fray. Alcott got to 7 under during the final round, but made a three-putt bogey on the 167-yard 16th.

Turner, who led entering the final round, made double-bogey 6 on the 17th to drop from 6 under to 4 under. She then made eagle 3 at the 18th to thrust herself back to 6 under.

Berteotti needed to birdie the 18th to keep playing, but she flew her third shot, a wedge, over the green, 30 feet from the hole. Her chip shot was on line but finished less than a foot from the cup.

As it was, the playoff had everything. It had sheer numbers. Only three times before had there been a playoff involving five players.

It had star power.

Inkster had won eight times in five seasons, including the 1984 Nabisco-Dinah Shore and the du Maurier Classic, both majors.

King had 12 career victories, including the Nabisco-Dinah Shore.

Jones had almost crashed into the winner's circle in a big way in 1984, falling one shot short of forcing a playoff with Hollis Stacy at the U.S. Open. She'd finally won her first tournament in '87, and 1988 would turn out to be an exceptional year for her. She won three times.

Lopez? Just her name said it all.

Inkster was the first player in at 7 under, but not without a lot of difficulty. Playing the 18th in regulation, she hooked her approach to the green—also 220 yards and struck with The Ginty—behind a skybox and almost into the river.

Inkster received line-of-sight relief from tournament marshals, chipped to 12 feet from the cup, and holed the birdie putt.

Lopez was next. At 18, she nearly holed her third shot, a wedge, before tapping in a 10-inch putt for birdie.

Jones was on 18 in two shots, then birdied after her 20-foot eagle attempt touched the edge of the cup before sliding past.

King had the last shot at winning in regulation. All she needed was to hole a 12-foot birdie putt that broke left to right.

Standing in the scorer's tent, Inkster and Jones couldn't bear to watch, covering their eyes. Lopez couldn't bear not to watch, staring as King's putt stopped inches short of the cup.

Inkster won the draw to see who would hit first. She slapped her drive to the center of the fairway, 220 yards from the center of the green, in almost the exact spot from which she had played moments before.

Lopez and Jones were in the fairway, but too far from the green to go for it with their second shots. However, King blew her tee shot 20 yards past Inkster.

After Lopez and Jones laid up, Inkster's caddie handed her The Ginty. The shot soared about 205 yards, bounced, then began rolling towards the pin. It slowed, then grazed the right edge of the cup before changing directions and coming to rest six feet past the hole.

"Misread it, huh?" Inkster would joke later after being told how close she had come to pulling off golf's rarest shot, the double-eagle.

Stunned, King still managed to hit her shot 25 feet from the hole, giving herself a chance to make eagle and put some pressure on Inkster.

Lopez and Jones could do no better than par. King's eagle attempt missed, and she tapped in for birdie. Inkster's putt for the win was in the hole from the moment she struck it.

Juli Inkster tries to coax a putt during the Crestar Classic at Sleepy Hole in Portsmouth.

making memories

Steve Melnyk accepts a large piece of hardware for his efforts in winning the 1970 Eastern Amateur Championship at the Elizabeth Manor Country Club in Portsmouth. Melnyk won in a four-way sudden-death playoff the included Tom Kite .

NOT BAD FOR AN INSURANCE MAN

Steve Melnyk was scheduled to be in Tennessee the third week of August 1970, making appearances as part of his public-relations duties for Florida's Gulf Life Insurance Company. That's where the 22-year-old had gone to work after graduating from the University of Georgia the previous year.

But Melnyk was priming to defend his U.S. Amateur championship in Portland, Oregon, in early September. He told his boss he "needed some serious competition."

The boss figured the one thing better than having a U.S. Amateur champion working for the company was having a two-time U.S. Amateur champion. He changed the destination on Melnyk's itinerary from Tennessee to Portsmouth's Elizabeth Manor Country Club and the 14th annual Eastern Amateur championship.

Melnyk won, outlasting 20-year-old Tom Kite, former U.S. Junior Champion Eddie Pearce, and 40-year-old clothier Moss Beecroft of Newport News

on the third hole of a sudden-death playoff that Kite figured never should have happened.

Kite, then a University of Texas golfer who had played a full slate of national amateur events that summer and had finished no lower than fourth—but no higher than second—made a double-bogey 6 on the 72nd hole to let Melnyk, Pearce, and Beecroft back in the game.

There were extenuating circumstances to Kite's collapse. As he stood on the 18th tee, the ominous late-afternoon rumblings that usually preceded a violent thunderstorm grew louder and louder as lightning raced down the river towards the golf course.

Guarding a one-shot lead and trying to get in the clubhouse before the storm broke, Kite drove his tee shot into the water. He dropped and hit his next shot into the rough, burying it in mud. Then the storm hit.

When Kite returned to the course an hour later, he chipped to 30 feet from the cup, then two-putted for 6. Melnyk, playing in Kite's threesome,

Steve Melnyk tees off during the 1970 Eastern Amateur Championship at Portsmouth, a tournament he won by defeating Tom Kite, Eddie Pearce, and Moss Beecroft in sudden death.

could have won outright, but he made bogey on 18 as the four men finished at 3-under-par 277.

Melnyk and Beecroft birdied the first hole of the playoff, eliminating Kite and Pearce.

"They're out there playing my tournament," Kite said glumly as he waited for Melnyk and Beecroft to finish. "I felt like I could reach out and grab this title, but something always happens."

On the third hole, Melnyk left his approach 25 feet from the cup. Beecroft was five feet closer.

But with the rain pouring down, Melnyk punched his ball into the hole. Beecroft left his match-extending putt short.

"I never wanted to win a tournament more than this one," Melnyk said later. "I haven't been playing much because of business commitments, and it kills me to see these other guys playing week after week and winning.

"I guess I'm envious, really. I've had to swallow a lot of pride."

Melnyk made no bones about the fact he didn't consider himself the favorite to win the tournament, which annually attracted the best amateur talent in the nation.

There were 200 players of all ages, experience, and backgrounds entered. Melnyk hadn't played competitively in two weeks, and finishing 31st in The Porter Cup was hardly his idea of a successful performance.

By almost everyone's calculation, the pre-tournament favorites were Lanny Wadkins and Allen Miller. It was considered the strongest Eastern Am field in the history of the tournament. Thirty years later, it still holds its own with any Eastern Amateur field.

Half of the top 20 finishers went on to play the PGA Tour. Melnyk was one of them until he became a network television analyst.

Other than Melnyk, the field included four college All-Americans, four Walker Cup players, the USGA Junior champion, and the winner of the Florida Open.

Wadkins, from Richmond, was a 20-year-old Wake Forest student, a Walker Cup member the preceding year, as well as defending State Amateur champion and defending Eastern Amateur champion.

Miller, another Walker Cup member, arrived in Portsmouth having just won the Canadian Amateur by 10 strokes. The 22-year-old Georgia graduate had also captured the Dogwood, Southeastern, and Northeast Amateur titles.

Then there was Bruce Ashworth, the star of the University of Houston's NCAA championship team and runner-up in 1969, and teammate John Mahaffey, that year's NCAA individual champion.

Vinny Giles, who had finished second in three consecutive U.S. Amateurs and was a five-time State Amateur champion, was on hand.

So was 17-year-old Gary Koch, victorious in the National Pee Wee, Florida Junior championship (twice), the Babe Zaharias Junior, the Orange Bowl Junior, the Florida High School championship, and the Florida Open.

He was joined by Pearce, a USGA Junior champion at age 16, the 36-hole medalist in previous year's Eastern Amateur and the current Florida Open champion.

And there was a new kid on the scene, a 16-year-old Virginia Junior Champion named Curtis Strange.

Despite all that talent, the first-round leaders were a couple of youngsters virtually no one knew anything about.

Richard Woulfe was a 20-year-old member of the Michigan State golf team. George Haines

was a teacher at a suburban Philadelphia Quaker prep school.

Both shot 5-under-par 65, two shots better than Beecroft, Mark Hayes, and Koch and one stroke off the course record.

Haines fashioned his round despite never having seen Elizabeth Manor. He didn't arrive at the course until 7 o'clock the night before. He went to the range, hit "about 100 wedges," then slept until shortly before his late-afternoon tee time.

"I figured maybe I could just keep it in play, then come back tomorrow," explained Haines, who played two seasons on the University of Pennsylvania golf team and was the 1968 New Jersey State champion. "I've been playing over my head since the Fourth of July. I've got to start telling myself that I can play with these guys."

The next two rounds belonged to Kite.

He had qualified for the U.S. Amateur in Dallas on Tuesday, taken a midnight flight, and arrived at the golf course as the sun was peeking over the Elizabeth River on Wednesday.

Highly displeased with his putting after an opening-round of 1-under 69, Kite returned to the putting green for a 90-minute workout in the broiling sun before calling it a day.

And while he wasn't perfect on Friday, Kite used just 29 putts and left three others on the lip in gaining the top spot on the leader board with a second-round 66 and 36-hole total of 135.

That tied the lowest 36-hole score in tournament history, while the cut score, 7-over-par 147, was also the lowest in the history of the tournament and five strokes better than the previous year.

"I could have really had a super round if I had been concentrating on making putts," said Kite, in what seemed a curious analysis of his day. "Instead, I was working on my putting stroke."

Former U.S. Open champion Tom Kite, here driving during the 1999 Michelob Championship, has come a long way since his sudden-death play-off loss to Steve Melnyk in the 1970 Eastern Amateur.

Kite's lead was anything but secure. Another Texan, Tom Jenkins, was tied for second with Hayes, only a stroke behind. Miller and Pennsylvania native Jim Simons were only two shots behind

Then came a logjam. Haines, Melnyk, Lanny and brother Bobby Wadkins, and Koch all were in at 138, the score defending champ Lanny Wadkins had sported at the midway point the year before.

Kite needed only 29 putts again Saturday—seven one-putt greens—in shooting a 2-under 68 that just wasn't up to his standards. Still, his record 54-hole total of 203 left him with a two-shot lead

over Pearce. Simons, Melnyk, and Jenkins were three behind.

"I hit my drives so bad, and I got bad lies in the rough," Kite fumed. "It was the shakiest round I've played all season. In match-play tournaments, you figure the winner is going to have six matches—five great ones and one he just gets by in. In medal play, it's usually three great rounds and one so-so. I just hope this was my bad one."

Pearce, who was to begin college life at Wake Forest in a couple of weeks, made an eagle 3 from eight feet on the 487-yard 10th hole. Riding high, he

then dropped a 70-foot birdie putt on the next hole.

Melnyk was giddy following a third round in which he canned six birdie putts of 15 feet or less. But he also made a double-bogey from a bad lie in a bunker, endured a three-putt bogey, and had short birdie putts on the 15th and 17th holes that hit the cup and spun out.

"I hit it great," Melnyk said. "Not bad for an insurance man."

making memories
Jack Isaacs found his game and his fame
late in life.

A LATE, BEAUTIFUL BLOOMER

J ack Isaacs turned a mid-life crisis into a spectacular career.

In 1948, Isaacs was 40 years old and facing a devilish dilemma. Golf was his life, but he had reached a competitive plateau. He wasn't scoring like he thought he should be. His peers respected him, but he had never won anything of substance in the state. He was contemplating a new career.

"My game was too much like that of a lot of people," he said in a 1965 interview. "If I was to win anything, I had to improve."

Isaacs, a Richmond native, knew the odds were against him. Back then, few players improved their games after age 40. Of course, few players at that age took the time to break apart their game and begin anew.

Isaacs did, examining his weaknesses and plotting how to turn them into strengths.

He bought two large practice mats, then hit 1,500 balls every day for several months. Friends would come by his pro shop at Langley Air Force Base in Newport News and watch him hit ball after ball while standing beneath an overhang. His cousin Charlie Isaacs, the 1928 State Open winner, remembers seeing Jack standing on a rubber mat inside his garage, pounding shots into a mattress he'd hung.

"Finally, I got my game like I wanted to have it," he recalled. "And I began to play better."

And how.

Isaacs won five Virginia State Open championships, then known as the Virginia Association of Golf Professionals Open.

The first was in 1949 at Ocean View Golf Course in Norfolk. He won in 1950 at Danville Golf Club. He won in 1956 and '58 at Ingleside in Staunton.

His last Open title, in 1961, came after an 18-hole playoff with amateur Claude King of Virginia Beach at Chandler Harper's Bide-A-Wee Golf and Country Club in Portsmouth.

Harper was the odds-on favorite to win for the seventh time, but many thought Isaacs, who had competed in every State Open since 1928, would be his primary challenge. The Langley AFB pro figured to use the event as a

Jack Isaacs (far left) won the 1961 VPGA State Open at Bide-A-Wee in Portsmouth. Isaacs is in pretty good company with Portsmouth's Chandler Harper (second from the left), Sam Snead, and Tom Strange of Virginia Beach.

putt greens. Still, he finished with a 5-over 77, necessitating the third 18-hole playoff in the event's 34-year history.

For most of the day, the two matched each other stroke for stroke. Isaacs had nine one-putt greens and just 25 putts in all. King countered with seven one-putt greens and 29 short strokes total.

Tied through 16 holes, Isaacs broke through with birdies on the final two holes to fire a 1-over 73 and win by two.

Isaacs also won three Maryland State Opens, the Florida Open, and in 1953, made an amazing leap into the semifinals of the PGA Championship.

"Jack was calm and easy-going," Harper said. "He rarely got perturbed or very excited. He got more out of his golf game than any man I've ever known."

The shining moment in Isaacs' career undoubtedly was the 1953 PGA Championship at Oakland Hills in Birmingham, Mich.

Then the head pro at Langley AFB, where he designed 27 holes and worked for 20 years, Isaacs advanced to the semifinals by beating, in order, Snead, Harper, Labron Harris, Henry Ransom and Dick Mayer.

Isaacs' semifinal match was against tiny Felice Torza, a 140-pounder known as "Tiger Boy." Isaacs, then 44, and Torza were both at par for their regulation 36 holes. They halved the first two holes of sudden death before Torza won with a par on the 39th hole.

Known as "The Quiet Man" because of the loose, easy, methodical manner in which he played, Isaacs competed in 25 U.S. Opens and PGA Championships, two Masters and three British Opens. He left Langley AFB for Tequesta in Florida, then returned to Virginia as pro at Willow Oaks Country Club in Richmond in 1965.

He died in 1982 at the age of 73.

tune-up for upcoming trips to the Sam Snead Invitational Golf Festival in White Sulphur Springs, West Virginia., and the British Open in July at England's Royal Birkdale.

By the final round on Sunday, the tournament was shaping up as predicted. Isaacs and Harper were battling for the lead, though they both trailed King, a superb player who would later try the PGA Tour.

After days of heavy rain, high winds swept through the Portsmouth golf course, sending scores skyrocketing. Isaacs, trailing by two shots at the start of the day, saved par from 25 feet behind the green on 18 to finish the final round with a 3-over 75 and 293 total.

King, a high school golf coach, struggled with his irons. He hit just one green in regulation on the back nine, but compensated for it with seven one-

making memories

Keith Decker won the 1996 State Open at
Willow Oaks CC in Richmond by seven strokes.

DECKER'S STATE OPEN: NO ACCIDENT

Keith Decker was accustomed to success.

The stocky hotel-furniture salesman from tiny Fieldale had won the Virginia State Amateur in 1988 and 1991. He had won the State Mid-Amateur championship in 1990, '91, and '95. He had been named the Virginia State Golf Association player of the year in '91. In 1995, he had been part of the Virginia team that won the first U.S. Golf Association State Team championship in Lake Nona, Florida.

Yet, something was missing.

He had never won the Virginia State Open.

Decker came to Willow Oaks in Richmond in 1996 with reason to believe that could change. He had played there on three previous occasions, finishing second in 1994 to professional Jerry Wood.

In addition, the 6,684-yard course suited Decker's game perfectly. He liked to play the ball with a right-to-left draw. Willow Oaks had just two holes that required left-to-right play.

Finally, Willow Oak's greens were similar in speed to those on his home course, Forest Park in Martinsville.

Decker and Rick Schuller of Leesburg shared the lead after 36 holes at 6-under-par 138. John Stone and Simon Cooke trailed by one stroke. There was a seven-way tie at 140. Twenty-eight players were five shots or less from the lead.

He had developed a routine of rising early, eating breakfast at the same restaurant, and then arriving at Willow Oaks an hour before his tee time to practice.

Two hundred yards from the front entrance to the course, Decker was stopped in traffic, waiting for the driver of the car ahead of him to make a left turn.

"I just happened to be looking in my rear-view mirror and I saw that this car behind me is not stopping and I see these guys talking to each other," Decker said. "I braced myself, because I knew that there was no way he'd be

Keith Decker relaxes at Ford's Colony during the 1999 State Open. Decker won the '96 Open at Willow Oaks with rounds of 69-69-66-72, for a sparkling total of 276.

After a couple of shaky holes, Decker made birdies at Nos. 5 and 6 to draw back to even for the day. The birdie 3 at No. 6 was especially gratifying. It's the hardest hole on the course, and Decker tamed it with a booming drive, a 5-iron to eight feet, and an easy putt.

"My confidence level rocketed after that," he said.

Decker's 12-under-par total of 276 was seven strokes better than Teachey, Stone, and Cooke. It was the largest margin of victory since Robert Wrenn lapped the field by 12 in 1991, also at Willow Oaks.

Members at Forest Park Country Club threw a party for the new Open champion. Decker's portrait now hangs in the clubhouse.

"They are the best people in the world," Decker says. "They thought it was great. Fieldale got a lot of publicity. Martinsville got a lot of publicity. The people there have always been very supportive of me."

Ironically, the only other accident in which Decker was involved happened two years later, also in Richmond.

"And, again, I'm looking in my rear-view mirror and see it coming," he says with a smile. "I figured it must have been the car. People couldn't see it. So I traded it in a couple of months after the second accident. Now I've got a big sports utility vehicle that's going to hurt somebody else, by gosh, if they hit me again."

able to stop in time."

Amazingly, Decker wasn't injured in the wreck. Neither were his clubs, which were in the trunk.

"The guy couldn't have been nicer," Decker said. "He was apologizing all over the place. It loosened me up more than it shook me up."

That became clear when Decker finally reached the course. After making two pars, be began hitting the ball so close to the flag that he couldn't help but make birdie.

He birdied Nos. 3-5 with the longest putt being 10 feet. After a bogey on No. 6, Decker regained that stroke with a two-foot putt on the eighth hole. He birdied 10, 12, and 16 and rolled in a 25-foot putt to save par on the par-3 15th hole.

When it was all over, Decker had fashioned a 6-under-par 66. Whereas 28 players had been within five shots of him at the start of the day, now only one player, amateur Mark Teachey, was within six strokes.

"I've shot lower rounds in the third and fourth rounds of other tournaments," he said. "But given the pressure of being in the State Open, as prestigious as that title is, it meant a lot to me. I'd had a little taste of it before when I finished second, and I was trying hard.

"I guess all the excitement was over with prior to the round."

Although the media gave him something to think about that night in his hotel by reminding him that Greg Norman had blown the Masters that year with a similar lead heading into the final round, Sunday was anticlimactic.

making memories

John Rollins hits the range at the 1999 Nike Dominion Open at the Dominion CC in Richmond. Rollins won the 1995 and 1996 State Amateur championships, one at the Cascades, one at The Virginian in Bristol.

ROLLINS ROLLS IN STATE AMATEURS

Meadowbrook Country Club in Richmond has produced three State Amateur champions: Lanny and Bobby Wadkins and the man who achieved a feat that eluded both Wadkins.

John Rollins, who spent the 1999 season on what is now the Buy.Com Tour, set himself apart by winning back-to-back State Amateur titles in 1996 and 1997.

There isn't a long history of Virginians successfully defending the amateur title. Since Chandler Harper won the 1933 and '34 State Amateurs, only four players have done it: Giles (1968-69), Strange (1974-75), Tom McKnight (1984-85), and Rollins.

That's fast company.

"I feel really good being able to say that I did something they didn't do," Rollins said in reference to the Wadkins brothers following his 7-and-6 rout of Dale Powell of Chatham in the 1997 final at The Virginian in Bristol. "Everybody knows that back in the late '60s and early '70s, Lanny was 'The Man.'"

Unwittingly, Lanny played a role in Rollins' first Amateur victory, an 8-and-6 thumping of Troy Ferris of Norfolk at the Cascades in Hot Springs. He was visiting The Homestead and, unaware the Amateur was being played, dropped by the course to see some friends.

Rollins and Ferris hadn't teed off when VSGA officials asked Wadkins to present the winner with the Schwarzschild Trophy.

"It was unreal," Rollins recalled. "I had no idea he was going to be there. For him to present the trophy to me, being from Meadowbrook, a Ryder Cup captain, a player with a great career, made it so special."

Wadkins helped make it so. He handled the presentation with class, addressing both players publicly, consoling Ferris by saying, "I've been on both sides. I've lost in the state finals and I've won. I know how you feel, and I can appreciate much more how [Rollins] feels."

Maybe that's because Rollins, a student at Richmond's Virginia Commonwealth University and the Colonial Athletic Association player of the year, disposed of Ferris in Lanny-like fashion.

John Rollins (left) hoists the Schwarzschild Trophy after winning the 1996 State Amateur. Lanny Wadkins makes the presentation.

That was the play Rollins needed. He won the next three holes and the title shortly after the two made the turn.

"I've never been beaten that badly in match play," Ferris said later. "The whole week, I was never down by more than one hole. Today, I didn't make a putt all day, and John didn't make a mistake all day. He played super."

Rollins' victory was more remarkable because until he started the tournament, he had never seen the Cascades. Yet he tamed a 6,600-yard, par-70 course that is the country's finest mountain layout.

"I had a good friend who played a lot of golf at the Cascades, and he told me some of the things to watch out for, especially how those mountain greens were," Rollins said. "I went there knowing what the course looked like, even though I had never played there."

The State Amateur capped a fruitful season for Rollins. He won the Colonial Athletic Association individual championship and two other tournaments. VCU reached the NCAA regional tournament for the first time. Rollins finished the season ranked among the top college players in the country.

Rollins qualified for the PGA Tour in 2000.

Rollins's first match, against Lexington's David Brogan, went 19 holes. Rollins defeated one of the best amateurs in the state with a birdie on the first hole of sudden death.

Next up was Glenn Mullian of Richmond. That match went 19 holes, with Mullian coming from behind to force the playoff. Again, Rollins won with a birdie on the first hole.

The rest of his matches were far more decisive, capped by the rout of Ferris.

Rollins played the front nine of the scheduled 36-hole final in 3-under par. Meanwhile, Ferris made nine consecutive pars, normally enough to be even or perhaps hold a lead. Instead, the Campbell College student trailed by three and finished the morning session 4-down.

"I was playing pretty solid golf," Rollins said. "Troy was playing well, but he couldn't get any momentum. Getting out there in 3 under took a lot of pressure off me."

Ferris came back briefly in the afternoon to trim his deficit to three, but Rollins won the par-5 fifth hole after hitting his second shot under a tree, chipping out into the rough, then maneuvering a brilliant pitching wedge five feet from the hole and saving par.

making memories

Kandi Kessler-Comer won the Virginia State Junior, Virginia State Amateur, and Virginias Women's title (Virginia and West Virginia) in 1984. Kessler-Comer, shown here putting, is now the director of golf at Glenmore CC in Keswick.

KANDI KESSLER, KID TIGER

No one in Virginia women's golf has enjoyed a season to rival Kandi Comer's performance in 1980-81.

She was Kandi Kessler then, a shy 17-year-old from Charlottesville who had turned to golf six years earlier because severe allergies kept her from her first love, horseback riding.

At 14, she offered a glimpse of what was ahead by becoming the youngest player to win the State Girls' Junior title.

In 1980, Kessler lapped the field, winning the women's State Amateur, a second Girls' Junior title and, shortly after turning 18, the Virginias Women's championship.

It was a brilliant 12-month stretch, the first time in state history that one player had won what some referred to as the Grand Slam of women's state titles.

"It all kind of just happened," said Comer. "I never went into it with the idea of winning them all. It was never a goal. I was just a very competitive person. I didn't even know there was a 'Grand Slam' until people started talking to me about it."

"Kid Tiger" was her nickname, with the emphasis on "Kid."

Kessler began her run with an easy victory in the State Junior. Playing at Salisbury Country Club in Midlothian, the West Albemarle High School student breezed home by eight shots over runner-up Debbie Zahand of Westwood CC in Vienna after a pair of 75s.

In the State Amateur, Kessler beat 22-year-old Liz Rowland of Portsmouth 7 and 6 in the 36-hole match-play final at the Cascades Course at The Homestead. In doing so, she became the first high school player ever to take the crown.

"The Cascades was always one of my favorite places to play," Comer said. "I knew if I won there, I could pretty much win anywhere, because I'd won on a great golf course."

Trailing by one hole on the back nine of the morning round, Kessler

Kandi Kessler-Comer won two tournaments on the LPGA's Futures Tour before becoming a club professional.

began rattling off one par after another on one of the toughest layouts in America. It was more than Rowland, a former gymnast attending Arizona State, could handle.

Kessler pulled into a tie with a par-4 on the 367-yard 12th hole, took the lead with a birdie-3 on the 322-yard 14th, then went to lunch 3-up by making par on the 202-yard 15th and 145-yard 18th holes.

Months later, just a couple of days before the 1981 Girls' Junior, Kessler capped her "Grand Slam" with a much closer victory in the Virginias Women's Championship at Hermitage CC in Richmond.

Featuring players from Virginia and West Virginia, the 54-hole stroke-play tournament ultimately came down to a battle between Kessler and Richmond's Jane Mack, then a two-time State Amateur winner and 1978 Virginias champion.

"People liked to set Jane and me up to be rivals, but we weren't," Comer said. "We were actually very good friends."

Kessler began the final round one stroke behind West Virginian Ann Jarrett and one stroke

ahead of Mack. However, Jarrett took herself out of the mix early by playing the first five holes in 6 over par.

Meanwhile, Kessler went out in 1-under 35. She picked up a spectacular birdie 3 on No. 10 when she cracked a 5-wood out of the rough to six feet from the hole.

After 13 holes, she led Mack by five. Mack drew to two shots back with a birdie at 17, but Kessler kept that margin from shrinking even more with a nervy three-foot par putt.

Kessler, who would win the State Am again in 1984 by defeating Ann Patrick of Richmond 4 and 3, began her college career at South Carolina, then transferred to North Carolina after one year.

She was a three-time All-ACC selection for the Tar Heels and an All-American as a senior. In 1986, *Golf Digest* rated her as the ninth-best women's amateur in the United States, and she was selected to play for the Curtis Cup team against Great Britain at Prairie Dunes Country Club in Kansas.

Kessler seemed destined for a successful career as a touring professional. But she played just two seasons on the LPGA Futures Tour before quitting while she was ahead.

With fiancé Mike Comer looking on, Kessler won back-to-back tournaments, then announced that she was through.

"I was on the 18th green needing to two-putt from 10 feet to win for the second week in a row," she recalled. "I had left the first putt four feet short, and I couldn't believe how nervous I was that I'd miss the second one. When I made it, I told myself, 'If you can't enjoy yourself when you win, what's the sense of playing?'"

Comer, who had played in five U.S. Opens, finishing 14th at Plainfield CC in New Jersey in 1987.

Today, she is the director of golf at Glenmore Country Club in Keswick.

MOSS BEECROFT: BETTER WITH AGE

Moss Beecroft's career in senior golf would be memorable, even if it weren't slightly quirky.

The Newport News resident, who was born in 1930, won the State Senior Championship in 1999 by beating Stan Fischer of Richmond 2 and 1 at The Homestead's Cascades Course.

For Beecroft, it was a record sixth victory in the tournament. While it marked his return to the top of Virginia's over-50 circuit, the victory also resurrected memories of the most unusual winning streak in Old Dominion golf history.

Beecroft dominated State Senior competition from 1986 to 1994, but only in even-numbered years.

He defeated Charlie Mattox of Charlottesville in 20 holes in 1986; Robert Lewis of Fairfax in 19 holes in '88; Arman Fletcher of Roanoke 2-up in 1990; Ken Newlin of Nokesville 5 and 4 in '92; and Don Foster of Salem 4 and 2 in 1994.

"It really was an amazing coincidence," Beecroft said. "I don't know how it came about, but once it started, it just kept going."

In 1999, however, Beecroft was practically perfect for the first nine holes of the final, carding a 1-under-par 34 that earned a 2-up advantage. That grew to 3-up after Beecroft birdied No. 10. He went 4-up, and seemed in total control, after a birdie at the 12th.

Fischer, a former University of Virginia quarterback who was playing in his fourth consecutive Senior final, fought back. After scoring a conceded eagle 3 on the 16th hole, he had trimmed Beecroft's lead in half.

But his attempt at making another eagle 3 at No. 17 fizzled when he hit his second shot into a green-side trout pond and could make only par. When Beecroft halved the hole, the title was his.

"In the twilight hours of a mediocre career, that was certainly nice," Beecroft said.

Mediocre? Hardly.

Moss Beecroft hits off the first tee of the James River Country Club in Newport News. Beecroft has dominated State Senior competition.

In 1992, he was low amateur at the U.S. Senior Open at Saucon Valley, 13 shots better than the next nonprofessional.

"I remember that the most because I felt like I didn't have any fluky rounds," said Beecroft, who shot 70-75-70-76-291.

A year earlier, Beecroft nearly pulled off a victory in the U.S. Senior Amateur at Crystal Downs Country Club in Frankfort, Michigan.

The greens were treacherous all week, Beecroft remembered, and "I got away with a lot of stuff until the final" against Bill Bosshard.

Beecroft needed three putts each on holes 7-11 and fell 5-down. Bosshard won 5 and 4.

"I handed it to him on a silver platter," Beecroft said.

Beating Bosshard wouldn't have been easy under any circumstance, but Beecroft entered the final just minutes after a tense, emotional, 1-up semifinal victory.

"I barely had time to get a bowl of soup," he said. By contrast, Bosshard had breezed through his semifinal match and was fresh for the 18-hole final.

"I'm not sure I agree with playing the semifinals and final on the same day," Beecroft said. "I think that any golfer who gets to that point in a national championship wants to be at his best for that match, and I told the USGA that."

Beecroft became serious about golf while in prep school at Woodberry Forest, whose campus featured a nine-hole course designed by Donald Ross. Beecroft, state pole-vault champion at the time, didn't own a set of clubs, so he borrowed his roommate's.

"I guess it's just my competitive nature, but from the first time I played, I always thought of competing. Otherwise, why do it?"

His first taste of success came in the 1967 Kenridge Invitational at Farmington Country Club in Charlottesville, which has convened the state's best amateurs in an annual competition since 1936. He knocked off Farmington's Buddy Loving in the semifinals then defeated George Fulton of Roanoke 3-and-2.

"That was a biggie for me," Beecroft said. "Fulton was a very notable player in the state."

Fulton *was* an accomplished player. The 1954 State Amateur champion, Fulton was appearing in his 10th Kenridge final.

Tournament officials decided beforehand to award the winner that year with something special: a sparkling blue blazer.

Beecroft owns five men's clothing shops, the irony of which wasn't lost on the good-natured Fulton.

"I'd give $1,000 for that blazer," Fulton told Beecroft.

"Put it up and it's yours," came the reply.

Later, Beecroft told the gallery that he would wear the blazer with great appreciation for what it meant to be a Kenridge champion.

THE NEW FRONTIER

Virginia golfers have been afforded a unique opportunity during the past seven years. With the exponential popularity of golf, the number of golfers playing the game has increased by leaps and bounds.

The landscape of Virginia golf has kept pace. From Northern Virginia to Virginia Beach, new layouts have popped up all over.

The era of upscale daily-fee courses began with the opening of Lee's Hill Golfers Club in 1993. The Fredericksburg course is routed through a series of Civil War battle trenches occupied by Gen. Robert E. Lee's Confederate troops in 1862 after the battle of Fredericksburg.

Architect Bill Love of Ault, Clark and Associates created a picturesque 18 holes that meanders through the Massaponax River basin. Carved out of the thick woods, Lee's Hill offers narrow fairways, none of them parallel with one another. Water comes into play on six holes, 57 bunkers catch errant shots, and severe doglegs on nine holes force golfers to use every club in the bag.

Williamsburg entered the fray in 1995 with the opening of The Colonial Golf Course. Brainchild of owner Francis Fenderson, The Colonial was the first daily-fee course amid the resort explosion in Williamsburg.

Golfers are made to feel welcome from the time they arrive. The impressive brick clubhouse has the grandeur of an exclusive country club, including a first-rate restaurant.

The architectural gem created by Lester George winds through picturesque woodlands and natural wetlands. In addition to the 18-hole layout, The Colonial offers an excellent practice area and a unique three-hole practice course.

From five different teeing areas, golfers experience five different courses in one at The Colonial. Only low handicappers need attempt to play the course from the "Colonial" tees. Measuring 6,809 yards, the championship course offers a long and difficult test where trouble lurks everywhere. The 60 bunkers, five uninviting water hazards, and expansive wetlands provide several opportunities for scores to balloon.

Lee's Hill Golfers Club in Fredericksburg opened in 1993. The fifth hole is a short, 150-yard par 3 with an intimidating pond situated between tee and green.

The ninth green with the clubhouse in the background at The Colonial Golf Course in Williamsburg is a 428-yard par 4 from the "Colonial" tees.

Virginia golf made another big splash in 1995 with the opening of the Augustine Golf Club in Stafford. From the time the club opened, enthusiasts have gushed about this wonderful design. The accolades have come from various regional and national golf publications.

This golf and housing community located south of Washington was the pet project of owner Tadahiko Nukui of Nukui International.

Named after George Washington's father, Augustine was designed by Jack Nicklaus protégé Rick Jacobson. He created a magnificent par-71, 18-hole layout through the hardwood forests and natural wetlands and creeks of northern Virginia.

The unusual hilly terrain for this area presents golfers with a selection of elevated teeing areas. The course starts with a bang. The first three holes make Augustine one of the more difficult starts in all of Virginia golf. Water comes into play

The pristine par-4 ninth hole at Augustine Golf Club in Stafford is a medium-length golf hole with a generous fairway but a small green.

sorts group opened two gems designed by Mike Strantz: Royal New Kent Golf Club in Providence Forge and The Legends of Stonehouse in Toano.

Overnight, Virginia became a mecca for avid golfers looking for that "must play" short list of courses around the country. Both courses opened with such fanfare that travelers from all over the world started to include Virginia as a golf destination.

Stonehouse received the highest award for new courses in the United States in 1996 from several national golf publications. There are plenty of legends about the land the course was built on.

It has been said that Captain John Smith lived at the first stonehouse. The land was also rumored to have been home to Nathaniel Bacon, a local hero and renegade, for a time. Historians say it's bunk, but there are even stories that claim the legendary pirate Blackbeard buried stolen treasure on this land.

Stonehouse is cut from thick woodlands. Deep gorges create a severe hilly terrain where precarious forced carries make golfers think about every shot. Golfers are hard-pressed to see more than one hole at a time. The course is a wild, exciting roller-coaster ride from start to finish.

Stonehouse is more than a golf course. It's an experience. Every hole is memorable and unique. Huge bunkers, 93 in all, can swallow ball and golfer alike.

It is difficult to choose any one hole to define this course, but the par 3s at Stonehouse rival any on an inland course in the United States. The third hole is the first of a breathtaking series. From the distant tee boxes, elevated on their individual stone walls, golfers take aim at an amphitheater green surrounded by huge grassy mounds.

If golfers don't reach the green with their tee shot, making par is almost impossible. A stream meanders along the length of the hole, wrapping

on each. Oddly enough, there is only one bunker among these holes.

The course doesn't let up after the opening trio. Wetlands play a part in all but one of the remaining holes.

Playing from the right set of the five teeing areas at Augustine can mean the difference between a successful score or a nightmare.

"Signature hole" is a term that can be used often at Augustine. Perhaps the most inspiring hole

on the course is the second, an intimidating par 4 that measures 456 yards from the back tees. Water flows down the left side and forces golfers to carry two shots over the hazard to reach the green.

If you survive the course, you can embellish the round in the impressive 14,000-square-foot clubhouse. A full-service restaurant with indoor and outdoor seating overlooks the 18th green.

Virginia golf really took off in 1996.

Just outside Williamsburg, the Legends Re-around the left side of the green before heading off into the woods again. Chipping onto the green from the severe downslopes of the mounding behind the green is a daunting task.

The third hole is difficult, but the par-3 17th hole seems even more demanding. Golfers must hit an accurate tee shot from an elevated tee to an elevated green. In between is a deep ravine that reminds some players of the Grand Canyon. The only saving grace is the gigantic green. NASA could land the space shuttle on this green, that measures 65 yards deep and 57 yards wide. A four-putt is not out of the question.

After the round, you can relax inside the new clubhouse. The spacious facility is made of stone inside and out, accented with huge wooden beams.

Stonehouse's sister course that opened later in the same year provides an even more demonic traipse through the Virginia countryside, molded to resemble Irish links terrain.

The second of Strantz's creations is Royal New Kent. Stonehouse took honors in 1996, and Royal New Kent stole the show nationally in 1997. It has since cemented itself among the top 100 courses in the United States.

The Latin word "Invicta" means unconquerable, a label that couldn't be more appropriate. From the "Invicta" tees, the course measures 7,291 yards. The course rating of 76.5 and a slope of 147 makes Royal New Kent the most difficult in the Commonwealth.

What makes it so difficult? There are 129 bunkers. Most have more sand than some beaches. Water comes into play on six holes. Blind tee shots give way to blind approach shots on many of the holes. Giant mounding and tall native fescue grasses make balls difficult to find and even harder to play.

The breathtaking 187-yard, par-3 15th hole is another difficult test at The Legends of Stonehouse in Toano. A deep ravine and a crowned green make this hole a small target to hit.

Royal New Kent is a rare beauty among inland courses in the United States. It has sweeping vistas and a unique character.

From the first tee, you would swear you are playing golf in Ireland. Impressive stone walls snake across the countryside, giant hills hide most of the fairway, and the wind whips across the open landscape, rustling the tall fields of grasses.

Hidden pot bunkers swallow up many a tee shot. There are 17 bunkers on the par-5, fifth hole.

Elevated greens make long holes even longer, and greens average 40 yards in depth.

It all adds up to 18 spectacular golf holes. As long as golfers aren't there trying to qualify for the PGA Tour, the experience can be a special one.

Southeastern Virginia was not the only part of the state to usher in great golf in 1996.

Raspberry Falls Golf and Hunt Club in Leesburg opened as a Gary Player signature design. This Scottish links-style course is spread out along

Golfers tee off from the 173-yard tee box at the par-3 seventh hole at Royal New Kent in Providence Forge, an Irish links-style layout that puts a premium on shot-making accuracy. The seventh hole has extreme pot bunkers and a hazardous creek protecting the large green.

rolling farmland one would never expect to find on the outskirts of the nation's capital.

Player created a course of mammoth proportions. From the back tees, the course measures 7,191 yards.

The wide-open space allows wind to whip across the entire layout, making it all that more demanding. Add seven holes where water comes into play, and 75 stacked-sod bunkers and Raspberry Falls is a complete test of golf.

The ninth hole is a spectacular par 5 that finishes away from the clubhouse. While reachable in two, it requires a booming tee shot and an equally precise fairway wood. The reward for two accurate shots is a chance for eagle. The hazards around the green make a double-bogey or worse possible. A creek and multiple deep bunkers, including one named "The Citadel" guard a super-sized green.

This hole is bested in greatness by the breathtaking 18th, an even longer par 5. The hole begins at one of the highest points on the course, with five teeing areas carved out of the hills like giant steps. A smart layup still leaves a precarious third shot into a narrow green sandwiched between a creek and five deep bunkers, the most difficult named "Rogue's Hollow." A visit there is certain doom.

The 18th finishes behind an impressive clubhouse decorated with plaids and tweeds. Inside, the staff redefines wonderful service.

In 1999, the Kiskiack Golf Club opened for its first full season and put to rest the possibility that the growth in golf courses had ceased.

Named after the American Indian tribe that roamed the land west of Colonial Williamsburg, this smart layout was designed by John LaFoy. He left most of the hilly landscape as it was, routing the course around two lakes.

The course is in immaculate condition from tee to green, creating quite a contrast to the blue lakes that surround the first, second, and ninth holes on the front nine and the 17th and 18th holes on the back.

The signature hole at Kiskiack comes early. The par-3 second hole is a masterpiece. For the long hitters playing from the gold and green tees, a 200-yard carry over water makes hitting a multi-tiered green guarded by two bunkers a formidable challenge.

The ninth hole also deserves mention for its pristine beauty and dramatic design. From elevated tees, this 506-yarder has golfers wondering how to play the hole. Water juts into the fairway on the left and the right, pinching the emerald greenery to almost nothing. Big hitters may attempt to carry the water, while shorter gunners must lay up. The second shot uphill toward the green has seven bunkers to dodge.

Fred Couples put his architectural stamp on Virginia with two courses that opened in 1999, both designed in collaboration with award-winning architect Gene Bates. The Westfields Golf Club in Clifton opened first.

A creek runs in front of the well-protected green complex of the long 550-yard, par 5 18th hole at Raspberry Falls Golf & Hunt Club in Leesburg. You won't find many with the courage or the game to go for this one in two.

The 506-yard, par 5 ninth hole at the Kiskiack Golf Club in Williamsburg is a difficult hole made more so by an uphill second shot to the green. Water protects the fairway landing area on both sides, and seven large bunkers protect the approach to the green.

Forty-eight bunkers and only four holes protected by water offer minimal resistance, and the landing areas are generous enough to allow golfers of all skill levels a fairly painless outing. The course plays longer than it looks, and the scores mysteriously add up quickly.

The stately clubhouse adds to the overall pleasure of the Westfields experience.

There are many wonderful holes at Westfields; but the most picturesque is the short par-4 16th, where a narrow green is guarded by water and a large bunker.

The other Couples Signature course is Heron Ridge, a long links-style layout just 10 miles from the Virginia Beach oceanfront.

The front nine is devoid of trees as it spreads out along flat land with sand and water everywhere. The ninth hole, a behemoth 554-yard par 5, defines the front side.

The mammoth 554-yard, par 5 ninth hole at the Heron Ridge Golf Club in Virginia Beach marks the end of a nine-hole, links-style layout nearly devoid of trees, and where wind whips across the landscape to wreak havoc on golfers.

The back nine runs through extensive groves of oaks and pines.

In all, 14 holes are affected by a vast expanse of water and wetlands, where errant shots are sure to drown. The course is subject to the whims of the seaside wind.

Players, beware. The Heron Ridge measures 7,017 yards from the back tees. Let Freddie and the low handicappers have it. There are four other tee areas designed for players of every skill.

The final addition to Virginia golf in 1999 is the first PGA Tour venture in the Middle Atlantic region. The Tournament Players Club at Virginia Beach opened to much fanfare.

Legendary golf architect Pete Dye and Hampton Roads native and touring professional Curtis Strange collaborated on the project.

The links-style course stretches to a gigantic 7,432 yards from the back tees. Even the gold tees offer a stiff test at 6,974 yards.

Five holes border woodlands at the extreme edge of the property, but they offer only a momentary diversion on a course routed through wide-open spaces. Huge sandy waste areas and extensive water hazards rule the day.

The single-level brick clubhouse fits into the Virginia landscape perfectly. The four-star restaurant, plush locker rooms, and a pro shop brimming with merchandise outstrip even the TPC's gaudy reputation.

The new breed of Virginia courses doesn't end with these 10. However, they set a standard only the most extraordinary will be able to match.

The 479-yard, par 4 second hole of the TPC at Virginia Beach is a gigantic test of a golfer's power. The links-style hole has a hole-long waste area running up the left side of the fairway.

PRESIDENTS AND VIRGINIA GOLF

Virginia, the mother of presidents, has welcomed its share of "First" visitors to its golf courses.

Bill Clinton has played many a leisurely Saturday round at Army-Navy Country Club in Arlington. He has also played with two-time U.S. Open winner and 2001 Ryder Cup captain Curtis Strange at Kingsmill Golf Club in Williamsburg.

George Bush favored the Robert Trent Jones Golf Club in Gainesville, site of two Presidents Cups, though he once played the course at the Marine base in Quantico.

Lyndon Johnson and Richard Nixon were partial to Burning Tree Country Club in Maryland, which was the most popular presidential golf hideout until its male-only membership policy made it a political landmine. However, Johnson wasn't averse to an occasional round at Army-Navy.

Gerald Ford, who helped dedicate the Golf Hall of Fame at Pinehurst, North Carolina, just days after pardoning Nixon, shot the lowest round of his presidency—81—at The Cascades in Hot Springs.

Given their proximity to the White House, Army-Navy and Washington Golf and Country Club have received most of the presidential play. But The Homestead Course and the Cascades Course in Hot Springs have enjoyed a long relationship with the White House, and the Golden Horseshoe Golf Club in Williamsburg shouldn't be forgotten, either.

Presidential involvement in golf, and presidential golf experiences in Virginia, got off to a slow start. William McKinley had a brief, unhappy fling with the game that lasted less than two rounds. It began in Bluff Point, New York, in 1897 and ended for good on the Homestead Course two years later.

Herbert Hoover, Harry Truman, and Jimmy Carter ignored the game. There is no evidence that Ronald Reagan ever played in Virginia during his term of office.

Then there were the rest. I found the older anecdotes to be the most interesting; proof positive that McKinley's experience on Virginia's fairways was, to say the least, atypical.

William Howard Taft, the 27th president, had a gargantuan appetite for everything, especially golf.

His immersion in the game was every bit as deep as Dwight Eisenhower's, and was critical to the sport gaining a foothold in the United States. Golf had been introduced in this country only 20 years before Taft was elected.

Shortly before Taft's inauguration, famous golfer and friend Walter J. Travis visited with the president-elect. He was dazzled by Taft's ambition to popularize the game.

"There is good reason to hope that by virtue of his example a vast number of men who are actively engaged in various professional and business pursuits may be led to see if there is anything in this so-called 'old woman's game,'" Travis told the *New York Times.* "Mr. Taft says he sees no reason why the game should not be as equally democratic here as in the home of its birth. In Scotland and in many parts of England and Ireland, nearly every one [sic] plays."

Soon after Taft was sworn in, newspapers began reporting stories of unprecedented congestion on courses throughout the nation.

"It is almost impossible to play on the public courses on Saturdays, Sundays and holidays," said Tom White, the keeper of the Van Cortlandt golf course in New York. "The fact that golf is President Taft's favorite game is undoubtedly responsible for this great increase . . . It is just an indication of the way people allow those in high places to set the fashion for them, in other things besides dress."

The 355-pound Ohio native, who occupied the White House from 1909 to 1913, once created a national scandal while on vacation at The Homestead. Instead of spending the entire Fourth of July in patriotic observance of Independence Day, Taft played golf.

William Howard Taft's enthusiasm for golf helped sell the game to the American people. Although his weight hovered around 355 pounds, Taft's scores were unusually good for someone his size. He averaged in the high 80s to low 90s.

He once refused to meet the president of Chile because his arrival conflicted with a scheduled round of golf.

Taft was criticized unmercifully for devoting more time to golf than to the issues of state. It never eroded his love of the game.

In November 1911, Taft returned to The Homestead near the end of what seemed like a presidential odyssey.

He had been out of Washington for seven weeks. Starting in Beverly, Massachusetts, Taft arrived at Hot Springs via Seattle, San Francisco, Los

Angeles, and 205 other cities, towns, and villages. The president traveled more than 18,000 miles, passed through 26 states, and made 305 speeches. Nearly five million people saw him pass by on his special train.

At 8:30 a.m., Taft's car pulled into Hot Springs. By 11, he was on The Homestead course with Major Archibald Butt, a military aide who was a frequent links companion.

"Mr. Taft had not played golf for so long that he found himself in none too good form for the first few holes," the correspondent for *the New York Times* wrote. "But his game strengthened after that and he held his score down to 94. . . . The President was not accompanied by a gallery, though a large crowd was at the first tee and would have followed but for a gentle hint from Major Butts [sic]."

Taft left the White House while in his mid-50s. He lived another 15 years, serving as chief justice of the Supreme Court, law professor at Yale, and unofficial ambassador of golf to his own country.

WOODROW WILSON once described golf as "an ineffectual attempt to put an elusive ball into an obscure hole with implements ill-adapted to the purpose." Sounds like he didn't particularly care for it. In reality, the 28th president was a fanatic.

Wilson, a native Virginian who was president from 1913 to 1921, played almost every day and was especially fond of Washington Golf and Country Club. Weather was rarely a deterrent, and Wilson normally played as many holes as he could in the 60 to 90 minutes he allotted himself. If there was snow on the ground, Wilson played with a ball painted red by a Secret Service agent.

In December 1917, Wilson's friend Col. Ed-

Woodrow Wilson, president from 1913 to 1921, was among the most avid golfers ever in the White House. He averaged six rounds of golf a week, even during his term. He often played at Washington G & CC in Arlington. He wasn't much off the tee, but despite his awkward form, was a decent putter.

ward Thomas Brown wrote to his wife that "I have played golf almost every morning this week with the President. We leave the House promptly at 8:30, arrive at the course in ab't twenty minutes, play twelve holes, and back in the car at 10:15 or 10:20,

the difference being attributed to my loss of balls.

"I don't think the President has ever lost a ball in his life. He doesn't play what 'we golfers' call a long game, but his direction is simply remarkable."

So were Wilson's average scores. He almost never broke 100. In true *Tin Cup* style, he once took a 26 on the second hole at Washington G&CC, flailing away at the ball until he got it to stop on a severely sloped green.

The press wasn't anxious to embarrass Wilson before the world, and occasionally they made him out to be more skilled than he actually was.

In a 1914 interview with Samuel Blythe, Wilson recalled a round he'd played at Piping Rock on Long Island. The next day, it was reported that he shot 80.

"The fact was, that day was one of the worst golf days I have had since I began, and it took me 146 strokes to make the round," he said. "Golf is my physical and mental barometer."

Wilson, who suffered a stroke two years before the end of his second term, played most often with White House physician Cary Grayson. It was Grayson, a rear admiral in the Navy, who prescribed that the game be incorporated in Wilson's daily health regimen.

In *Woodrow Wilson: An Intimate Memoir*, Grayson wrote how he used Wilson's teaching background to argue that the president should play a full round on weekends:

"I told him that as teachers had Saturdays for holidays, he, as a former teacher, ought to take at least a portion of Saturday for golf, and so he formed the habit of having an early breakfast on Saturday morning, followed by a game of golf."

In his correspondence, Wilson made no bones about the impact the rigors of the job and his personal tribulations had on his score.

In 1918, the British tank *Britannia* was brought to the White House. One day Wilson took a ride, and as he climbed out, he scalded his right hand on a hot pipe.

The president's solution to the problem was to begin golfing using just one hand. In a May 1918 note to daughter Jessie, Wilson confided, "My hand is practically well again, though I have to put ointment on it every morning and wear a glove during the day. I am now playing golf with two hands, though not very well."

Wilson's first wife, Ellen, died in the White House in 1914. In March of the following year, Wilson met Edith Bolling Galt, a widow who was friends with the president's cousin, Helen Bones.

It appears to have been love at first sight. The president and his golf game barely held up when they were not together.

"My game is picking up a bit now," Wilson wrote to her in August 1915. "It suffered a collapse after you went away from me at Cornish. I *could* not get my attention concentrated on the ball. My thoughts were 'over the hills and far away' and my nerves were, to say the least, not wholly or perfectly under control. Don't you see that you will *have* to come and stay with me at the earliest possible moment—in order to improve my game *in life?*"

They were married in December of 1915 and honeymooned at The Homestead, where they played golf every day. The new first lady frequently accompanied her husband and Grayson on the course once they returned to Washington.

W A R R E N G. H A R D I N G, who served from 1921 to 1923, was already a member of Washington Golf and Country Club before he was elected.

According to *A History of Washington Golf and Country Club: A Century of Tradition*, the club's Board of Directors wrote Harding a letter after the 1920 election requesting that he detail any special desires he had now that he was president.

"[Harding] replied that he wished nothing that had not been supplied to him as a member in the past or which was not now available to other members," authors Tim Hackler and Amanda Robb wrote, quoting the club's annual report. "When told that Club members would expect to treat him just as President Wilson had been treated—namely, with the same attention and courtesy accorded to other members, but no more—he replied heartily that was exactly what he wanted."

In 1921, Harding participated in a tournament for national newspaper correspondents at Washington G&CC. The *New York Times'* account of his play that day indicated that Harding finished with a net-76 that, like players of all skill levels, could have been better.

"One man who had followed the play for the eighteen holes was prepared to submit a list of 'ifs,' many of them based on inexcusable errors of judgment or stroking, which proved that the President, with his handicap, easily should have carried off first honors," said the *Times* story, which carried no byline. "But the President would listen to no condolence. He had done his best to win and that was all there was to it."

There was no doubting Harding's enthusiasm for the game—and placing a more-than-occasional wager on the outcome. But in his case, it was truly a gamble. A preelection news account of Harding's membership in an informal group known as the "Senate Society for the Promotion of Golf" said he "has no extraordinary form, but a youthful swing."

In February 1923, when Harding ended more than two months of confinement because of cold weather, illness, and the pressures of the job to

Warren G. Harding continued the trend of presidential golfers during his tenure at the White House (1921-23). Another president whose playing and practice did not net good results, Harding had trouble breaking 100.

play golf at Columbia Country Club in Maryland, the *New York Times* found the story significant enough to run on the front page.

By the time F R A N K L I N D E L A N O R O O S E V E L T became president in 1933, he had been suffering from poliomyelitis for 12 years and had long since had to abandon golf.

Franklin D. Roosevelt (1933-1945) was a powerful player before he was stricken with polio at the age of 39, long before he entered the White House. His length off the tee kept his game respectable. He usually scored in the 80s and even won a club championship at Campobello Golf in Maine.

That didn't deter him from enjoying a sport in which he had taken an active interest from childhood. Father James Roosevelt had designed a six-hole course on the family estate at Hyde Park in New York around 1890. Young Franklin presumably cut his teeth there and at the family retreat on Campobello Island off the coast of Maine.

Roosevelt played frequently while serving in the Wilson Administration, though there is no record of him and Wilson playing together. Roosevelt was noted for his long, majestic drives, and his average score was in the 80s.

Although Eleanor Roosevelt once was quoted as saying that, after her husband was struck down by polio, he never again even mentioned the word "golf," that's not even remotely true, as a 1936 story from Farmington Country Club in Charlottesville confirms.

In town on presidential business on July 4, Roosevelt was treated to a putting exhibition by State Amateur contestants Morton McCarthy of Norfolk and Bobby Riegel of Richmond, the tournament's eventual winner.

A limousine carrying the president and first lady pulled onto the course and parked just a few feet from the 10th green.

The president never left the car, but watched intently, encouraging the players to strike their putts "accurately and smoothly now." Accounts indicate that he genuinely enjoyed the performance of both men.

"I have some golf background," he told them, "because my father built the course at Hyde Park back in 1889. It looks like you have wonderful greens here."

Calling D W I G H T D. E I S E N H O W E R a golf fanatic would be like describing Einstein as bright. There was no limit to his mania.

Within days of taking office in 1953,

Eisenhower was practicing his short game on the White House lawn. Later, he approved the construction of a putting green and a sand trap just outside the Oval Office. The floor of the Oval Office was horribly pockmarked from Eisenhower having tromped over it wearing his golf shoes.

Eisenhower went virtually nowhere without some piece of golf equipment, and he never missed an opportunity to squeeze in a round. It's estimated that, while president, Eisenhower played golf 800 times.

A few months after entering the White House, word got out that Ike was having problems breaking 90. The subject became a topic of national debate, with Eisenhower finally stating the obvious: The pressures of the job, and the severity of the nation's problems were taking a toll.

One Eisenhower aide, never named, leaked a story that Eisenhower was on his way to a match at Burning Tree Country Club when acting special counsel Bernard M. Shanley hurried into his office with a matter that demanded immediate attention.

When they were done, Shanley is reported to have said, "I'm sorry to have held you up, Mr. President. Have a good game."

To which Eisenhower replied: "Thanks, Bern. My golf would be a lot better if someone would do something about the price of beef."

Three days after that story appeared, Eisenhower was in Norfolk and played at the Sewell's Point Golf Club. He shot 43-44-87 on the par-72 course and unleashed a 250-yard drive on the third hole. He fired the low score in his unidentified foursome.

"People who play this course regularly consider 87 a pretty good score," Sewell's Point pro Johnny O'Donnell, that year's State Open titlist, told the Associated Press.

Security was so tight for the president's visit

that virtually no one saw him play. One club member, Dr. Royal T. Somers, shook Eisenhower's hand, but Ike wasn't around long enough to make small talk with anyone else.

Ironically, the round came on the same course that Eisenhower's good friend, Arnold Palmer, would play his first match after turning pro following his 1954 U.S. Amateur victory. The combination of Eisenhower's insatiable passion for the game and Palmer's swashbuckling style resulted in a national golf boom the likes of which had never been seen before.

Eisenhower also had a friendship with Sam Snead, the two playing occasional rounds both at Burning Tree and at The Greenbrier Resort in West Virginia.

In *Slamming Sammy*, Snead wrote that he once tried to give the president some pointers:

"Mr. President, I think if you turned a little more . . . here, hit another one."
He said, "You know my pro, Ed Dudley?"
I said, "Yes, sir."
"Well, all he ever tells me is turn, turn, turn, turn!"
It seemed like Ike was losing sleep over the fact that his short backswing was causing him to lose power on his drives. The problem was so obvious, I didn't hesitate to give him my advice: "You've got to stick your butt out more, Mr. President."
His bodyguards couldn't believe I'd said that to the President of the United States. I couldn't believe it either, but Ike was too intent on his game to notice.

Eisenhower suffered a heart attack in 1954—hours after finishing 27 holes at Cherry Hills in Denver—ileitis in 1956, and a mild stroke in 1957. After each, he was back on the tee within a few months.

Walter Hall, the former pro at the Kennedy home course in Hyannis Port, Massachusetts, once

President Dwight D. Eisenhower often played golf in impressive company. Here, Eisenhower sits with Byron Nelson (far left), Ben Hogan, and Clifford Roberts (far right), longtime chairman of the Masters, after a round of golf at Augusta National. While in Washington, Ike played two or three rounds a week; but on vacation, he often played 36 holes a day at Augusta National, where he was a member.

said that J O H N F. K E N N E D Y would have consistently scored in the 70s if he had played three times a week. There is little doubt that Kennedy was the finest golfer to inhabit the White House, with average scores in the high 70s to low 80s.

"I never played a full eighteen holes with him," Hall said in 1961, while preparing to compete in a PGA senior event in Dunedin, Florida. "He always was too busy. It would be five or seven or nine holes usually . . . He really moves the ball. He hits a longer drive than I do. And he's a real competitor.

"His concentration is wonderful. He was a senator then and usually there were people tagging along talking business with him. When he'd come up to his ball he'd forget everything but making the shot."

According to close friend Bill Battle of Ivy, Kennedy had a rhythmic swing that looked like the product of years of intense range work. In reality, it was the product of amazing natural athletic ability, especially considering the severe back injury Kennedy suffered while playing football at Harvard.

Battle, who Kennedy would later name Ambassador to Australia, advised his friend on numerous campaign issues, including his choice for vice president.

Their first of several conversations on the subject took place on July 4, right before the 1960 Democratic Convention. The Kennedy clan was spending a weekend at the family compound on Cape Cod. Battle and his wife were invited.

"Jack and I were playing golf with Bobby Kennedy, and Jack asked me, 'Who do you think I should take as vice president?'" Battle recalled. "It was his shot. He was standing over the ball when I said, without hesitation, 'Lyndon Johnson.'"

Pres. John F. Kennedy (1961-1963) was probably the best of all the presidential golfers, scoring in the high 70s, low 80s. Two things kept him from being even better: A bad back, which kept his practice to a minimum, and such insistence on keeping his passion for the game a secret that he rarely played.

Eisenhower that the admittedly pro-Kennedy *New York Times* found it necessary to editorialize on the subject in December 1960.

A good many reasons can figure into a man's decision to give (golf) up . . . But a reason you hardly ever hear anymore, and ought never to hear, is that a man expects to be too busy at the White House to play golf, except on vacations. There have been a lot of jokes about presidential golf . . . it is possible that jokes about the president playing golf are in oversupply . . . But the nation might well worry its conscience over whether it has been having so much uncharitable fun with presidential golf that it has made a trip around the course a political liability too great for a president to bear. That would be absurd.

One little-known fact about Kennedy is that he played at Fauquier Springs Country Club in Warrenton on April 9, 1961, and April 16, 1961.

The course, built in 1957, sits on sulphur springs frequented by many of the early presidents as a retreat. The nation's fifth president, James Monroe, owned a cabin on the property. The original hotel was burned to the ground by Yankee soldiers during the Civil War, rebuilt, and burned to the ground again.

There is no physical evidence at the club that he was ever there and no knowledge of his score. The club's president, Bob Foley, was a 16-year-old boy and member of the club when Kennedy came to play. Foley and friend Jimmy Wines were the two final choices to caddie for Kennedy; Wines was chosen.

"He came in a black sedan with maybe one or two other cars," Foley remembered. "There was no pomp to it, no entourage. He arrived just like anyone else who wanted to play golf there."

"I'll never forget this. Jack never flinched, just hit the ball, turned to me and said, 'Why would he take it? He's the most powerful man in Washington now.' And I said, 'Yep, he is, but if you win, he won't be. It's one thing if he's the majority leader with a Republican president. But if he's a majority leader with you as president, a strong president, he'll be nothing but a messenger boy to the Senate.'

"I knew Jack had thought of that, but his way was to make you think it was your idea. Then I told him, 'Furthermore, you need him in the South if you're to have any chance.'"

Kennedy was extremely secretive about his passion for the game. The Democrats had blasted Eisenhower for spending too much time on the links during his presidency. Kennedy didn't want to be painted with the same broad brush.

Kennedy played so rarely compared to

Clockwise from top left: Pres. Lyndon B. Johnson (at Golden Horseshoe), Pres. Ronald Reagan (with wife Nancy) President Bill Clinton, and Pres. George Bush.

APPENDIX
TOURNAMENT RESULTS

WOMEN'S AMATEUR RESULTS

Year	Winner/Runner-up	Score	Site
1922	Mrs. J.W. Zimmerman, Lexington	3 and 2	Homestead Course
	Mrs. Jean S. Jones, Richmond		Hot Springs
1923	Margaret Lucado, Lynchburg	2 up	Homestead Course
	Mrs. J.W. Zimmerman, Lexington		Hot Springs
1924	Margaret Lucado, Lynchburg	4 and 3	Homestead Course
	Mrs. Ashby Jones, Richmond		Hot Springs
1925	Mrs. A.L. Myatt, Hampton	2 and 1	Princess Anne CC
	Mrs. J.C. Spitz, Richmond		Virginia Beach
1926	Mrs. Jean S. Jones, Richmond	default	CC of Virginia
	Mrs. J.C. Spitz, Richmond		Richmond
1927	Louise Branch, Richmond	3 and 1	Norfolk CC
	Mrs. W. Barham Jones, Norfolk		Norfolk
1928	Mrs. J.C. Spitz, Richmond	3 and 2	Norfolk CC
	Mrs. W. Barham Jones, Virginia Beach		Norfolk
1929	Mrs. Jean S. Jones, Richmond	4 and 3	CC of Virginia
			James River
	Martha Martin, Richmond		Richmond
1930	Clara Priddy, Richmond	19 holes	Homestead Course
	Mrs. A.E. McClure, Roanoke		Hot Springs
1931	Mrs. H.C. Kersten, Richmond	4 and 3	Farmington CC
	Mrs. T.A. Balthis, Richmond		Charlottesville
1932	Mrs. David H. Clark, Va. Beach	4 and 3	Princess Anne
	Mrs. Jean S. Jones, Richmond		Virginia Beach
1933	Mrs. Kennon Rodwell, Virginia Beach	3 and 2	Roanoke CC
	Mrs. H.C. Kersten, Richmond		Roanoke
1934	Lily Harper, Portsmouth	5 and 4	Cavalier CC
	Mrs. George Schenk, Norfolk		Virginia Beach
1935	Lily Harper, Portsmouth	19 holes	Hermitage CC
	Mrs. David Clark, Alexandria		Richmond
1936	Lily Harper, Portsmouth	3 and 2	James River CC
	Mrs. N.H. Allen, Newport News		Newport News
1937	Lily Harper, Portsmouth	3 and 2	Homestead Course
	Susie Ingalls, Hot Springs		Hot Springs
1938	Lillian Wood, Richmond	4 and 3	CC of Virginia
	Mrs. Grayson Dashiell, Richmond		Richmond
1939	Mrs. Lily Harper-Martin, Portsmouth	7 and 5	Princess Anne
	Mrs. George Owens, Richmond		Virginia Beach
1940	Mrs. Lily Harper-Martin, Portsmouth.	8 and 6	Chamberlin CC
	Mrs. N.H. Allen, Newport News		Hampton
1941	Mrs. Lily Harper-Martin, Portsmouth.	2 and 1	Hermitage CC
	Mrs. George Owens, Richmond		Richmond
1942-45	NO TOURNAMENTS, WORLD WAR II		
1946	Mrs. J.W. Reynolds, Richmond	6 and 5	Ingleside CC
	Mrs. R.C. Hockaday, Newport News		Staunton
1947	Mrs. J.W. Reynolds, Richmond	19 holes	Ingleside CC
	Mrs. J.B. Cralle, Roanoke		Staunton
1948	Mrs. J.W. Reynolds, Richmond	5 and 4	Roanoke CC
	Mrs. George Owens, Petersburg		Roanoke
1949	Sydney Elliott, Charlottesville	5 and 3	Princess Anne CC
	Mrs. J.R. Hall, Richmond		Virginia Beach
1950	Mrs. J.B. Cralle, Richmond	8 and 7	Homestead Course
	Mary Patton Janssen, Charlottesville		Hot Springs
1951	Mrs. Wm. Pollard, Charlottesville	10 and 8	Farmington CC
	Mary Patton Janssen, Charlottesville		Charlottesville
1952	Sydney Elliott, Charlottesville	7 and 6	Washington G&CC
	Mrs. A.B. Bower, Richmond		Arlington
1953	Sydney Elliott, Charlottesville	10 and 8	Homestead Course
	Mrs. Charles Egenroad, Arlington		Hot Springs
1954	Mrs. Margaret Allen, Arlington	5 and 4	Cavalier Y&GC
	Virginia Edwards, Fredericksburg		Virginia Beach
1955	Mrs. Margaret Allen, Arlington	5 and 4	Homestead Course
	Mrs. A.B. Bower, Richmond		Hot Springs
1956	Mrs. Margaret Allen, Arlington	5 and 4	Homestead Course
	Sydney Elliott, Charlottesville		Hot Springs
1957	Mary Patton Janssen, Charlottesville	6 and 5	Princess Anne
	Mrs. Charles Egenroad, Arlington		Virginia Beach
1958	Mary Patton Janssen, Charlottesville	12 and 11	Cascades Course
	Mrs. Charles Egenroad, Arlington		Hot Springs
1959	Mary Patton Janssen, Charlottesville	13 and 11	Hermitage CC
	Donna O'Brien, Richmond		Richmond
1960	Mary Patton Janssen, Charlottesville	15 and 13	Cascades Course
	Sydney Elliott, Charlottesville		Hot Springs
1961	Mary Patton Janssen, Charlottesville	8 and 6	Farmington CC
	Connie Gorsuch, Roanoke		Charlottesville
1962	Mary Patton Janssen, Charlottesville	1 up	Cascades Course
	Robbye King, Arlington		Hot Springs
1963	Robbye King, Arlington	2 and 1	Cascades Course
	Mrs. William Pollard, Charlottesville		Hot Springs
1964	Mrs. William Pollard, Charlottesville	3 and 2	Cascades Course
	Robbye King, Norfolk		Hot Springs
1965	Mrs. Barbara Hughes, Richmond	3 and 1	Cascades Course
	Jane Mack, Richmond		Hot Springs
1966	Robbye King, Arlington	3 and 1	Cascades Course
	Mrs. Helen Rawls, Suffolk		Hot Springs
1967	Mrs. Barbara Hughes, Richmond	4 and 3	Cascades Course
	Mrs. Robert Trebilco, Arlington		Hot Springs
1968	Mrs. Richard Canney, Centreville	7 and 5	Cascades Course
	Mrs. Ralph Petrone, Blacksburg		Hot Springs
1969	Mrs. Robbye King-Youel, Charlottesville	6 and 5	Cascades Course
	Mrs. Barbara Hughes, Richmond		Hot Springs
1970	Mrs. Robbye King-Youel, Charlottesville	3 and 1	Cascades Course
	Candy Sibbick, Martinsville		Hot Springs
1971	Mrs. Robbye King-Youel, Charlottesville	37 holes	Cascades Course
	Mrs. Richard Canney, Centreville		Hot Springs
1972	Mrs. Robbye King-Youel, Charlottesville	2 up	Cascades Course
	Candy Sibbick, Martinsville		Hot Springs
1973	Pamela Clark, Alexandria	2 and 1	Cascades Course
	Jane Mack, Richmond		Hot Springs
1974	Candy Sibbick-Robertson, Charlottesville	7 and 6	Cascades Course
	Mrs. Barbara Hughes, Richmond		Hot Springs
1975	Nancy Hollenbeck, Arlington	2 up	Cascades Course
	Mrs. Kay Schiefelbein, Alexandria		Hot Springs
1976	Mrs. Kay Schiefelbein, Alexandria	3 and 2	Cascades Course
	Liz Waynick, Roanoke		Hot Springs
1977	Jane Mack, Richmond	37 holes	Cascades Course
	Mrs. Robbye King-Youel, Charlottesville		Hot Springs
1978	Jane Mack, Richmond	5 and 4	Cascades Course
	Mrs. Kay Schiefelbein, Alexandria		Hot Springs
1979	Mrs. Kay Schiefelbein, Alexandria	4 and 2	Cascades Course
	Mrs. Robbye King-Youel, Charlottesville		Hot Springs
1980	Kandi Kessler, Charlottesville	7 and 6	Cascades Course
	Liz Rowland, Portsmouth		Hot Springs
1981	Liz Waynick, Roanoke	2 and 1	Cascades Course
	Kathy Ayers, Waynesboro		Hot Springs
1982	Jane Mack, Richmond	6 and 5	Cascades Course
	Robin Andrews, Galax		Hot Springs
1983	Anne Patrick, Richmond	2 up	Cascades Course
	Liz Waynick, Roanoke		Hot Springs
1984	Kandi Kessler, Charlottesville	4 and 3	Cascades Course
	Anne Patrick, Richmond		Hot Springs
1985	Donna Andrews, Lynchburg	4 and 3	Cascades Course
	Penny Stallins, Salem		Hot Springs
1986	Donna Andrews, Lynchburg	2 and 1	Cascades Course
	Fran Hensley, Martinsville		Hot Springs
1987	Donna Andrews, Lynchburg	3 and 2	Cascades Course
	Jane Mack, Richmond		Hot Springs
1988	Donna Andrews, Lynchburg	5 and 4	Cascades Course
	Susan Slaughter, Floyd		Hot Springs
1989	Donna Andrews, Lynchburg	22 holes	Cascades Course
	Donna Martz, Broadway		Hot Springs
1990	Donna Martz, Broadway	3 and 2	Cascades Course
	Mrs. Kay Schiefelbein, Alexandria		Hot Springs
1991	Vikki Valentine, Virginia Beach	3 and 2	Cascades Course
	Sherry Zaleski, Manassas		Hot Springs
1992	Jane Mack, Richmond	2 and 1	Cascades Course
	Sara Cole, Roanoke		Hot Springs
1993	Anne Patrick, Richmond	1 up	Cascades Course
	Dot Bolling, Salem		Hot Springs
1994	Amy Ellertson, Richmond	7 and 6	Cascades Course
	Natalie Easterly, Richmond		Hot Springs
1995	Amy Ellertson, Richmond	7 and 5	Cascades Course
	Fran Hensley, Martinsville		Hot Springs
1996	Lee Shirley, Salem	4 and 3	Cascades Course
	Maggie Balch, Richmond		Hot Springs
1997	Lee Shirley, Salem	2 up	Cascades Course
	Amy Ellertson, Richmond		Hot Springs
1998	Lee Shirley, Salem	1 up	Cascades Course
	Catalina Durall, Glen Allen		Hot Springs
1999	Mimi Hoffman, Alexandria	2 and 1	Glenrochie CC
	Chris Epperly, Newport News		Abingdon

VIRGINIA STATE AMATEUR CHAMPIONS

	Winner/Runner-up	Score	Site
1911	Wm. H. Palmer Jr., Richmond	N/A	CC of Virginia
	H.H. Meade, Richmond		Richmond
1912	James McMenamin, Hampton	82-88-170*	Norfolk CC
	Wm. H. Palmer Jr., Richmond	84-86-170	Norfolk
1913	James McMenamin, Hampton	82-85-167	Hampton Roads GC
	Otho Parramore, Hampton	82-86-168	Hampton
1914	Wm. H. Palmer Jr., Richmond	156	Hermitage CC
	W.P. Wood, Richmond	163	Richmond
1915	Matthew Paxton Jr., Lexington	78-82-160	Roanoke CC
	Rives Fleming, Richmond	83-85-168	Roanoke
1916	Matthew Paxton Jr., Lexington	152	Lexington GC
	Wilson Wallace, Richmond	159	Lexington
1917	J. Pope Seals, Richmond	79-83-162	CC of Virginia,
			Westhampton
	Rives Fleming, Richmond	86-85-171	Richmond
1918	Silas M. Newton, Richmond	77-82-159**	Oakwood CC
	J. Pope Seals, Richmond	82-77-159	Lynchburg
1919	J.S. Barron, Norfolk	4 and 3	Norfolk CC
	Silas M. Newton, Richmond		Norfolk
1920	J.S. Barron, Norfolk	153***	Old Point Comfort
	Matthew Paxton Jr., Lexington	153	Hampton
1921	H.H. Hume, Norfolk	77-81-158****	CC of Virginia
	Frank Jones, Richmond	85-73-158	Richmond
	Dr. Dorsey Taylor, Richmond	79-79-158	
1922	Silas M. Newton, Richmond	11 and 10	Homestead
	H. Crim Peck, Lexington		Hot Springs
1923	H. Crim Peck, Lexington	3 and 1	Homestead
	Elmore Hotchkiss Jr., Richmond		Hot Springs
1924	Paul Jamison, Roanoke	3 and 2	Homestead
	A.L. Hawse, Richmond		Hot Springs
1925	Major E.L. Naiden, Hampton	2 and 1	Lakeside CC
	H.H. Hume, Norfolk		Richmond
1926	J. Taylor Crump, Richmond	2 and 1	Cascades
	Dr. Rice Warren, Charlottesville		Hot Springs
1927	Charles Mackall, Charlottesville	5 and 3	Princess Anne
	Jack Howard, Richmond		Virginia Beach
1928	Billy Howell, Richmond	9 and 7	Cascades
	J. Davis Ewell, Richmond		Hot Springs
1929	Pat Dillon, Virginia Beach	2 up	Princess Anne
	Charles Nelson, Richmond		Virginia Beach
1930	Chandler Harper, Portsmouth	2 up	Cascades
	Billy Howell, Richmond		Hot Springs
1931	Billy Howell, Richmond	9 and 8	Hampton Roads GC
	Chandler Harper, Portsmouth		Hampton
1932	Billy Howell, Richmond	9 and 7	CC of Virginia James
			River
	Jimmy Watts, Lynchburg		Richmond
1933	Chandler Harper, Portsmouth	10 and 9	Farmington CC
	Lansing Eubank, Richmond		Charlottesville
1934	Chandler Harper, Portsmouth	7 and 5	Princess Anne
	Aulick Burke, Petersburg		Virginia Beach
1935	Billy Howell, Richmond	6 and 5	Cascades
	Bobby Riegel, Richmond		Hot Springs
1936	Bobby Riegel, Richmond	4 and 3	Farmington CC
	Frank Sutton, Richmond		Charlottesville
1937	Dick Payne, Norfolk	9 and 7	Cascades
	Walter Cushman, Charlottesville		Hot Springs
1938	James O. Watts, Lynchburg	10 and 9	Cascades
	Walter Cushman, Charlottesville		Hot Springs
1939	Wynsol Spencer, Newport News	3 and 1	Princess Anne
	Morton McCarthy, Norfolk		Virginia Beach
1940	Sam Bates, Norfolk	9 and 8	Cascades
	Charley Kent, Richmond		Hot Springs
1941	Walter Cushman, Charlottesville	2 and 1	Cascades
	George Payton, Hampton		Hot Springs
1942	Jack Kamilton, Newport News	1 up	Cascades
	George Payton, Hampton		Hot Springs
1943-45	No tournaments, World War II		
1946	Edmund Gravely, Richmond	6 and 5	CC of Virginia James
			River
	Jack Hamilton, Newport News		Richmond
1947	Jack Hamilton, Newport News	4 and 3	Boonsboro CC
	Dave Ewell Jr., Richmond		Lynchburg

Year	Winner / Runner-up	Result	Site
1948	Wynsol Spencer, Newport News / Dick Payne, Norfolk	6 and 5	Cascades, Hot Springs
1949	Jack Hamilton, Newport News / Wynsol Spencer, Newport News	3 and 2	Cascades, Hot Springs
1950	Dick Payne, Virginia Beach / Wynsol Spencer, Newport News	2 up	Cascades, Hot Springs
1951	Connie Sellers, Roanoke / George Fulton, Roanoke	4 and 3	Cascades, Hot Springs
1952	George Gosey, Lynchburg / Runt English, Roanoke	7 and 6	Cascades, Hot Springs
1953	Wynsol Spencer, Newport News / George Gosey, Lynchburg	2 and 1	Cascades, Hot Springs
1954	George Fulton, Roanoke / Buddy Loving, Charlottesville	4 and 3	Cascades, Hot Springs
1955	Wynsol Spencer, Newport News / Lt. Larry Hurst, Oceana	5 and 4	Cascades, Hot Springs
1956	Wayne Jackson, Newport News / Harry Easterly Jr., Richmond	1 up	Cascades, Hot Springs
1957	Robert Q. Wallace, Norfolk / Tom Strange, Norfolk	5 and 3	Cascades, Hot Springs
1958	Jimmy Flippen, Danville / Walter Lawrence, Richmond	4 and 2	Cascades, Hot Springs
1959	Wynsol Spencer, Newport News / Jordan Ball, Virginia Beach	2 up	Cascades, Hot Springs
1960	Ned Baber, Richmond / Wright Garrett, Danville	39 holes	Cascades, Hot Springs
1961	Bobby Loy, Norfolk / Barclay Andrews, Roanoke	3 and 1	Cascades, Hot Springs
1962	Vinny Giles, Lynchburg / Sam Wallace, Williamsburg	6 and 5	Cascades, Hot Springs
1963	Nelson Broach, Richmond / Orville Hamlin, Blacksburg	7 and 6	Cascades, Hot Springs
1964	Vinny Giles, Lynchburg / Charlie McDowell, Virginia Beach	2 and 1	Cascades, Hot Springs
1965	Wayne Jackson, Hampton / Tim Collins, Christiansburg	6 and 5	Cascades, Hot Springs
1966	Vinny Giles, Lynchburg / Nelson Broach, Richmond	7 and 6	Cascades, Hot Springs
1967	Sam Wallace, Williamsburg / Billy Deemer, Blacksburg	7 and 5	Cascades, Hot Springs
1968	Vinny Giles, Richmond 70-70-70-65-275 / Wayne Jackson, Hampton 68-71-79-72-290		Cascades, Hot Springs
1969	Vinny Giles, Richmond / Wayne Jackson, Hampton	1 up	Cascades, Hot Springs
1970	Lanny Wadkins, Richmond / Bobby Wadkins, Richmond	6 and 5	Cascades, Hot Springs
1971	Vinny Giles, Richmond / Lanny Wadkins, Richmond	3 and 2	Cascades, Hot Springs
1972	Bobby Wadkins, Richmond / Curtis Strange, Virginia Beach	2 and 1	Cascades, Hot Springs
1973	Carl Peterson, Virginia Beach / Harry Lea, Danville	1 up	Cascades, Hot Springs
1974	Curtis Strange, Virginia Beach / Skeeter Heath, Hampton	3 and 2	Roanoke CC, Roanoke
1975	Curtis Strange, Virginia Beach / O.D. Gardner, Newport News	8 and 7	Cedar Point CC, Suffolk
1976	Skeeter Heath, Hampton / John Bruce, Danville	11 and 10	Chatmoss CC, Martinsville
1977	Neff McClary, Springfield / Billy Sibbick, Martinsville	1 up	Washington G&CC, Arlington
1978	Sam Wallace, Williamsburg / John Cuomo, Richmond	3 and 2	James River CC, Newport News
1979	Steve Smith, Martinsville / Pete Van Pelt, Fairfax	3 and 2	Cascades, Hot Springs
1980	Mark Lawrence, Richmond / Gil FitzHugh, Fairfax	3 and 2	Willow Oaks, Richmond
1981	George MacDonald, Virginia Beach / Dan Keffer, Roanoke	10 and 9	Danville GC, Danville
1982	Jeff Horn, Richmond / John Cuomo, Richmond	2 and 1	Cedar Point, Suffolk
1983	David Tolley, Roanoke / David Mankin, Fincastle	6 and 5	Blacksburg CC, Blacksburg
1984	Tom McKnight, Galax / Mike Pratt, Richmond	4 and 3	CC Petersburg, Petersburg
1985	Tom McKnight, Galax / J.P. Leigh, Chesapeake	3 and 2	Fairfax CC, Fairfax
1986	Brett West, Virginia Beach / Sam Stein, Richmond	4 and 2	Cascades, Hot Springs
1987	Vinny Giles, Richmond / Steve Douglass, Norfolk	1 up	Golden Eagle, Irvington
1988	Keith Decker, Fieldale / Dicky Linkous, Roanoke	3 and 1	Danville GC, Danville
1989	Tom McKnight, Galax / Vinny Giles, Richmond	4 and 3	CC of Virginia James River, Richmond
1990	Hank Klein, Richmond / Mike Grant, Radford	1 up	Birdwood GC, Charlottesville
1991	Keith Decker, Fieldale / Gary Strickfaden, Virginia Beach	4 and 3	Golden Eagle, Irvington
1992	Allen Barber, Yorktown / Keith Decker, Fieldale	5 and 4	Golden Horseshoe, Williamsburg
1993	David Partridge, Richmond / Simon Cooke, Richmond	5 and 4	James River CC, Newport News
1994	Scott Inman, Springfield / David Brogan, Lexington	3 and 1	RTJ Golf Club, Gainesville
1995	David Partridge, Richmond / Scott Inman, Springfield	3 and 2	Stoney Creek, Wintergreen
1996	John Rollins, Richmond / Troy Ferris, Norfolk	8 and 6	Cascades, Hot Springs
1997	John Rollins, Richmond / Dale Powell, Chatham	7 and 6	The Virginian, Bristol
1998	Jay Fischer, Suffolk / Pat Tallent, Vienna	2 up	Golden Eagle, Irvington
1999	Steve Marino, Fairfax / Keith Decker, Fieldale	5 and 4	Boonsboro CC, Lynchburg

* Won playoff, 79-86
** Seals disqualified during 18-hole playoff for undisclosed violation
*** Won 18-hole playoff, 80-81
**** Won 18-hole playoff, 82 to 89 to 94

EASTERN AMATEUR RESULTS
AT ELIZABETH MANOR CC, PORTSMOUTH

Year	Winner/Runner-up	Score
1957	Tom Strange	284
	Jordan Ball	286
1958	Ward Wettlaufer	286
	Claude King	289
1959	Ward Wettlaufer	284
	Horace Ervin	292
1960	Deane Beman	283
	William Chapman	289
1961	Deane Beman	281
	Ed Justa	282
1962	Charles Smith	275
	Deane Beman	282
1963	Deane Beman	282
	Wright Garrett	285
1964	Deane Beman	282
	Bill Campbell	285
1965	George Boutell	279*
	Jim Grant	279
1966	Marty Fleckman	277
	George Boutell	281
1967	Hal Underwood	277
	Vinny Giles	279
1968	Robert Barbarossa	286
	Hal Underwood	287
1969	Lanny Wadkins	278
	Bruce Ashworth	281
1970	Steve Melnyk	277*
	Tom Kite	277
	Morris Beecroft	277
	Eddie Pearce	277
1971	Ben Crenshaw	280
	Joey Dills	282
1972	Ben Crenshaw	281
	Danny Edwards	283
1973	Vinny Giles	285*
	Bob Byman	285
	Dallas McCoy	285
	David Strawn	285
1974	Andy Bean	272
	Gary Koch	277
1975	Curtis Strange	268
	Bob Byman	278
1976	Vance Heafner	284
	Scott Hoch	287
1977	Buddy Alexander	282
	John Jones	283
1978	Vance Heafner	281
	Tommy Carlton	287
	Scott Hoch	287
1979	Greg Chapman	281
	Steve Smith	283
	Scott Hoch	283
1980	Mike West	280
	Clarence Rose	282
1981	Steve Liebler	282
	George MacDonald	285
	Joey Sadowski	285
	Mike Pratt	285
	Kevin Klier	285
1982	John Inman	279
	Todd Anderson	281
	Steve Jurgensen	281
	David Leveille	281
1983	J.P. Leigh	280
	William Musto	282
1984	Fred Wadsworth	277*
	James Estes	277
1985	Phillip McCormick	271
	Bryan Sullivan	272
1986	Ralph Howe III	279*
	Tim Loustalot	279
1987	Jay Nichols	274
	Bob Goettlicher	275
1988	O.D. Vincent	273
	Steve Douglass	274
	Rick Williams	274
	Ryoken Kawagishi	274
1989	Les Porter	278
	Jason Wiedner	278
1990	Jon Hurst	268
	Mark Leetzow	278
	Jeff Barlow	278
1991	Jason Wiedner	273
	Jean-Paul Hebert	274
	Jim Furyk	274
1992	David Howser	274
	John Pettit	278
	Chris Haarlow	278
	Ronald Whittaker	278
1993	Tom McKnight	269
	Kelly Mitchum	270
1994	Steve Liebler	276
	Tony DeLuca	277
1995	Tom McKnight	274*
	Lee Eagleton	274
1996	Jason Buha	205*
	Tom McKnight	205
1997	Tom McKnight	270
	John Rollins	277
1998	Arron Oberholser	274
	Tom McKnight	278
	(Moved to 6,940-yard, par-72 Bide-A-Wee, Portsmouth)	
1999	Wayne Perske	279
	Joshua Habig	281

*won sudden-death playoff

VSGA SENIOR RESULTS

Year	Winner/Runnerup	Score	Site
1948	Fred Gill, Petersburg ‡	n/a	n/a
1949	Harry Thompson, Richmond ‡‡	n/a	n/a
1950	Coleman Hunter, Richmond	n/a	n/a
1951	Cy Young, Lexington‡‡‡	n/a	n/a
1952	H.W. Blandford, Newport News	n/a	n/a
1953	John Chappell, Richmond	n/a	n/a
1954	Herman Richardson, Richmond‡‡‡‡	n/a	n/a
1955	Fred Reuning, Bristol	n/a	n/a
1956	H. Gordon Adkins, Newport News	n/a	n/a
1957	Dr. Paul T. Goad, Roanoke	n/a	n/a
1958	Ray Croslin, Radford		
1959	E.D. Mustard, Charlottesville / Fred Reuning, Bristol	5 and 4	The Cascades, Hot Springs
1960	John Connolly, Fairfax / E.D. Mustard, Charlottesville	1 up	The Cascades, Hot Springs
1961	E.D. Mustard, Charlottesville / Smith Ferebee, Richmond	3 and 2	The Cascades, Hot Springs

Year	Champion / Runner-up	Score	Venue
1962	Smith Ferebee, Richmond	6 and 5	The Cascades
	Marvin Giles Jr., Lynchburg		Hot Springs
1963	E.D. Mustard, Charlottesville	1 up	The Cascades
	Crockett Carr, Roanoke		Hot Springs
1964	William Smith, Charlottesville	6 and 5	Cascades
	Don Kelsey, Blacksburg		Hot Springs
1965	Ed Evans, Lynchburg	4 and 3	Cascades
	Donald O'Brien, Richmond		Hot Springs
1966	George Beamon, Suffolk	5 and 4	Cascades
	Joe Harding, Richmond		Hot Springs
1967	Stan Holm, Norfolk	306	Cascades
	Edwin King, Richmond		Hot Springs
1968	Harry McCready, Portsmouth*	75-78-78-79-310	Cascades
	Joe LaSalle, Alexandria	75-77-80-78-310	
1969	Carson Logan, Portsmouth	3 and 2	Cascades
	George Gosey, Lynchburg		Hot Springs
1970	Dick Payne, Norfolk	6 and 5	Cascades
	Paul Severin, Richmond		Hot Springs
1971	Dick Payne, Norfolk	6 and 4	Cascades
	William Smith, Charlottesville		Hot Springs
1972	Dick Payne, Norfolk	7 and 6	Cascades
	Ed Loveless, Arlington		Hot Springs
1973	Paul Severin, Richmond	3 and 2	Cascades
	Dick Payne, Norfolk		Hot Springs
1974	James O. Watts, Lynchburg	9 and 7	Cascades
	Burr Melvin, Newport News		Hot Springs
1975	Landon Buchanan, Roanoke	1 up	Cascades
	Dick Payne, Norfolk		Hot Springs
1976	Aulick Burke, Bristol	3 and 2	Cascades
	Bill Robertson, Langley AFB		Hot Springs
1977	Ed Loveless, Arlington	2 up	Cascades
	Paul Severin, Richmond		Hot Springs
1978	Robert Flanagan, Arlington	1 up	Cascades
	Harry Easterly Jr., Richmond		Hot Springs
1979	Burr Melvin, Newport News	6 and 5	Cascades
	Bill Robertson, Hampton		Hot Springs
1980	Bill Robertson, Hampton	2 and 1	Cascades
	Johnny Johnston, Roanoke		Hot Springs
1981	Phil Grant, Hampton	2 and 1	Cascades
	George Costain, Lynchburg		Hot Springs
1982	Blair Nicely, Lexington	2 and 1	Cascades
	James O. Watts, Lynchburg		Hot Springs
1983	Bill Robertson, Hampton	1 up	Cascades
	Paul Severin, Richmond		Hot Springs
1984	Robert Lewis, Fairfax	19 holes	Cascades
	Hugh Botts, Fairfax		Hot Springs
1985	Jim Gunn, Alexandria	1 up	Cascades
	Arnold John, Roanoke		Hot Springs
1986	Moss Beecroft, Newport News	20 holes	Cascades
	Charlie Mattox, Charlottesville		Hot Springs
1987	Arman Fletcher, Roanoke	19 holes	Cascades
	Harry Easterly Jr., Richmond		Hot Springs
1988	Moss Beecroft, Newport News	19 holes	Cascades
	Robert Lewis, Fairfax		Hot Springs
1989	Henry Kerfoot, McLean	1 up	Cascades
	Moss Beecroft, Newport News		Hot Springs
1990	Moss Beecroft, Newport News	2 up	Cascades
	Arman Fletcher, Roanoke		Hot Springs
1991	Ken Newlin, Nokesville	3 and 1	Cascades
	Arman Fletcher, Roanoke		Hot Springs
1992	Moss Beecroft, Newport News	5 and 4	Cascades
	Ken Newlin, Nokesville		Hot Springs
1993	Jim Alexander, Lynchburg	4 and 3	Golden Horseshoe Williamsburg
	Bob Moyers, New Market		
1994	Moss Beecroft, Newport News	4 and 2	Cascades
	Don Foster, Salem		Hot Springs
1995	Claude Williamson, Waynesboro	5 and 4	Cascades
	Bob Moyers, New Market		Hot Springs
1996	Stan Fischer, Richmond	2 and 1	Cascades
	Bob Moyers, New Market		Hot Springs
1997	Claude Williamson, Waynesboro	20 holes	Cascades
	Stan Fischer, Richmond		Hot Springs
1998	O.D. Gardner, Newport News	4 and 3	Kingsmill River Course, Williamsburg
	Stan Fischer, Richmond		
1999	Moss Beecroft, Newport News	2 and 1	Cascades
	Stan Fischer, Richmond		Hot Springs

† Age limit was set at 45, match-play format
†† Small field in '48, format changed to stroke play
††† Format returned to match play
†††† Age limit raised to 50, two days of qualifying
* McCready won on 1st extra hole

PRESIDENTS CUP
ROBERT TRENT JONES GC, GAINESVILLE

1994 Matches
United States 20, International 12

First Day: Four-Ball: US 5, International 0; Corey Pavin/Jeff Maggert (US) def. Steve Elkington/Vijay Singh, 2 and 1; Jay Haas/Scott Hoch (US) def. Fulton Allem/David Frost, 6 and 5; Davis Love III/Fred Couples (US) def. Nick Price/Bradley Hughes, 1 up; John Huston/Jim Gallagher Jr. (US) def. Craig Parry/Robert Allenby, 4 and 2; Tom Lehman/Phil Mickelson (US) def. Frank Nobilo/Peter Senior, 3 and 2.

Foursomes: United States 2, International 2; Hale Irwin/Loren Roberts (US) def. Frost/Allem, 3 and 1; Haas/Hoch (US) def. Parry/Tsukasa Watanabe, 4 and 3; Nobilo/Allenby (Int.) def. Pavin/Maggert, 2 and 1; Elkington/Singh (Int.) def. Mickelson/Lehman, 2 and 1; Price/Mark McNulty (Int.) HALVE with Love/Gallagher; Totals: United States 7, International 2.
Second Day: Four-Ball: International 3, United States 1; Allem/McNulty (Int.) def. Gallagher/Huston, 4 and 3; Watanabe/Singh (Int.) def. Haas/Hoch, 3 and 1; Parry/Hughes (Int.) def. Roberts/Lehman, 4 and 3; Couples/Love (US) def. Nobilo/Allenby, 2 up; Price/Elkington (Int.) HALVE with Mickelson/Pavin Totals: United States 9, International 6.

Foursomes: United States 3, International 2; Frost/Senior (Int.) def. Irwin/Haas, 6 and 5; Pavin/Roberts (US) def. Parry/Allem, 1 up; Singh/Elkington (Int.) def. Maggert/Huston, 3 and 2; Love/Gallagher (US) def. Nobilo/Allenby, 7 and 5; Mickelson/Lehman (US) def. Hughes/McNulty, 3 and 2; Totals: United States 12, International 8.

Third Day: Singles: United States 8, International 4; Irwin (US) def. Allenby, 1 up; Haas (US) def. McNulty, 4 and 3; Gallagher (US) def. Watanabe, 4 and 3; Mickelson (US) HALVE with Allem; Singh (Int.) HALVE with Lehman; Senior (Int.) def. Huston, 3 and 2; Hoch (US) HALVE with Frost; Maggert (US) def. Hughes, 2 and 1; Nobilo (Int.) HALVE with Roberts; Couples (US) def. Price, 1 up; Love (US) def. Elkington, 1 up; Parry (Int.) def. Pavin, 1 up

1996 Matches
United States 16, International 15

First Day: Four-Ball: United States 4, International 1; Fred Couples/Davis Love III (US) def. Greg Norman/Robert Allenby, 2 and 1; Ernie Els/Mark McNulty (Int.) def. Scott Hoch/Mark Brooks, 2 up; Phil Mickelson/Corey Pavin (US) def. Vijay Singh/Jumbo Ozaki, 2 and 1; Mark O'Meara/David Duval (US) def. Steve Elkington/Frank Nobilo, 3 and 2; Tom Lehman/Steve Stricker (US) def. Nick Price/Peter Senior, 4 and 2.

Foursomes: United States 3, International 2; Kenny Perry/Justin Leonard (US) def. Price/David Frost, 3 and 2; O'Meara/Duval (US) def. Nobilo/Craig Parry, 2 and 1; Elkington/Singh (Int.) def. Lehman/Stricker, 2 up; Mickelson/Pavin (US) HALVE with Els/McNulty; Couples/Love (US) def. Norman/Allenby, 1 up. Totals: United States 7, International 2.

Second Day Four Ball: International 3, United States 2; Price/Elkington (Int.) def. Leonard/Norman, 2 up; Norman/Allenby (Int.) def. Stricker/Pavin, 1 up; Perry/Hoch (US) def. Parry/Nobilo, 2 and 1; Ozaki/Singh (Int.) def. Love/Couples, 2 and 1; O'Meara/Duval (US) def. Els/McNulty, 4 and 3; Totals: United States 9, International 5.
Foursomes: International 4, United States 1; Senior/Frost (Int.) def. Pavin/Mickelson, 3 and 2; Nobilo/Allenby (Int.) def. Love/Brooks, 3 and 2; Price/McNulty (Int.) def. Perry/Leonard, 3 and 1; Norman/Els (Int.) def. Lehman/Stricker, 1 up; O'Meara/Hoch (US) def. Elkington/Singh, 1 up; Totals: United States 10, International 9.

Third Day Singles: United States 6, International 6; Parry (Int.) def. Brooks, 5 and 4; Duval (US) def. Senior, 3 and 2; O'Meara (US) def. Price, 1 up; Frost (Int.) def. Perry, 7 and 6; Stricker (US) def. Allenby, 6 and 5; Hoch (US) def. McNulty, 1 up; Love (US) def. Ozaki, 5 and 4; Elkington (Int.) def. Leonard, 1 up; Els (Int.) def. Mickelson, 3 and 2; Norman (Int.) def. Pavin, 3 and 1; Nobilo (Int.) def. Lehman, 3 and 2; Couples (US) def. Singh, 2 and 1.

MICHELOB CHAMPIONSHIP RESULTS

Anheuser-Busch Golf Classic

Year	Winner	Score	Runner-up	Score
1981	John Mahaffey	72-67-70-67-276	Andy North	278
1982	Calvin Peete	66-68-69-203*	Bruce Lietzke	205
1983	Calvin Peete	66-75-66-69-276	Tim Norris	277
1984	Ronnie Black	69-69-66-63-267	Willie Wood	268
1985	Mark Wiebe	70-69-64-70-273**	John Mahaffey	273
1986	Fuzzy Zoeller	70-68-72-64-274	Jodie Mudd	276
1987	Mark McCumber	65-69-67-66-267	Bobby Clampett	268
1988	Tom Sieckmann	69-66-66-69-270**	Mark Wiebe	270
1989	Mike Donald	67-66-70-65-268**	Tim Simpson	268
			Hal Sutton	268
1990	Lanny Wadkins	65-66-67-68-266	Larry Mize	271
1991	** Mike Hulbert	66-67-65-68-266	Kenny Knox	266
1992	David Peoples	66-69-67-69-271	Bill Britton	272
			Ed Dougherty	
			Jim Gallagher Jr.	
1993	Jim Gallagher Jr.	66-68-70-65-269	Chip Beck	271
1994	Mark McCumber	67-69-65-66-267	Glen Day	270
1995	Ted Tryba	69-67-68-68-272	Scott Simpson	273

Named Changed to Michelob Championship at Kingsmill

Year	Winner	Score	Runner-up	Score
1996	Scott Hoch	64-68-66-67-265	Tom Purtzer	269
1997	David Duval	67-66-71-67-271**	Grant Waite	271
			Duffy Waldorf	271
1998	David Duval	65-67-68-68-268	Phil Tataurangi	271
1999	Notah Begay	67-70-69-68-274**	Tom Byrum	

* The 1982 tournament was shortened to 54 holes because of weather.
** Wiebe, Sieckmann, Donald, Hulbert, Duval, and Begay won in sudden-death playoffs.

CRESTAR SENIOR CLASSIC RESULTS

United Virginia Bank Senior Classic

Year	Winner	Score	Runner-up	Score
1983	Miller Barber	281 (-7)	Rod Funseth	282
			Don January	282
			Roberto De Vicenzo	282
1984	Dan Sikes	207 (-9)	Lee Elder	208
1985	Peter Thomson	207 (-9)	George Lanning	211
1986	Chi Chi Rodriguez	202 (-14)	Don January	205

Name changed to Crestar Classic

Year	Winner	Score	Runner-up	Score
1987	Larry Mowry	203 (-13)	Gary Player	204
			Bob Charles	204
1988	Arnold Palmer	203 (-13)	Lee Elder	207
			Larry Mowry	207
			Jim Ferree	207
1989	Chi Chi Rodriguez	203 (-13)	Jim Dent	204
			Dick Rhyan	204
1990	Jim Dent	202 (-14)	Lee Trevino	203

VIRGINIA PGA OPEN RESULTS

Year	Winner	Score	Site
1958	Jack Isaacs, Langley	69-68-72-73-282	Ingleside, Staunton
1959	Al Smith, Danville	68-66-74-74-282	Bide-A-Wee, Portsmouth
1960	Chandler Harper, Portsmouth	69-72-67-70-278	Ingleside, Staunton
1961	Jack Isaacs, Langley	71-73-74-75-193*	Bide-A-Wee, Portsmouth
1962	Mac Main, Danville	67-68-67-67-269	Ingleside, Staunton
1963	Tom Strange, Virginia Beach	68-67-70-73-278	Blue Bills, Roanoke
1964	Tom Strange, Virginia Beach	68-71-73-69-281	Cavalier, Virginia Beach
1965	Bob Mitchell, Danville	71-67-72-72-282	Arnold's Ranch, Disputanta
1966	Tom Strange, Virginia Beach	69-73-74-73-289**	Bide-A-Wee, Portsmouth
1967	Chandler Harper, Portsmouth	65-73-67-71-276***	E. Shore CC, Onancock
1968	Chandler Harper, Portsmouth	68-71-71-70-280	Fredericksburg CC
1969	Chandler Harper, Portsmouth	74-71-77-72-294	Keswick, Charlottesville
1970	Chandler Harper, Portsmouth	70-73-74-72-289	Keswick, Charlottesville
1971	Claude King, Norfolk	67-71-71-74-283	Waynesboro CC
1972	a-Nelson Long Jr., Hot Springs	71-71-71-72-286	Lake Wright, Norfolk
1973	Herb Hooper, Richmond	71-73-71-76-291	Evergreen, Haymarket
1974	a-John Bruce, Danville	74-70-70-72-286****	Red Wing, Virginia Beach
1975	a-John Bruce, Danville	71-68-70-72-281	Leesburg G&CC
1976	a-John Bruce, Danville	70-72-71-70-283	Fredericksburg CC
1977	a-John Bruce, Danville	77-72-69-77-295	Ivy Hill, Lynchburg
1978	a-Bobby Inman, Ports.	77-70-70-70-287	Salisbury CC, Richmond
1979	a-Tony DeLuca, Vienna	67-67-68-71-271	Lake Wright, Norfolk
1980	Billy King, Roanoke	73-74-66-76-289	Bide-A-Wee, Portsmouth
1981	Bobby Wadkins, Richmond	70-68-73-69-280	Countryside, Roanoke
1982	Bobby Wadkins, Richmond	65-69-72-68-274	Lake Wright, Norfolk
1983	Bobby Wadkins, Richmond	71-74-72-69-286	Lake Monticello, Palmyra
1984	Woody FitzHugh, Great Falls	66-67-69-68-270	Meadowbrook, Richmond

* won 18-hole playoff vs. Claude King, Virginia Beach, 73-75
** won 18-hole playoff vs. Herb Hooper, Richmond, 72-73
*** won 18-hole playoff vs. Herb Hooper, Richmond, 66-68
**** WON 18-HOLE PLAYOFF VS. MAC MAIN, FARMVILLE, 71-75

CRESTAR-FARM FRESH CLASSIC RESULTS

United Virginia Bank Golf Classic at 6,526-yard, par-72, Elizabeth Manor CC, Portsmouth

Year	Winner	Score	Runner-up
1979	Amy Alcott	286 (-2)	Susie McAllister
1980	Donna Caponi	277 (-11)	Nancy Lopez

Moved to 6,672-yard, par-72, Sleepy Hole, Suffolk

Year	Winner	Score	Runner-up
1981	Jan Stephenson	205 (-14)	Sally Little, Janet Alex
1982	Sally Little	208 (-11)	Kathy Whitworth
1983	Lenore Muraoka	212 (-4)	Stephanie Farwig, Debbie Massey, Alice Miller
1984	Amy Alcott	210 (-6)	Cathy Marino
1985	Kathy Whitworth	207 (-9)	Amy Alcott
1986	M. Spencer-Devlin	214 (-2)	Barb Thomas, Jody Rosenthal
1987	Jody Rosenthal	209 (-7)	Cindy Hill

Name changed to Crestar Classic

| 1988 | Juli Inkster* | 209 (-7) | Nancy Lopez, Betsy King, Rosie Jones |

Moved to 6,570-yard, par-72, Greenbrier CC, Chesapeake

| 1989 | Juli Inkster | 210 (-6) | Beth Daniel, Liselotte Neumann |
| 1990 | Dottie Pepper-Mochrie | 200 (-16) | Chris Johnson |

Name changed to Crestar-Farm Fresh Classic

| 1991 | Hollis Stacy | 282 (-6) | Patty Sheehan, Tammie Green, Elaine Crosby |
| 1992 | Jennifer Wyatt | 208 (-8) | Donna Andrews |

* won in sudden-death playoff

VIRGINIA STATE OPEN WINNERS

Year	Winner	Score	Site
1924	Elmer Loving, Virginia Beach	75-86-75-76-312	Hermitage, Richmond
1925	Pat Petranck, Petersburg	73-77-79-74-293	Roanoke CC, Roanoke
1926	Pat Petranck, Petersburg	74-77-80-79-310	Hermitage, Richmond
1927	Jimmy Thompson, Richmond	77-76-77-78-308	CC of Virginia, Richmond
1928	Charlie Isaacs, Richmond	76-84-72-75-307	Princess Anne CC, Virginia Beach
1929	Roland Hancock, Lynchburg	70-73-74-217*	Hermitage, Richmond
1930	a-Harry Thompson, Richmond	73-75-77-71-296	Westwood GC, Richmond
1931	a-Buddy Clement, Roanoke	82-78-83-78-321	Truxton Manor, Norfolk
1932	a-Chandler Harper, Portsmouth	73-68-75-78-294	Westwood GC, Richmond
1933	Bobby Cruickshank, Richmond	72-70-74-69-285	CC of Virginia James River, Richmond
1934	Bobby Cruickshank, Richmond	72-70-74-74-290	Hermitage, Richmond
1935	Bobby Cruickshank, Richmond	70-75-71-73-289	Old Dominion GC, Newport News
1936	Bobby Cruickshank, Richmond	68-70-72-67-277	Old Dominion GC, Newport News
1937	Bobby Cruickshank, Richmond	78-70-72-69-289**	Farmington, Charlottesville
	Ernie Ball, Charlottesville	68-72-76-73-289	
1938	Chandler Harper, Portsmouth	71-72-70-71-284	Old Dominion GC, Newport News
1939	Bobby Cruickshank, Richmond	69-75-74-78-296	Danville GC, Danville
1940	Chandler Harper, Portsmouth	71-70-72-283	Boonsboro CC, Lynchburg
1941	Chandler Harper, Portsmouth	66-71-69-68-274	Ocean View, Norfolk
1942-45	NO TOURNAMENTS, WORLD WAR II		
1946	Sam Snead, Hot Springs	69-66-68-72-278***	Cavalier Y&GC, Virginia Beach
	Chandler Harper, Portsmouth	72-68-72-63-278	
1947	George Payton, Hampton	67-65-66-66-264	Cavalier Y&GC, Virginia Beach
1947	George Payton, Hampton	67-65-66-66-264	Cavalier Y&GC, Virginia Beach
1948	Johnny O'Donnell, Norfolk	72-71-70-67-280	Hampton CC, Hampton
1949	Jack Isaacs, Langley Field	65-68-72-70-275	Ocean View, Norfolk
1950	Jack Isaacs, Langley Field	74-71-72-71-288	Danville GC, Danville
1951	Johnny O'Donnell, Norfolk	70-70-70-72-282	Cascades, Hot Springs
1952	Chandler Harper, Portsmouth	66-68-71-71-276	Cavalier, Virginia Beach
1953	Johnny O'Donnell, Norfolk	70-71-70-73-284	Ingleside CC, Staunton
1954	Johnny O'Donnell, Norfolk	72-72-69-73-286	Cascades, Hot Springs
1955	Johnny O'Donnell, Norfolk	71-64-68-69-272	Ocean View, Norfolk
1956	Jack Isaacs, Langley Field	75-73-72-71-291	Ingleside, Staunton
1957	a-Tom Strange, Virginia Beach	69-68-69-68-274****	Ocean View, Norfolk
	Shorty Oatman, Norfolk	63-69-68-74-274	
1958	Al Smith, Danville	75-78-68-221	CC of Virginia James River, Richmond
1959	Joe Cannon, Charlottesville	69-71-75-215‡	Farmington, Charlottesville
	Clare Emery, Arlington	70-74-71-215	
1960	Al Smith, Danville	68-68-69-205	Danville GC, Danville
1961	Claude King, Virginia Beach	72-72-73-217‡‡	James River CC, Newport News
	a-Ron Gerringer, Newport News	72-76-69-217	
1962	Claude King, Virginia Beach	72-69-75-216	Boonsboro CC, Lynchburg
1963	Claude King, Virginia Beach	70-68-68-206	Roanoke CC, Roanoke
1964	Herb Hooper, Williamsburg	68-72-70-210	Princess Anne CC, Virginia Beach
1965	Bobby Mitchell, Danville	78-68-72-218	CC of Virginia James River, Richmond
1966	Herb Hooper, Richmond	71-73-71-215	Hidden Valley CC, Salem
1967	Tom Strange, Virginia Beach	71-74-145*	Chatmoss CC, Martinsville
1968	Chandler Harper, Portsmouth	72-69-73-214‡‡‡	Elizabeth Manor, Portsmouth
	Bill Calfee, Portsmouth	72-68-74-214	
1969	a-Vinny Giles, Lynchburg	69-69-68-206	Roanoke CC, Roanoke
1970	a-Rick Bendall, Danville	69-73-70-212	James River CC, Newport News
1971	Lanny Wadkins, Richmond	68-68-69-205	CC of Virginia James River, Richmond
1972	Jennings House, Va. Beach	71-72-143*	CC of Petersburg, Petersburg
1973	Bruce Lehnhard, Haymarket	74-71-73-218	International Town and CC, Fairfax
1974	a-Vinny Giles, Richmond	70-69-70-209‡	Danville GC, Danville
	a-Chip Heyl, Sterling	71-69-69-209	
1975	a-Chip Heyl, Sterling	70-74-68-212	Lake of the Woods CC, Locust Grove
1976	a-Mike Pratt, Danville	70-71-72-213	Blacksburg CC, Blacksburg
1977	Bob Post, Locust Grove	65-68-73-206	Cavalier Y&GC, Virginia Beach
1978	a-Robert Black Jr., Vienna	72-67-72-211	Reston GC, Reston
1979	a-Stephen Smith, Martinsville	73-70-66-209	Chatmoss CC, Martinsville
1980	Clem King, Charlottesville	71-69-72-212	Kingsmill GC, Williamsburg
1981	a-Tony DeLuca, Vienna	73-71-72-216	Westwood CC, Vienna
1982	a-Bill Sibbick, Martinsville	70-73-72-215	Chatmoss CC, Martinsville
1983	Robert Wrenn, Richmond	67-68-70-205	Staunton CC, Staunton
1984	Mark Carnevale, Williamsburg	67-68-69-204	Danville GC, Danville
1985	a-Tom McKnight, Galax	71-72-66-70-279	Farmington CC, Charlottesville
1986	Woody FitzHugh, Great Falls	70-67-71-70-278	Willow Oaks, Richmond
1987	Tim White, Richmond	67-74-74-70-285	Brandermill CC, Midlothian
1988	Woody FitzHugh, Great Falls	66-72-69-73-280	Stonehenge G&CC, Midlothian
1989	Robert Wrenn, Richmond	73-74-66-71-284‡‡‡‡‡	Willow Oaks, Richmond
	a-Gill FitzHugh, Fairfax	68-72-72-72-284	
1990	Bruce Lehnhard, Locust Grove	72-73-67-70-282	Willow Oaks, Richmond
1991	Robert Wrenn, Richmond	68-68-63-69-268‡‡‡‡‡‡	Willow Oaks, Richmond
1992	Craig Gunn, Danville	69-69-72-70-280	Willow Oaks, Richmond
1993	a-Vinny Giles, Richmond	68-69-69-72-278	Willow Oaks, Richmond
1994	Jerry Wood, Martinsville	65-69-72-70-276	Willow Oaks, Richmond
1995	Rob McNamara, Charlottesville	69-71-69-67-276*	Willow Oaks, Richmond
	Frank Ferguson, Fairfax	68-71-68-69-276	
1996	a-Keith Decker, Fieldale	69-69-66-72-276	Willow Oaks, Richmond
1997	Jerry Wood, Martinsville	68-68-71-69-276	Willow Oaks, Richmond
1998	Rick Schuller, Centreville	70-73-68-68-279	Ford's Colony, Williamsburg
1999	a-Faber Jamerson, Appamattox	66-68-73-70-277	Ford's Colony, Williamsburg

* rain-shortened
** Won 18-hole playoff, 72-74
*** Won 18-hole playoff, 64-67
**** Won 18-hole playoff, 64-67
‡ Won with birdie on first extra hole
‡‡ Won with par on first extra hole
‡‡‡ Won on 2nd extra hole
‡‡‡‡ Won on 3rd extra hole
‡‡‡‡‡ Won with par-4 on 3rd extra hole
‡‡‡‡‡‡ Tournament record

PHOTOGRAPHER'S ACKNOWLEDGMENTS AND
PHOTO CREDITS

I need to thank Ruth and Roger Franklin, my parents. They have given me the strength to succeed, perservere, and follow my dreams. They have been there for me every step of the way, especially allowing me to fulfill my dream of becoming a photographer and introducing me to golf, a sport I dearly enjoy and respect. Their unending love has been a great, inspiration.

Jim Ducibella, the author, for having the confidence in me to allow me to illustrate this wonderful book project of his.

I must also thank Bert Goulait, Cliff Owen, Jeff Snyder at Penn Camera, Jackie Snead, Erika Keenan, Conan Owen, Paula Hank at The Homestead, Mark Epstein, Linda Epstein, Presidential Libraries: Woodrow Wilson, Franklin D. Roosevelt, John F. Kennedy, Lyndon B. Johnson, and Ronald Reagan. Also, Frank & Shellie Ferguson at Washington Golf & CC, Francis Fenderson, Mike Pizzetti, Richard & Sue Franklin, my grandmother Irene and late grandfather Frederick Franklin, grandma York, Dick & Barbara Smith, Duke Parziale, Ron Coderre, Paul Desrosiers, Linda Miller, Dave Buell, Joel Richardson, Joe Silverman, Barker Davis, Deanne Street, Ralph Alswang at The White House, Donna Andrews (especially her dear mother, Helen), Vinny Giles, Chandler Harper, Sam Snead, Curtis Strange, Sarah Strange, Lanny Wadkins, Moss Beecroft, Bobby Mitchell, Carol Godwin at Colonial Williamsburg, Glen Byrnes at Golden Horseshoe, the Mike Williams family, the Virginia Sports Hall of Fame, my boss at *The Times*—Alan Zlotky and deputy director Chuck Weiss for cutting me some slack during this extensive project, Bill Leddon and Scott Rowlands—scanning experts who helped me out, The Library of Congress, Sue Ducibella, Frank Herzog, Renee Ross, Ellen—for that first set of Titleist DCI's, the folks at TPC Virginia Beach, the staff at Bide-A-Wee, Ken Kerr at The Virginian, Cary Sciorra at Robert Trent Jones GC, Rob McNamara, Wayne Hall, and the staff at Farmington CC, the helpful people at Kingsmill Resort, Art Utley for showing me around Richmond and his help in tracking down a great number of photos, Vicki Kronis, everyone at Ford's Colony, Kandi Comer, Robbye King-Youel, Bill Battle, Harry Easterly, David Sutherland, Syracuse University, the Syracuse University Division of International Programs Abroad, Wintergreen Resort, Mike Eave at Imagers in Atlanta, Georgia, Weymouth Crumpler at James River Country Club, for all of those at SPI Publishing, especially Mike Pearson, Jennifer Polson, Danielle Dupuis, and Christina Cary and the entire staff of the VSGA especially David Norman and Harold Pearson who let me access their extensive photo archives.

The help from every one of the above persons made this project possible. The moral support, professional help, and invaluable time given, especially those who helped find photos from years gone by, I cannot even begin to thank you enough.

Ross D. Franklin